HUMAN RIGHTS OF DALITS
SOCIETAL VIOLATION

HUMAN RIGHTS OF DALITS
Societal Violation

G.S. BHARGAVA
R.M. PAL

GYAN PUBLISHING HOUSE
New Delhi-110002

Human Rights of Dalit: Societal Violation

ISBN : 9788121206488

Published in 2010 in India by
Gyan Publishing House
5, Ansari Road, Daryaganj,
New Delhi - 110002
Phone : 011-47034999, 9811692060

e-mail : books@gyanbooks.com
gyanbook@vsnl.com
website : gyanbooks.com

Printed at : Gian Ridhi Offset Printers, Delhi

CONTENTS

1

A DALIT INTERFACE

This volume owes itself largely to a two-day national workshop on "Human Rights and Societal Changes with reference to the Scheduled Castes (SCs) and the Scheduled Tribes (STs)" jointly organised at Chennai (Madras) on 3rd and 4th August, 1996, by the Dalit Liberation Education Trust (DLET) Madras, and the National Human Rights Commission (NHRC). The then Lok Sabha Speaker, P.A. Sangma, inaugurated it by lighting the customary lamp followed by insightful observations. With his vast experience in activating the Scheduled Tribes in the north-east, Mr. Sangma weighed the merits and demerits of reservations for the social amelioration and economic development of the tribal communities. He also cautioned against overdoing reservations, especially in respect of the STs.

The organisational and financial responsibility of the workshop was on the sturdy shoulders of Mr. Henry Thiagaraj, managing trustee of the DLET, who had brought to bear on it his characteristic efficiency and natural charm. Backed by his dedicated band of hard-working personnel of the DLET, he was singularly responsible for the success in projecting the idea behind the workshop.

Bishop Azaria of DLET welcomed the participants.

The NHRC Chairperson, Justice Ranganath Mishra, delivered the opening address outlining the background of the workshop and its purpose. The keynote address was delivered by Professor Sibnarayan Ray, the well known intellectual and radical humanist. NHRC members, Mr. Virendra Dayal, Justice V.S. Malimath and Secretary-General R.V. Pillai actively participated in the workshop deliberations, chairing discussion sessions and intervening in the proceedings. Mr. Pillai also presented a paper.

The four sub-themes for discussion were carefully selected to ensure a structured consideration of the main topic. They were : 1. Social Policy and Societal Changes with reference to Dalits (the popular nomenclature for SCs and STs) ; 2. Appraisal of Legislative Measures for the Uplift of Dalits ; 3. Religious and Social Practices and Human Rights of Dalits, and 4. The Concept of National Human Rights Movement and Dalit Uplift.

Dr. R.M. Pal, Editor, *PUCL Bulletin*, co-ordinator of the workshop, introduced the subject and raised a number of questions and problems for consideration by the participants.

The distinguished participants included well-known scholars, academics, activists both Dalits and non-Dalits, and civil servants.

The DLET deserves thanks from all the participants for providing this platform for a dialogue—the first to be ever held in which a statutory institution (NHRC) took active part.

The workshop was the beginning of an effort for mutual understanding between the NHRC and Dalit scholars and activists to facilitate and promote greater interaction between the two. It is hoped the Commission will pursue with vigour the societal aspect of protection and promotion of human rights. By all accounts, it was a good beginning.

The volume is divided into two sections : the first section is a comprehensive account of the workshop proceedings and the second includes writings by G.S. Bhargava, R.M. Pal, Henry Thiagaraj and Air Commondore G.N. Baindur (Retd.) on aspects relevant to the central theme of the exercise, namely societal changes and Dalit uplift in the context of promotion of human rights. We are conscious of repetition of arguments and data in the papers presented at the workshop but have not purposely edited them to preserve the original flavour of the deliberations. However, where statistical data and charts are repeated, they have been abridged. Many of the writings included in the second section have appeared in newspapers and periodicals and are being published with the courtesy of the respective publications.

New Delhi
10, May, 1999

G.S. Bhargava
R.M. Pal

2

INTRODUCTION

Why is it that the thoughtful section of our people, as also victims of injustice and torture are highly critical of the caste system? Why are they angry? Why is it that the dominating section of our people are unwilling to bury the ugly relics of the system?

Way back in 1992, I had the privilege of sharing the platform in Delhi with Swami Agnivesh and Justice Krishna Iyer. Both of them delivered emotional speeches—Justice Iyer with tears in his eyes ! —before a highly educated gathering, mostly Dalits, on horrendous crimes committed on the SC/STs by upper caste Hindus. Justice Iyer recommended that there must be more judges—at least 50 per cent—from the SC/ST communities so that they could get justice. Swami Agnivesh angrily suggested that the SC/STs must be given fire arms to teach a lesson to the upper castes !

If constitutional provisions alone could have prevented crimes on grounds of birth they would not have increased, I pointed out. Taking to arms, of course, should be summarily dismissed. We might pause, therefore, I added, to look at the system that has sanctioned the indignities heaped on the SC/STs. Is it possible to reform the Hindu society so far as the caste system is concerned ? The Arya Samaj to which Swami Agnivesh belongs is no doubt against the caste system. But the problem arises when the Arya Samaj and Swami Agnivesh vehemently affirm their faith in the theory of *karma* which is at the root of keeping the down-trodden under perpetual bondage. It does not admit of revolt against tyranny ; it prevents one from shaping one's own destiny. We will note later what Lord Krishna has prescribed in this regard.

The issue relates to the institution of caste which has been the stumbling block of social justice and human rights, as also a clear acknowledgement of the fact that every human being, given favourable conditions, is capable of developing unlimited powers of intellect and will, and that those conditions have not yet been created for those who deserve them the most.

Let us note the approach of a humanist and liberal, Nissim Ezekil, who is well-known in the English speaking world as an outstanding Indo-Anglian writer, critic and academic of our time. Shortly after the seminar referred to above, I wrote a brief editorial note in the *PUCL Bulletin*, a monthly journal published by People's Union for Civil Liberties, on the subject suggesting that without demolishing the impregnable walls erected by the system "lock, stock and barrel respect for rights and liberties will remain a distant goal. Nothing short of a philosophical revolution can bring a change, and for that we need to have iconoclasts, not status-quoists and constitutional experts".

Nissim Ezekil wrote in reply : "As a regular reader since its inception, of the *PUCL Bulletin*, I would like to claim that I am in agreement with its basic concepts and arguments. Let us consider the relations of the caste system to the innumerable problems we face in India about civil liberties, which may in this case be referred to as normal rights in all human relationships". He then takes up the "statement" about demolishing the system, and the need for "a philosophical revolution". "Well, now, nothing I say be regarded as championing the mode of thinking common to status-quoists, but constitutional experts are still needed for validating necessary changes in society as a whole. And the philosophical revolution, which I am entirely in favour of, with its iconoclasts, will have to face multilingual and multicultural factors. We can neither wait for such a revolution nor do without it. So it seems to be a practical way of thinking about and within it to consider the possibility of persuasive arguments and liberal reforms which move in the direction of the ultimate goals. If, on the other hand we dismiss such a proposition as a shameful compromise, we have to, as the *PUCL Bulletin* editor does, consider it impossible 'to reform Hindu society so far as the caste system is concerned' .... All I am drawing attention to, and even insisting on, is the need for a strategy which will help us to spread our ideas without creating more enemies than friends ....I still believe it is possible to widen our appeal, to make it seem more reasonable and practicable". Mr. Ezekil recommends "that kind of revolution [which] may require patience as much as persistence, and not divide the forces at work into rival camps, with civil war as the inevitable consequence".

I have quoted Mr. Ezekil at length for he represents the liberals and secular humanists in the country who do not want India to fall apart, and also for his appeal to reason, for his robust optimism ; and we hope the perpetrators of societal violation of human rights, will join such a debate on the caste system. If, however, past history is any indication, as we shall see later, Mr. Ezekil's appeal to reason is unlikely to make any dent in the camp of the dominating section of the people.

Let us first give a brief look at the intellectual, moral, and religious support that has been given to the caste system, *varna-vyavastha* with a view to examining it in relation to the provisions of the Universal Declaration of Human Rights (UDHR) 1948. The Gita which is usually referred to as the guide to Hindu way of life, states (Lord Krishna telling Arjuna) : "The works of Brahmins, Kshtriyas, Vaishayas, and Shudras are different .... The work of the Shudra is service. They all attain perfection when they find joy in their work ... Greater is thine own work, even if this is humble, than the work of another, even if this be great. When a man does the work God gives him, no sin can touch this man. And a man should not abandon his work .... Because thou art in the bondage of Karma, of the forces of thine own past life ; and that which thou, in thy delusion, with a good will dost not want to do, unwillingly thou shalt have to do".

According to laws of Manu, Brahma created the Brahmin, the Kshatriya, the Vaishya and the Shudra from his mouth, his arms, his thighs, and his feet respectively ; and this he did "for the sake of the prosperity of the world". He assigned separate duties and occupations to them in order to "protect" this universe—the first three for teaching, protecting citizens, trading and lending money on interest respectively, and the last for serving the first three without being critical of them. The Dalits are described as *varna-sankara* born out of the intermixture of the "pure varnas" and they are outside the system. (Obviously they are not recognised even as persons by Manu). Furthermore, the laws prescribe that penance for a Brahmin for the killing of an animal or a Shudra is the same ; in fact the killing of a cow is more heinous than killing a Shudra.

It may also be noted that women, too, have received the same treatment in our scriptures. I may quote Professor Romila Thapar : "It is interesting that whereas these texts (*Dharma-Sastra* and similar literature) take great care to classify men with a minutiae of distinctions, women are generally treated as a unifirm category. Furthermore, the status of women as a whole is clearly defined, for they are unambiguously equated with the *Sudras* as for example in *Manu,* X1, 153. Even the *Gita* places women, *Vaisyas* and *Sudras* in the same category and describes them all as being of sinful birth (*Bhagavat-Gita,* IX. 32). According to another text the punishment for killing either a woman or a *Sudra* is identical (The law-book of Parasara, V1.32). Perhaps the most gruelling of all is the treatment of the widow, which at times borders on the inhumane and this is particularly disconcerting, coming as it does, from the *Sastras* of a culture which laid so much stress on respecting and caring for the aged. The subservience of women is precisely summed up in the Manu *Dharmasastra* where it is stated that a woman should never be independent. As a daughter she is under the surveillance of her father, as a wife of her husband and as a widow of her son (Manu, IX, 32)". ["Looking Back in History" by Romila Thapar in *Indian Women* ed. Devaki Jain, Publications Division, Government of India]. In short, "a woman is not fit for independence", declares Manu.

This is the system the Brahmanical religion has created which according to all thoughtful people should be demolished.

Now, where does the system stand in relation to the human rights situation ? The very first two Articles of the UDHR make it clear that freedom, equality, and fraternity are the very basis of human rights. "All human beings are born free and equal in dignity and rights" (Art 1). "Everyone is entitled to all the rights and freedoms without distinction of any kind, such as race, colour, sex, language, religion, political or other opinion, national or social origin, birth, ..." etc. (Art 2).

It is obvious that the caste system is inconsistent with the provisions of the UDHR, for our system gives different status to different persons on the basis of birth. Denial of eduction to some people including women violates Art 26(1) according to which, "everyone has the right to education..." Our system requires a person to join the occupation of the caste to which he is born, and this violates Art 23 (1) which prescribes that everyone has the right to work, to free choice of employment, to just and favourable condition of work and protection against unemployment. Compulsion of marriage within the caste alone is violation of Art 16(1) which says, "men and women of full age, without any limitation due to race, nationality or religion, have the right to marry and to found a family. They are entitled to equal rights as to marriage, during marriage and at its dissolution". Our system does not permit certain sections of the people including women to enter temples, to learn Sanskrit, to read religious books, to be priests. This is in contradiction with Art 18, "Everyone has the right to freedom of thought, ..." etc. Some people (the Dalits) are forced to live in the outskirts of village, and this violates Art 13(1), "Everyone has the right to freedom of movement and residence, ..." etc.

There are a number of other societal laws which are violative of human rights. A *begdar* (labourer), generally of lower caste, according to the laws of Manu, is obliged to work without payment. If a Brahmin forces a twice-born to work for him, he is to be punished; but if a Brahmin forces a Shudra to work for him, on payment or without, he is not to be punished.

Read between the lines, and it becomes clear that the upholders of the system, on the authority of the scriptures, seek to persuade the poor, the depressed, the oppressed, and the exploited to reconcile their lot to suffering, sacrifice, love and voluntary poverty—all that signify complete surrender and the absence of the spirit of revolt.

Let us be clear. Caste divides and gives rise to divisiveness and dissension. The system erected impregnable walls between groups of human beings. It has ordained that social hierarchy is to be determined by birth—under divine sanction. Social hierarchies and occupation-based heredity exist in other societies also, but this divinely sanctioned hierarchy is exclusively ours. A further difference is that under our system one must find joy only in the work that has been allotted to him or her by birth ; and if you do the allotted work you will be rewarded in the next life. If you go against this injunction you are committing a sin—you must be punished. Does not this explain why the SC/STs are punished by the upper castes through the *Ranveer Sena* in Bihar for daring to walk with their heads erect ?

Debate and dialogue have never been one of our traditions. Our tradition has been one of monologue. During the freedom movement, an attempt was made by Rabindranath Tagore and Gandhi to start a debate on Gandhi's programme to attain swaraj. In no time the "debate" ended with Gandhi's conferring "Gurudev" on Tagore, and Tagore's "Mahatma" on Gandhi. Buddhism was expelled from the country but not before the Brahmanical religion declared Buddha an "Avatar" ! Very recently Amartya Sen has been dismissed with 'Bharat Ratna" and whole life free tickets by Air India and Indian Airlines ! Let him go on talking whatever he likes about his thesis (for which he got the Nobel prize) of the need for compulsory basic education ; now that we have made him a Bharat Ratna it is not necessary to implement this social welfare programme ! We could not care less about his views, namely that we are far behind other countries in the field of basic education because of the hierarchical system of our society ! What a shame, that we dump our great men in this manner. (One wonders if Amartya Set got an eerie feeling when he got the Bharat Ratna !)

The great humanist, Tagore warned us long ago, in the beginning of this century : " In trying to avoid collisions (India) set up boundaries of immovable walls, thus giving to her numerous races the negative benefit of peace and order but not the positive opportunity of expansion and movement. India has made grave errors in setting up the boundary walls too rigidly between races, in perpetuating in her classification the results of inferiority ; often India has crippled her children's mind and narrowed their lives in order to fit them into her social forms". There has hardly been any debate and discussion on what this humanist said against the hierarchical system ; not even between Tagore and Gandhi. One of the reasons for this kind of mindset is that we have always felt uncomfortable at truth being hurled at us ; we have never acknowledged the existence of dark and horrendous corners in our system. Let us be sure : we can never close the doors on such corners unless we first, at least, recognise the existence of these corners.

We are told that the caste system does not exist any more, or has started disappearing—told even by well-meaning liberals. Has caste identity really disappeared ?

There is no limit in our country to holding up a fiction to obscure facts. Let us not pretend that the system has vanished from our society. We must accept the ground reality, namely that, even though the Indian constitution is not based on the laws of Manu and the *Gita,* and has abolished untouchability and has made provisions for equality before law, the immovable walls remain. The constitution has merely prescribed, but has not given any description of the ground reality. Social reformers like Swami Agnivesh and Justice Krishna Iyer must pay adequate attention to this aspect of our society—the caste system—so that the objectives of the UDHR and our own Constitution become realisable. Constitutional provisions, are of course, important—a civil society must have them, as Nissim Ezekil has suggested—but without a philosophical revolution, which alone can ensure uprooting of the system, a change for the better does not appear to be attainable.

There are a number of well-meaning liberals—Gandhians, radical humanists and human rights activists—who follow the Christian dictum, namely that, a gentleman is one who does not inflict pain on others. They do not inflict pain on the SC/STs ; as a matter of fact they are ashamed of the fact that this kind of discrimination exists in our society. These well-intentioned people who cherish the true values of democracy suggest that there should be a vigorous reformist movement, along with constitutional movements and provisions, to eradicate the evils of the system. They may, however, peep into our history. All attempts to reform the Brahmanical religion—even to make it a non-Sanskritic religion—including religious and social reformist movements, have failed. Buddha tried and appeared to succeed but only to be expelled from the country. Nanak, Kabir and their colleagues and disciples also made brave, but futile, attempts. During the British regime, a number of rationalists and reformists, specially in Bengal and Maharashtra, fought relentlessly. And yet, no less a man than Ishwar Chandra Vidyasagar at one stage, while fighting the cause of widow remarriage, got so exasperated by the cunning arguments put forward by Sanskrit scholars and Pandits against widow remarriage, that he felt constrained to exclaim in utter disgust : "Oh unfortunate women, what sin have you committed that you should have been born in India where men have no sensitivity ! [*Courtesy* The Statesman, *10 April, 1999*]—**R.M. Pal**

3

THE FIRST DIALOGUE

Ranganath Misra

This is the first dialogue that the National Human Rights Commission (NHRC) has welcomed with a view to focusing attention to the problems related to societal violations of human rights of Dalits. It is a matter of great pain and shame that even after five decades of independence people are lynched to death and burnt alive in the name of caste. Even in Tamil Nadu Dalits are killed by upper caste people.

I am happy that we in the NHRC accepted Dr. R.M. Pal's suggestion that the NHRC must take the human rights problem of Dalits (both SCs and STs) on its agenda and provide a platform for a continuous dialogue. The next step that we took was to join the DLET (Dalit Liberation Education Trust) in organising this workshop. I am also happy that we accepted Dr. Pal's advice to hold the workshop at a place outside Delhi. We thank Mr. Henry Thiagaraj and Bishop Azaria of the DLET for organising this workshop.

Dr. Pal has brought together eminent scholars, academics, and social activists—*those who matter and* people who are aware of the problem in its intensiveness. I and my colleagues in the NHRC look forward to the deliberations with great expectations.

We have indulged in empty talks for the last five decades ; we have made no progress so far as the cause of the Dalits and Adivasis are concerned. When cementing was necessary, we were engaged in watering and when water was necessary we were cementing.

We should have come together ; instead we are divided. I have always been impressed by what Dr. Pal has been saying, namely, that caste has been creating divisiveness and dissension. We have not taken the reality into account.

Equality must become a reality. The very first Article of the Universal Declaration of Human Rights declares that human beings are born free. This workshop will contribute towards realising the ideal of equality.

We must have a casteless society. But legislation alone is not the solution to the problems of the Dalits, especially for crimes like untouchability. The sense of equality should be shared and enjoyed by one and all and is not meant to be confined to the Constitution or to be used in some judicial orders.

It pains me when we receive reports, almost daily, that Dalits and Adivasis have been killed and burnt alive. Education has not helped us to recognise human beings as persons. Mr. Thiagaraj has provided us this platform to go into the problem and we must thank him and DELT for this brain-storming session.

I have seen the list of participants. They are our most distinguished intellectuals and activists. The country depends on them for finding a solution to the problem. It is precisely because of this that DELT and NHRC have joined together. Let me repeat, the country relies heavily on you.

4

CLOSE THE DOOR ON THE HORRENDOUS PAST

(introductory remarks)

R.M. Pal, Coordinator of the Workshop

Those of us who are concerned about the uplift of Dalits, and are engaged in an analysis of our social system which has been, and is, responsible for human rights violations, have every reason to be grateful to the DLET and the NHRC for making it possible for us to meet in Madras [now renamed Chennai].

I would like to raise a few questions and problems—some of them appear to be intractable ; it is in this background I proposed to Mr. R.V. Pillay, Secretary General, NHRC that it might consider having at least a brain-storming session on the subject to which reference was made by NHRC in its 1994-95 annual report. I have been writing on this subject in the PUCL Bulletin and elsewhere for the last several years. I have maintained that our social system has been, and is, responsible for the most atrocious forms of human rights violations. In a complex country like ours, all other forms of violations—child labour, custodial rape, torture, death, female infanticide, name any thing—stem from this.

1. It is generally agreed that we have to create in India, where about 80 per cent of the people are Hindus, a purposive, secular society. Is it possible so long as the ugly relic of the past, namely the caste system, persists?

2. How does one explain the fact that every attempt—Buddha to reformers of our time—to reform and reorganise the basis of our system has broken down without making any serious dent in the impregnable walls? I am aware of the fact, however, that Hinduism is a very complex religion. I am also aware of the fact that there is a lot of scope to theological flexibility along with the social rigidity in it.

3. In spite of the changes—many perceptive analysts maintain, however, that these changes are superficial—that we see today, is the hold of the system any less than it was in the past? Has caste identity disappeared?

4. How does one explain the fact that in the recent past, far from caste showing any signs of breaking down, there has been a strengthening of caste feeling?

5. What lessons can one draw from the political awakening of Dalits today? Has it weakened the hierarchical system? Will it promote the cause of Dalit uplift? And will there be any change for the better in the human rights situation?

6. What has been the role of our intellectuals in perpetuating caste feeling and in finding justification for the system?

7. Is there any movement from inside Hindu society which aims at putting an end to the hierarchical order ordained by the system? Again, if we want a social revolution, in the context of establishing a secular society where the dignity of the individual will be respected, can it take place before a philosophical revolution has disrupted the authority of traditional values? We seem to be caught in a vicious circle. For example, can superstitions be dispelled by legislation? Have we shown any indication that we are brave enough to make iconoclastic laws?

8. What has been the role of the doctrines of Karma, Transmigration of Soul, Maya, and so on, specially in relation to uplift of Dalits?

9. Will we succeed in establishing a society of our dream even if we have the comprehensive legislation with the determined purpose of breaking up the system? Or do we need a movement with a scientific approach and reason which will in time establish a society based on equality and fraternity? (Legislation has been

limited to abolition of untouchability without even a debate, not to speak of dismantling, on the source of untouchability).

I am sure, all of us present here are agreed on at least one point, namely, that rights are not protected by laws alone. What is needed is sensitivity on the part of society. In the absence of sensitivity and conscience, can legislation help?

If we want significant change, and want to eradicate "ancient wrongs", an expression used by the NHRC, we need to have movements, to be led by creative thinkers like you present here. Such movements, creative movements grow only in an atmosphere like the present one—where some of the best minds of our country will deliberate on the subject in this workshop. People of my age fondly hope that such a movement for human rights and uplift of Dalits which depend on answers that I have raised, will lead to a peaceful revolution to uproot anything that stands in the way of demolishing "ancient wrongs" and the uplift of human beings. Such a movement will have formidable foes : the vested interest in perpetuating and glorifying an unequal system; religion to glorify the system ; philosophers and social anthropologists who sing its praise. The fact, however, remains that without such a movement our society cannot be rendered purposive and placed on the road to progress.

Lastly, we must at least acknowledge the fact that we have a dark past, a horrendous past, for if we do not accept this basic truth, how can we close the door on that past ? For that we need to raise our voice of reason.

I may add that but for DLET, specially Mr. Henry Thiagaraj and Bishop Azaria this workshop could not be held. We are all grateful to them. I would also record my thanks to the NHRC.

5

HUMAN RIGHTS OF SC/STs—a radical break with Tradition and dismantling of the pernicious Caste system—Inaugural address

P.A. Sangma

I find from the programme agenda of the Workshop that several crucial subjects relevant to the Scheduled Castes and Scheduled Tribes and their uplift have been listed for discussion. The subjects include social policy and societal changes, legislative measures, religious, social practices, etc. They have been designed to be discussed within the framework of the concept of human rights. Right now, wide-ranging social, economic and political changes are taking place in our democratic policy. They have significant implications for the uplift of the Scheduled Castes, the Scheduled Tribes and the backward classes. The workshop agenda is, indeed, contextual. My congratulations to the organisers of this workshop.

The Preamble to our Constitution enjoins that justice, liberty, equality and fraternity shall be secured for all citizens. It is also patent in this mandate that justice shall cover social, economic and political spheres. The principle behind the constitutional concept of justice and equality is one of equity. Equity is very much more than arithmetical equality. Our people are entitled to liberty in terms of freedom of thought, expression and faith. And, the foundation of the concept of fraternity is dignity of the individual.

India has also actively and very constructively participated at the international level in giving shape to the international Bill of Human Rights which consists of the Universal Declaration of Human Rights, The International Covenant on Civil and Political Rights, and The International Covenant on Economic, Social and Cultural Rights. These instruments, inter-alia, envisage that right to liberty and equality is the birth right of all and is inalienable; that there shall be no discrimination on any ground—race, colour, sex, language, religion, political or other opinion, national or social origin, property, birth or other status; that right to life and security of person shall be enjoyed by all; and that the right to economic and social rights include the right to work, the right to equal pay for equal work, the right to form and join trade unions and the right to education, etc.

India has also ratified these Human Rights instruments. The detailed provisions of our Constitution are also consistent with these instruments. Right to equality before law; prohibition of discrimination on grounds of religion, race, caste, sex or place of birth; equality of opportunity in matters of public employment, abolition of untouchability; right to freedom of speech, expression, association and movement; protection of life and personal liberty, prohibition of forced labour and employment of children; right to freedom of religion; protection of minorities, etc., have been provided for as justiciable fundamental rights in Part III of our Constitution.

Coming to the question of uplift of the Scheduled Castes and the Scheduled Tribes in the above background, what looms large is the size of the problem. The population of India is nearly a billion, about one-fifth of humanity. The Scheduled Castes and the Scheduled Tribes amongst them are about 25 per cent of the total population, about 5 per cent of humanity. More than the size of our population, the problem is its incredible magnitude and complexity. In our country major religions were born—Hinduism, Buddhism, Jainism and Sikhism. There are more Muslims in India than in any other countries of the Middle-East and North Africa.

Since Independence, successive governments have taken several affirmative actions. The Untouchability Act of 1955 and

Protection of Civil Rights Act of 1976, consistent with Article 17 of the Constitution, have outlawed untouchability. The Bonded Labour System (Abolition) Act, 1976 has abolished forced labour. The Child Labour Prohibition and Regulation Act, 1976 prohibits employment of children in hazardous occupations.

The Central and State Governments, put together, invest over Rs.10,000 crore per annum for the benefit of the Scheduled Castes and the Scheduled Tribes.

We have also created institutional structures for the uplift of the Scheduled Castes and the Scheduled Tribes and the Minorities—the National Commission for the Scheduled Castes and the Scheduled Tribes, and National Minorities Commission, apart from the National Backward Classes Financial Development Corporation.

India may have participated in the establishment of Human Rights Instruments, may have constitutional provisions flowing from the concept of Human Rights; may have established a regime of laws to protect, and to positively discriminate in favour of the Scheduled Castes and the Scheduled Tribes. But if the practice of human rights is to be realised in the backdrop of this societal fabric, a radical break with tradition is required. And, if we are to bring about a sea-change in values and dismantle the old social order, the obvious remedy is education. With education comes enlightenment which, in turn, leads to generation of awareness. This alone can yield the upsurge that is required from amongst the Scheduled Castes and the Scheduled Tribes to match with the extent and intensity of State intervention in legislative and investment terms.

Education is very vital also for the smooth and non-violent transition of the Scheduled Castes and the Scheduled Tribes from the category of depressed classes into the category of the prosperous and the empowered. The disturbing phenomenon experienced in certain parts of our country is the growth of caste based private *senas* or militias. This is due significantly to the exploitation of the Scheduled Castes and the Scheduled Tribes by unscrupulous elements in society. If education is imparted, because of the enlightenment that comes with that, the Scheduled

Castes and the Scheduled Tribes will not subject themselves to such exploitation.

Of course, economic development is also very vital. The budget allocations for the Scheduled Castes and the Scheduled Tribes are largely meant for their economic development. The Central and State Governments have further evolved policies for reservation of jobs in public service. It should be realised that as of now public service does not provide jobs for more than 20 million people. At an average annual rate of occurrence of vacancy positions at about 3 per cent, the total annual intake will be only about six lakhs. At the reservation rate of 25 per cent, only about 1,50,000 people will be benefited annually. Thus while reservation is an affirmative action so far as it goes, it does not really present any practical solution to the problems of the Scheduled Castes and the Scheduled Tribes in employment. There are also limits to the growth of employment in public service. Employment opportunities will increasingly become available in the liberalising economy only in the private sector. For expediting these employment opportunities, skill is required. This skill can be acquired only through education.

Reservation, whether it be for the purpose of education or employment, in the long run, is also likely to keep the Scheduled Castes and the Scheduled Tribes back from genuine development.

Another important means of economic development is, of course, vesting depressed classes with rights over property. It is only ownership over some property that can help in even facilitating access to meaningful education. It is keeping this in view that land reforms measures have been taken in several parts of the country. While in some States land reforms have been implemented effectively, in many States they are yet to be implemented seriously. Greater effort is required in this area. At the same time, it should also be ensured that while implementing land reforms as a measure of distributive justice, land holdings are not reduced to uneconomic sizes. Uneconomic holdings could only result in sub-optimal farming, often reducing the new class of land owners to underemployed people.

Our processes of implementation of programmes often involve spreading of resources thinly over vast areas. It is desirable that the

Scheduled Caste and the Scheduled Tribe habitations are identified and different development agencies come together at the grassroots level and invest all their resources in a coordinated way in such identified habitations.

Appropriate monitoring mechanisms should also be established at the Central as well as State levels to monitor the delivery of services. It is a known fact that even though the order of investment on the Scheduled Castes and the Scheduled Tribes is about Rs. 10,000 crore per annum as of now, the reach of the benefits is not universal. There are complaints of leakages of resources in the process of implementation.

The majority of the Scheduled Castes and the Scheduled Tribes are agricultural labourers. Because of economic compulsions they send their children for work when they should be in schools. Child labour is self-perpetuating. Children who labour, lose education and therefore employment opportunities through education when they are adults. Without the means of income for want of education, they in turn may continue to send their children to work. Child labour would need to be terminated by voluntary action on the part of the parents. Mere governmental efforts to terminate child labour through legislative measures will not yield the desired results.

Educational and economic development of the Scheduled Castes and the Scheduled Tribes ultimately will enhance their electoral power particularly in view of their huge number. This, in turn, will help them to become political and governmental decision makers.

My prescription for the uplift of the Scheduled Castes and the Scheduled Tribes is :

- Creating awareness about the international instruments on human rights and their implications and about the Constitutional provisions, National laws and Government's affirmative actions;
- Creation of an upsurge by the Scheduled Castes and the Scheduled Tribes themselves through education and peaceful means so as to dismantle the pernicious caste system based on archaic values;

- Enhancement of work participation by the Scheduled Castes and the Scheduled Tribes through human capital development;
- Not to look upon reservation in public service as a panacea for unemployment;
- Competing for securing employment opportunities by availing themselves of benefits under the various developmental programmes of the Governments;
- Insisting on covergence of governmental resources and delivery of services in identified habitations of the Scheduled Castes and the Scheduled Tribes;
- Insisting on and participating in monitoring mechanisms to prevent leakage of governmental resources deployed for benefits to the Scheduled Castes and the Scheduled Tribes;
- Securing the future of the children by pro-active, non-participation in child labour practices; and through all these means getting access to power as political and governmental decision makers.

6

THE DALIT MOVEMENT : NOTES ON ITS PERSPECTIVE AND SUGGESTIONS FOR A PROGRAMME (Keynote Address)

Sibnarayan Ray

As I see it, the struggle of the Dalits in this country is part of a global movement which, if successful, promises to bring about what may prove to be the greatest socio-cultural revolution in the history of human civilization. It has been fashionable for some time among intellectuals in the West to talk about "the end of history". In actuality, history, at the end of this century, is entering a new and most momentous phase. Since the beginning of civilization about four or five thousand years ago, every organized society, based on division of labour, has been dominated by a succession of privileged minorities. They have invariably appropriated to themselves the lion's share of the benefits of civilization and deprived the overwhelming majorities of their rightful dues while making the latter do all the hard work and serve those in control of affairs. They have also systematically brainwashed the latter with the help of religions, myths, legends, *nitishastras,* rituals, and other cunning devises into accepting the legitimacy and immutability of this fundamentally unjust structuring of societies and distribution of wealth and benefits. This is as true of the ancient Egyptian, Chinese, Indian or Greco-Roman civilizations as of those which followed them in the Middle Ages, or those which still continue to dominate our so-called modern states.

For obvious reasons, our discussions here are to be primarily focused on the contemporary Indian context. Nevertheless, I think it will be a deadly error if we do not also keep in mind the global context and significance of the struggle in India. Over a century ago Mahatma Jyotirao Phule dedicated his historic work *Gulamgiri* to the fighters for the emancipation of the Negroes in America. He was already aware of the suppressed social forces in different countries of the world which were then just beginning to stir, but which promised to alter the course of history once they gained momentum. With the advantage of our hindsight we may say that the first clear and vigorous secular challenge to the elitistic and hierarchical notion of civilization came from the famous Declarations of the Rights of Man in the last quarter of the eighteenth century in America and France. The very notion of human rights as opposed to privileges is revolutionary in its far-reaching implication. Rights imply absolute equality in the eye of law, irrespective of religious, ethnic, sexual, politico-economic, or linguistic-cultural differences. It means that every human being is entitled to meet certain fundamental and universal needs, and the legitimacy of a social order rests on its recognition and protection of these natural rights. However, it has taken nearly two centuries for the Human Rights movement to find articulation on a global scale. Properly strengthened and developed, it will transform these Declarations into the true and reliable foundations of a new universal civilization in the next century.

A proper perspective for the emerging phase in human history is provided, I think, if we recognize that the denotation of the term Dalit is not limited only to the Scheduled Castes and Scheduled Tribes of India but in fact embraces what the term connotes, namely, the oppressed, or in the words of Frantz Fanon, "The Wretched of the earth". It includes within its fold everyone who is denied or deprived of his or her natural rights as a human being, whose dignity or self-respect is mauled and systematically violated, who is exploited and reduced to an instrument for serving the interest of the exploiters. The vast majority of women and men, even in the contemporary world, continue to be Dalits—suffering from poverty, disease, illiteracy, unemployment and under-employment, lack of housing and social security, and gross social injustice. The situation of the Dalits in India is part of this universal situation which is altogether unacceptable and must be radically changed.

At the same time, it is important to note that man makes history, that otherwise we would not have moved from the primitive phase of cave dwellers, hunters and nomads through many inventions, revolutions and socio-cultural transformations to our present day civilization. This process of the continuous remaking of ourselves and of history has been greatly accelerated in our age. Old and powerful empires have crumbled in our own lifetime. The end of the cold war has opened new possibilities and raised great expectations. Wars and revolutions in our century have been more frequent and on bigger scales than ever before. The struggles of the colonial peoples against the imperialists, of the blacks for equal right with the whites, of women for complete and unambiguous establishment of equal rights of the sexes in every sphere of life—all these are, like the Dalit movement in India, part of a great contemporary global movement towards the emergence of a new and superior civilization.

In India, the Dalits have had a few factors in their favour, but the obstacles and constraints against them have been, and continue to be, fearfully strong and pertinacious. The convulsions and catastrophes which preceded and accompanied partition and independence were followed by efforts to rebuild India, and it was fortunate that there were enlightened leaders at that time who succeeded in providing the new sovereign state with a secular democratic constitution which clearly committed itself to the principle of fundamental human rights. This meant, prima facie, that the traditional structuring of Indian society in which the principle of human rights had no place, and the ideology of *homo hierarchicus* and surmountable inequality from birth which gave it legitimacy, were rejected ; and they were replaced by commitment to the modern and revolutionary principles of liberty, equality and fraternity. Universal adult franchise was introduced for the first time in this country ; untouchability was abolished and its practice made punishable by law ; special protections and safeguards were provided for the Scheduled Castes and Scheduled Tribes who had suffered most under the traditional order. Nehru and Ambedkar were the two most outstanding leaders who contributed decisively to this fortunate development.

But although since independence several progressive laws have been enacted and steps taken to reduce the disabilities and promote the development of the Dalits in India, the actual experience of the last five decades have only helped to highlight the inadequacy of these measures and to expose the precarious situation of the Dalits. Laws in support of fundamental human rights are without question very important, but it is also clear that they are not, by themselves, sufficient to ensure enjoyment of these rights, or to establish a just, egalitarian and free society. Revolutionary transformations are needed in the minds of the people—in their attitudes, beliefs and behaviour—and these are rarely brought about by mere legislation. Two other essential elements required for effecting such a transformation seem to me to be education and organization. The Dalits have to organize themselves from the grass roots upwards to be effective in changing the structure of society and in overthrowing the hegemony of its hierarchic-elitistic culture. For this purpose, apart from everything else, a radical programme of education is indispensable.

The programme, as I see it both as a social thinker and as an educationist of half a century's personal experience, would have to be addressed to at least three objectives, which though very intimately related, nevertheless require to be spelled out separately. First, education for leadership from among the Dalits. This involves devising special courses which will impart to young Dalits adequate knowledge of the real situation in which they are placed, of the rights to which the Dalits are entitled under existing law and the lacunae which require to be removed, certain essential intellectual disciplines and skills necessary to deal with the complex problem of modern life, and principles of organization, cooperation and mobilization which would be necessary for building and strengthening the movement. Suitable course material will have to be prepared, competent writers and teachers to be found, dedicated young pupils to be selected and provided for. Courses of specified duration may be given through workshops, camps, intensive seminars, and other formal and informal ways of living and learning together. Secondly, compulsory education of all Dalits in their rights and circumstances, in the history of the long human struggle against social injustice, and towards developing their creative potentialities, critical faculty, spirit of enterprise and voluntary cooperation, and determination never to submit to injustice and degradation. Without this education no grass roots democracy will strike roots in this authority-ridden country nor will the Dalits succeed in restructuring society on egalitarian foundations.

Thirdly, the children of the traditional and contemporary elite groups also urgently require to be radically reeducated. History teaches us that radical transformation of an established social system with its entrenched culture and tradition may be brought about in more than one way. The more dramatic method is what is commonly called a "revolution" which involves the violent overthrow of the existing order by those who suffer most from its existence and operation. This option, illustrated by the French and Russian revolutions, may in certain situations prove unavoidable, but in terms of human suffering and wastage it is very costly. It also involves the terrible risk of replacing one oppressive regime by another which may prove to be even more tyrannical and unjust. However, this is not the only way. Great changes do take place relatively peacefully if those demanding such changes are fairly well organized and intellectually and morally equipped, and the people occupying positions of power and privilege prove to be perceptive and flexible enough to recognize the rightfulness of the new demands and cooperate in hastening those changes. This alternative, however, requires reeducating the elite groups so that they may be freed from their narrow outlook and learn to place the interest and welfare of the community above their own special privileges.

Here the Indian situation is somewhat paradoxical. On the one hand, the Constitution and not a few pieces of legislation which have followed it, bear witness to the enlightened outlook of a section of the Indian elite. On the other, there is also piling evidence of the unscrupulous use of violence and terror by the traditionally entrenched elite groups against the Dalits and dispossessed whenever the latter try even peacefully or on a small scale to resist injustice and oppression. Unless we are fatalistically reconciled to a perspective of civil war and violent upheavals, we have to make every effort to create an atmosphere where the elite groups would recognize the wrongness of their attitudes and behaviour, and seek to mend themselves. Here too I see the crucial importance of a radically new programme of general education, made compulsory and universal, which would imbue the children of the privileged classes with the ideals of liberty, equality and fraternity and make them conscientiously reject the unjust and immoral socio-cultural system which they have inherited from their elders. Our present educational system and courses are altogether unsuited to the above objectives.

What is suggested in these notes is no more than a sketch, and the perspective and proposals require to be carefully considered and their detailed implications have to be spelled out. I hope the workshop will help all of us to reach a better understanding of what steps are required to be taken, and produce proposals that may be taken up for implementation.

7

HUMAN RIGHTS AND THE DALITS

Gopal Guru

It is beyond dispute that the issue of human rights is of profound historical importance in the human endeavour of reconstructing society on egalitarian principles. However, among scholars and intellectual human rights activists, there does not seem to be any agreement on the definition and the scope of human rights. First, the disagreement on the definition and scope of human right is broadly located into the dichotomy between the universal and the specific.[1] Second, it is also located in the difference between societal violence and civilizational violence.[2] And finally, an attempt is being made by scholars to a creative interpretation which seeks to define in terms of "right to be human"[3] rather than human rights ; and a majority of the scholars seek to define human rights basically in terms of their violation by society on the one hand and the state on the other.[4]

This varied perception of human rights provides the context in which one can pose four questions particularly with special reference to the human rights of Dalits in the country. First, in the dichotomy between the universal and the specific where can one situate the issue of Dalit human rights ; second, does the Dalit discourse, if any, remain fettered within their specificity or does it come out of this specificity to be seen in terms of its universal applicability ; third, how does the Dalit discourse on human rights regard the framework of civilizational violence as more fundamental than societal violence? And finally, is the state-centered, legally-oriented framework of human rights adequate to understand the question of the violation of Dalit human rights? These are some of the issues that require serious follow-up.

In recent years there have been attempts to define human rights without reducing them either to an abstract universality or to the romanticisation of specificity. For example, a scholar and human rights activist like Nandita Haksar defines human rights as the expression of cultural politics based on the multiplicity of life.[5] Haksar, therefore, seeks to expand the scope of human rights, to include in human rights, right against illicit dumping of toxic and dangerous substances, right against external debt, the right to cultural values, the right of indigenous people to their own way of life and the right of disabled people.[6] However, Haksar rightly sounds a note of caution against politics which fall into the trap of romanticising the marginals; on the contrary, as she further says, one should deepen cultural politics that should be linked to a wider vision.[7]

D.R. Nagraj is one of the leading intellectuals making major theoretical intervention on Bahujan issues. Well-known creative writer, academic and human rights intellectual-activist, Dr. D.R. Nagraj died on 12 August 1998 at a very young age. He had attended the Madras workshop. However, he laments that dalit discourse is creating a sort of cultural vacuum. What he means by this vacuum is that dalit discourse, while focusing on human rights, does not address itself to the question of civilizational violence through which communities are being wiped out by the process of modernisation.[8] Therefore, he concludes, it is not enough to focus merely on societal violence but should keep civilizational violence in view. However, Nagraj's communitarian approach seems to be problematic when it is understood in terms of human rights because, how can one restore the community based occupation which by its very nature involves the violation of human rights, as they result in destroying the human dignity of a community, for example, scavenging. Secondly, the communitarian approach presupposes that the communities exist side by side harmoniously without any tension. This is not a tenable proposition, because the communities are historicity constituted through the constant struggle for and against domination. And it is this historicity that has always condemned the Dalits to seek the protection for human rights. Thus, the protection of community rights from the onslaught of modernity would not automatically ensure human rights to the Dalits. In view of the limitation of this communication approach one will have to take assistance either from Nandita Haksar or from Upendra Baxi who defines human rights in terms of right to be human. Both these scholars have discussed the human rights of the Dalits in India, though not in great detail. I am making an attempt to understand the human rights particularly of the Dalits in the light of the framework as developed by these scholars. However, it may not be a mechanical confirmation of the themes developed by Haksar and Baxi ; on the contrary it will be a critical reflection on the writings of the eminent scholars.

Nandita Haksar's framework is attractive because it offers a critique of the state which violates human rights and also offers a certain kind of visibility to the human rights of the Dalits which otherwise face the danger of being neglected or subsumed under the grand framework of either extreme culturalism and universalism, or economic reductionalism. This paper thus would like to understand the question of Dalit human rights in a different perspective which is influenced by the needs to understand it in terms of empirical, theoretical and ontological concerns.

First, it is important to take up the empirical dimension of human rights, particularly of the Dalits, as it is important to understand the intensity and the magnitude of their violation. It has been rightly argued by Haksar and many others that it is the state and the upper castes who are primarily responsible for the violation through unleashing violence on the Dalits. Thus, the right to the limb is constantly violated by the State and the upper castes. The violence by the upper castes becomes much more brutal particularly against the Dalits. This is evident from the killings of the Kotwal family in Latur district of the Marathwada region of Maharashtra. In this incident an upper caste mob spurred on by enraged caste feelings, broke open the door of a Dalit household and attacked two young sons and their father with deadly weapons killing all the three, then they dragged the bodies of the victims as decomposed bodies of dogs or cats are dragged out of the village. The frequent mass killings of Dalits by the Ranbir Sena of landlords in Bihar, the gorging out of the eyes of Gawai brothers in Akola district in Maharashtra and the violence on a Dahanam Dalit school girl in Tamil Nadu, are also examples of brutal violation of the Dalit right to life and limb.

The violation of Dalit human rights has another heinous dimension which involves the sexual exploitation of and sexual violence against Dalit women. Such violence ranges from putting a live lizard in the saris of the Dalit women in Osmanabad district in Maharashtra to the gang rape of Bhanwari Devi in Rajasthan. Even a cursory look at the SC/ST Commissioner's report or the Proceedings of People's courts, organised by certain action groups in Delhi and Bangalore or the investigative reports published in the *PUCL Bulletin* edited by Dr. R.M. Pal, one will come across innumerable cases of sexual violence perpetrated by high caste Hindus and the police.

However, it looks as though it is the male sexual urge and brutality which are behind such incidents involving the violation of the social honour of Dalit women, thus making the only dimension of the violation of the rights of Dalit women. What is lacking in such academic discourses or even in the perception of human rights activists, is that the sexual violence against Dalit women and also women from the minority community, have more than a gender bias. Because along with men high caste women also are found, in certain cases, to be responsible for destroying the social honour of Dalit women. This was evident when high-caste women in order to exonerate their men folk took to maligning the image of the victims by charging them with loose morals. Incidents like the killing of the Kotwals in Marathwada and the stripping and beating of Dalit women in some villages in Mul and Brahmpuri talukas of Chandrapur district in Maharashtra[9] and vicarious voyeurism by the high caste women of sexual violence by their manfolk on Dalit and other women confirm this fact.

One can look at this absence of feminie conscience as a reflection of the internalisation of patriarchal violence among upper caste women. This poses a serious question to feminist discourse and the feminist movement in the country.

Such violence should not be defined only in terms of its physical or sexual aspect but has to be understood in terms of its implications for intimidation of marginalised groups like the Dalits. Dalit people feel intimidated from speaking out in the presence of the high caste people who control public institutions and public assemblies. It is also true that the Dalit women feel as intimidated in the presence of men of their own communities as in the company of educated high caste women.

Thus, freedom of expression which is at the core of human rights is denied to the Dalits both by the state and the non-Dalit reactionary Hindus. This violation signifies the individualistic dimension of human rights. But what is needed is to include in the definition of human rights, not only the individual right to expression but the Dalit right to speak for the non-Dalits or right to take a normative lead even for non-Dalits. The need to broaden the definition through the inclusion of the Dalit right to acquire space in public discourse has become imperative specially after the Bhanwari Devi incident in Rajasthan. This case certainly involves the violation of the right to life but also the right to human dignity. In addition her gang rape also reflects the violation of the Dalit right to move away from the immediate to the abstract and acquire the public space.

In the feudal social order, the obstructionist Hindu Laws have arbitrarily determined the social location of people in a kind of tight caste hierarchy. In Marathi, for example, it came to be described as *apilya payrine waga* (meaning your boundaries are religiously fixed and you must respect the boundaries). This confinement of the social location of the oppressed has led to the total marginalisation of the Dalits and left them absolutely "dumb". The suppression of subjectivity ultimately not only facilitates the oppression but also leads to the higher castes assuming the right to undertake reforms on behalf of the marginalised sections. Thus the right to speak for all sections of society presupposes the supremacy of the high castes leading to Brahmanical ego fed on the strict maintenance of the social boundaries by the Dalits. Bhanwari Devi showed extraordinary courage in challenging the arbitrary boundaries by intervening into the high caste dominated discourse on patriarchy. She opposed child marriages among the high caste families. It hurt the ego of the high caste people and she had to pay the price for crossing the caste boundaries. The Bhanwari Devi case indicates the violation of human rights of the Dalits by denial to them space in public discourse. Thus, Dalits rights need to be understood not in individualist but collectivist terms.

The collectivist idea can be substantiated when one tries to understand the collective implication of the individual act of violation of human rights of the Dalits. In other words, human rights are denied to Dalits because of their group character ; Dalits receive discriminatory treatment because of the group character. To put it more bluntly, resistance of violation by a single Dalit person endangers the life and limb of the entire community. It is for this reason only that Dr. Ambedkar did not embark on any individual adventure and had to withdraw apropos of the Poona Pact involving Gandhiji, for otherwise, the entire Dalit community would have been engaged in the upper caste outrage of the 1930s. This "package deal violence" sparked by an individual act of crossing the traditional boundaries had led to mass violence against the Dalits of a village in Tumkar district of Karnataka in June, 1996. Similarly the Dalits of a village in Ambejogai taluka of Bhir district of Marathwada were terrorised and made to flee the village by non-Dalits.[10] Thus, the violation of rights acquires group character in as much as violence against individual gets compounded affecting the entire Dalit community. Thus the magnitude of the violation of rights particularly in caste ridden or ethnically divided societies begins with the violence unleashed against individuals but invariably leads to violence against the community.

The violation of Dalit human rights through violence against the Dalit community flows from the fascist ideology of the Hindutva forces and its political apparatus. Thus fascist ideology is also linked to the ideology and practice of untouchability which is technically the violation of the human dignity of the Dalits and was abolished by the Constitution fifty years ago. The fascist ideology of untouchability is based on a specious concept of "purity pollution line" and practises discrimination against the Dalit. Even at the risk of inviting the wrath of environmentalists, one must cite illustrations relating to 'man animal' comparison to indicate how the human dignity of the Dalits is violated by the Hindutva elements, and the State. Some animals are considered by this section of society to be secured while the "untouchables" are identified as sources of pollution. Dr. Ambedkar had said that the Black people or Afro-Americans in the U.S. are slightly better than the Indian Untouchables because the White people of America do not regard them as sources of pollution by touch. Even in the days before the abolition of slavery they were not kept beyond reach. On the other hand, when the Dalits of a village in the Chikkodi taluka of Belgaum district of Karnataka were forced by high caste Hindus to eat human excreta in 1992 they were regarded as sub-human.[11] In Maharashtra the government led by the Shiv Sena and BJP practises discrimination by prescribing school uniforms of different kinds for Dalits and the others. Khaki shorts and shirts constitute the uniform for non-Dalit pupils in the Zila Parishad schools in the State while Dalit pupils have to wear blue shirts and shorts. The identification by the colour of the dress of the Dalits is on account of historical association of blue with the Dalits. In the process the government is encouraging the high-caste Hindus to commit atrocities on the Dalits. The government has also withdrawn police cases against high caste Hindus under the 1989 Dalit Act (Prevention of Atrocities Against SCs Act). The reports of the Commissioner for SC/STs have listed several instances of treating the Dalits as pollutants by the high caste Hindus in different states of the country. The recent report by Harsh Mander'[12] is supportive of the SC/ST Commissioner's reports in this respect.

The role of the state in protecting human dignity of the Dalits seems to be very unsatisfactory in the sense that it has not been able to stop the practice of scavengers carrying night soil on their heads. Though these Dalits are enumerated as "mehtar" instead of "Bhangi" in the government records, they are treated by the Hindu society as filthy, polluting creatures. The stand of some of the so called voluntary organisations of environmentalist activists in opposing the government's efforts to mechanise the sanitary services is conducive to the continuance of the barbaric practice. It is quite possible that the government may have a vested interest in eliminating the practice by the use of wood pulp but the activists should not be insensitive to the human rights aspect by seeking the perpetuation of physical carrying of night soil by the scavengers. If they have an objection to the government's proposal they should suggest alternatives to it. Similarly, rag picking is considered environment friendly. It is done mostly by Dalit women who according to these activists do not consider rag picking as below human dignity.

Rag picking brings the human being into identification with dogs and pigs which feed on the garbage just as the rag pickers make their living out of the garbage. At the same time, the police and many householders consider the rag pickers as potential petty thieves so that there are instances of abuse and physical attacks on rag-picking Dalit women. Finally, the endorsement of rag picking by the upper caste perception is based on exteriority. The elitist and superficial perception of rag picking divides feminist consciousness. It becomes superficial, at times, a reactionary agenda for the simple reason that instead of criticising the economic system which forces a large section of society to make a living on garbage, it tends to legitimise the economic system by treating garbage or rag picking as environment friendly.

Thus, this kind of partial and sometimes negative view of human rights which treats rag picking as an attribute of the welfare liberal state makes us take a radical view of human rights, the post-modernist-statist view which is partial makes it imperative for scholars and human rights activists to develop a radical and integrated view of human rights. According to this view, along with the fulfilment of the non-material needs of the Dalits, like protecting the human dignity and promoting social fraternity the satisfaction of material needs also becomes a precondition for restoring the right to be human. For example, certain trades like tanning and sanitation carry the stigma of pollution to the practitioners, mostly Dalits. Or to put it slightly differently, as Harsh Manlar has noted, the dividing line between pollution and poverty is very thin, meaning those who are socially polluting are also necessarily steeped in poverty. Thus, the Dalit perspective would seek societal resources for concretising the right to be human. The right to be human should also enable the person to satisfy his or her most basic wants like food, shelter and clothing.

The Dalit perspective on the right to be human does not take a voluntaristic view that human rights are bestowed for all people to enjoy. On the contrary, it assumes that the right to be human, is not state constituted but is historically constituted through the constant struggle for "Manuski" (human treatment) led by Phule, Periyar, Ambedkar and many others. The right to be human, therefore, is not the result of charity of the mahatmas or the high caste pandits or an ad hoc approach to human rights of the liberal state, but is the outcome of Dalit struggle for parity. The parity principle within the Dalit perspective has to be organised around dignified conditions of human existence. In this context, the Dalit perspective on human rights is different.

Haksar's framework of human rights looks to be attractive because it offers a critique of the state which violates Dalit rights and also offer visibility to human rights, which, otherwise are quite often either neglected or are subsumed in the framework of an abstract universalism, extreme culturalism or economic reductionism.

The Dalit perspective is distinct because of its group character as against the legalistic, individualistic approach of the state towards the human rights of Dalits and other marginalised sections of society. Protecting a single individual does not necessarily and effectively make the entire Dalit community automatically secure. On the contrary as it happened in case of the 1989 Act recourse to the law by affected Dalit individuals against the higher castes in Marathwada region engulfed the entire Dalit community of the region in a widespread caste outrage after the decision to rename Marathwada University after Ambedkar in 1993. Similarly, the case of Bhanwari Devi in Rajasthan shows the limitations of the individualistic approach as it does not capture the deep structures of violation of human rights of the Dalit. The case of Bhanwari Devi at the surface level no doubt represents the violation of the right to expression of an individual. But what it does not really capture is that Bhanwari Devi's exercise of right to speak against child marriage leads to terrorisation of the entire community which would not dare to speak for others and would not dare to acquire the public space. Thus, the case of Bhanwari Devi suggests that the definition of human rights in the Indian context needs to be expanded to include in its gamut not only individual rights but the right of the community to move from the immediate to the abstract.

In other words, the Dalit perspective does not ignore specificity but at the same time has the potential to move towards universality. [*This is a revised version of the paper which Professor Guru presented at the Workshop.*]

REFERENCES

1. Haksar, Nandita, "Human Rights and International Solidarity", *Man and Development*, Vol. XVII, No. 3, 1995, pp. 10-20.
2. D.R. Nagraj made this point in his oral presentation in the national workshop on HR, jointly organised by the NHRC and the Dalit Liberation Educational Trust, Madras, at Madras on 3rd and 4th August, 1996. (The present workshop)
3. Baxi, Upendra, "Emancipation as Justice" in ed. Baxi and Parekh, *Crisis and Change in Contemporary India*, Delhi, Sage, 1995, p. 144.
4. This was the view that was predominantly expressed by the members of the NHRC in the workshop as mentioned above.
5. *Op. cit.* Haksar, p. 17.
6. *Ibid.*
7. *Ibid.*
8. *Op. cit.* Nagraj.
9. Report on the Mahila Dharmandhate Vorodhi Parishad (Marathi) 1987.
10. An interview with one of the victims of this village and the news was also covered by the local newspapers in the first week of July.
11. Mane, D.A., "Dalit Movement in Karnataka", in VAK ed. *Dalit Movement at the Crossroad*, VAK Publication, 1995.
12. Report by Harsh Manlar in *Asian Age*, Bombay.

8

CONSTRUCTING A CONCEPT OF DALIT-BAHUJANS AND HUMAN RIGHTS

Kancha Ilaiah

Not many Indian intellectuals have conducted a discourse on caste and human rights. The institution of caste blindfolded us so much that the very notion of civil and human rights was unimportant for nationalist intellectuals and leaders. There were two obvious reasons for avoiding attention to human rights during the freedom struggle: (1) that it would open a pandora's box of caste inequalities, (2) that it would expose how human beings treated other human beings as worse than animals.

In post-independent India because of movements and struggles led by Ambedkar and Periyar, Dalit bahujan intellectuals began to focus on Dalit bahujan human rights. In the post-emergency period, though many civil rights organisations emerged and some of them focused attention on exposing atrocities on the SCs, they did not conceptualise caste and human rights. The notion of atrocity on Dalit bahujans expressed itself by focusing attention on physical assaults like rape and murder, on the vulnerable sections of society and the human rights discourse treated it as violation of human rights. But the discourse should go beyond these parameters and dwell on caste and human rights.

Does not the very existence of caste, which raised the pernicious practice of untouchability to a principle by considering physical contact with the Dalits to be sinful or socially wrong, become a question of human rights? The right to be touched or the right to touch other individuals while moving or operating in the civil society, is very much a human right. The free play implicit in it is that human rights alone makes a 'civil' society 'civil'. The functioning of democratic institutions presupposes a free movement of human beings in the civil society. Secondly, a democratic civil society should ensure co-eating, co-existing and co-movement of human beings subject to observance of the laws against stealing and fraudulent acquisition of property. A civil society may punish a person who steals somebody's food or property but no civil society punishes a person for touching another person or his/her food in day-to-day activities. But the caste system does this invoking state structures. The caste system cuts *Kancham Pothu, Mancham Pothu, Vruthi Pothu* (food relationship, marriage relationship and occupation relationship in Telugu). These relationships in an advanced civil society cannot be determined by external factors like caste. It involves the human rights of the hierarchised castes because one caste constantly keeps violating the human rights of the other castes below it. In the process the notion of untouchability came into operation as a logical result. The idea of untouchability, both in theory and practice, mutilates the growth of human personality of more than twenty per cent of the people, namely, the SCs.

The concept of human rights should intervene to remove the basic hurdles in the process of human development of all people. In a rudimentary form Christianity and Islam introduced the notion of all-pervasive human rights into their societies way back in history. But the Brahmanical religion, on the contrary, did not allow the very notion of human rights to come into its orbit. It believed that except its own self no other social sections should have any rights, whatsoever. As a result of such a notion of Brahmanism the state institutions basically remained of *danda* wielders and the civil society produced gods who resolved human conflict only through violence. Even today the popular images of many Hindu gods appear in aggressive modes and not in benign human form. The notions of some being Devatas (deities) and others being Rakshasas as (demons) present a picture of dehumanisation and degradation of all producing castes of India. In fact, the Brahmanical language constantly reproduces the consciousness of violation of human rights of the Dalit Bahujans. The human rights movement, therefore, should grapple with these questions.

However, the first major effort of the human rights movement should be abolition of untouchability in this country, while carrying on a general campaign against the caste system itself. As long as untouchability exists, no civilised country can claim that human rights are safeguarded in that country. So far, the NHRC has been focusing only on the violation of human rights by the state agencies as against individuals. The widespread civil-societal violation of human rights centering on the caste system has yet to be addressed. It is now time for the NHRC to launch a massive campaign against untouchability. The government has been carrying on a massive campaign against polio to reach the message to the entire child population of the country. A similar campaign against untouchability is necessary, and it does not involve much money. Such a campaign in every nook and cranny of the country—urban and rural—will force the Indian society to re-examine the notion of the caste system and more particularly untouchability.

The second campaign should be on abolition of the practice of not sharing food with the SCs both in rural and urban areas. This pernicious practice is particularly widespread in rural India. Even today there are restaurants with separate tumblers and cups for Scheduled Caste users. In community functions in the village the SCs are not allowed to dine with the rest of the villagers. The so-called upper castes are debarred from the social and the familial functions organised by the SCs nor would they invite the SCs for their social gatherings. Educated Scheduled Caste persons in the villages are naturally put off by such a social environment. When they strive for a better human environment the casteist upper castes react violently resulting, in many cases, in violence against the protestors. Human rights organisations respond only at that stage and talk about violation of human rights of the Dalits. The NHRC should concentrate, at least from now on, on the cause rather than on the effect.

The third issue which is causing tension on the human rights front between the practitioners of the Brahmanical religion and the Dalit Bahujans is intercaste marriage. Irrespective of rural and urban differentiation, Dalit Bahujans marrying upper caste boys and girls leads to attacks on the Dalit Bahujans only. There are cases of 'public hanging of Dalit boys or girls and their parents' responsible for such marriages. There have also been cases of "public burning to death" of such brides and grooms. One does not come across such brutal killings for marrying persons from particular sections of the community in the human rights history of western countries. Inter-marriages between even blacks and whites in the U.S. have not resulted in such brutalities. So the roots of brutal violation of human rights of brides and grooms and their parents for inter marriages with upper castes lie in the institution of caste. The NHRC, therefore, should undertake a massive programme in support of intercaste marriages both in the rural and urban areas. It must ask for the establishment of institutions to monitor cases of violence in intercaste marriages.

Another form of attack on the cultural rights of the SCs, STs and a section of OBCs, including their right to their food habits, has begun. The Bharatiya Janata Party (BJP), for example, in its recent election manifesto said that if voted to power it would impose a complete ban on beef eating in India. Such a stand of a national political party violates the food rights of a major section of Dalit Bahujan people in India. Food habits over a period of time generate particular modes of food economy. The food culture—habits and tastes—of a particular group of people should not be controlled or changed by another group of people whether they operate in the form of a political party or a governing authority. The food tastes and habits of people give them an inalienable right to maintain, nurture and develop such food resources without harming the interests of other groups of people. The proposition to ban beef eating in India will have larger implications for the SCs, STs and the OBCs. This was the point that Dr. G.G. Swell, the tribal leader from North-East made in Parliament. I examined the detailed implications of the BJP's proposal in my article "Beef, BJP and Food Rights of People" (*Economic and Political Weekly, 15 June, 1996*). In view of the serious implications of such an attempt of the BJP, the NHRC and this workshop must pay a serious attention to this issue. The NHRC can take up the issue with the political parties, the Election Commission and the Government of India.

Beef, BJP and Food Rights of People

The BJP in its election manifesto told the nation that if it is voted to power it would impose a "complete ban on the slaughter of cows, calves, bulls and bullocks". In other words, it told the nation that it would impose a total ban on beef food of the Indian people. Such a position of the BJP emanates from its self-constructed notion that beef is the food of Muslims and Christians only, and beef food culture is an imposition of Islamic-Christian culture on the Indian people. The BJP realised that it can no longer brow-beat the minorities by setting up agendas of demolition of religious shrines, as such agendas were becoming counter-productive. It seems to have worked out a new agenda in banning beef food to brow-beat the minorities. Incidentally, what is not realised is that this agenda will boomerang much more than the other agendas the BJP earlier set—because this agenda is going to affect the food rights of about 45-50 per cent of Indians who are either occasional or regular beef eaters. Even a commonsense observation would indicate that in India the non-Muslim, non-Christian beef eaters outnumber even in simple arithmetic terms. The anti-beef ideology of the BJP emerges from its Brahminical Hindutva consciousness. Blind to the ground-level social reality, the BJP leadership is creating a notional myth that beef-eating—by killing 'sacred' cows and bulls—is a non-Indian cultural practice. It wants to sell the idea that pre-Muslim India did not have a beef-eating cultural practice at all. The BJP ideologues earlier attempted to sell a similar theory for caste system also—that caste is post-Mughal rule social structure. But it did not work. Its anti-beef agenda is going to face resistance from SCs and STs because as on today the SCs, STs and some castes among OBCs depend on beef food more than the minorities do. Of course, the very notion of beef food being a Muslim-Christian contribution, is a myth because even the BJP top leaders know that in pre-Buddhist India beef was an integral food of all Indians, including Brahmins.

The BJP may take up a campaign by constructing a theory that banning of beef is part of its 'true secularist' ideology. Its notion of 'true secularism' foregrounds certain animals—cows and bulls—

as being sacred animals, glowing over the fact that the notion is not shared by very many Dalit Bahujan castes at all. Yet the BJP wants to project the notion as an all-India non-Muslim, non-Christian notion and thus, impose it on all castes which do not share the cultural ethos of Brahminism at all. SCs, STs and several OBCs have been historically beef-eaters, and never believed in the theory that the cow is a sacred animal. That does not mean that they do not care for their cattle. Brahminical consciousness makes us forget that the beef-eating castes are also the cattle-rearing castes, and their love and affection towards these animals is more intimate than those of the castes which do not involve themselves in rearing cattle and yet construct a theory of sacred bovine animals. Love towards animals and eating their meat for survival is not a contradiction but a dialectical process. The essence of this process has been that human life is more important than animal life. The culture of consuming the flesh of certain animals got gradually internalised. How come a political party that aspires to rule a multicultural country like India does not understand that food habits which are part of our cultural practice cannot be changed by state agencies. Unlike drinking alcohol or playing cards, which continue in spite of social taboos against it, food habits are different. When a family or a social group eats certain food like beef there is no notion of taboo around it. It exists as a full cultural process. It also acquires the character of socio-political rights of people—the food rights of people. A political party or a government cannot suspend the food rights of people simply because the leadership of a ruling party does not like the taste of a particular food, or because it considers some animals sacred.

Over the centuries, even before the Muslim rulers came to India, the beef-eating SC castes, other Sudra castes and the pure vegetarian Brahminical castes lived side by side. The Brahminical dislike of beef food did not extend to the state banning beef or meat foods. In an era of advanced capitalism and universalisation of democracy if a party sets an agenda that it would ban a particular food on religious grounds, such a move is going to send signals that fascism of the worst kind is on the cards. Leave alone Muslims and Christians, for millions of SCs beef alone is the most proteinous food that they can afford. Veena Shatrugna of National Institute of Nutrition says, "beef contains 21 per cent proteins whereas rice contains only 6-8 per cent proteins". No vegetable protein content goes beyond 10 per cent. This was one of the reasons why the poorest of the poor continued to eat beef in spite of the ritualistic Hindu society condemning it.

Medically, it is a known fact that consuming high protein food is the best check for chronic diseases like tuberculosis. Tuberculosis is the most common disease that attacks human beings who are under-nourished. Thus among the SCs and STs, the beef food was singularly responsible for preventing tuberculosis, and also where cases of tuberculosis prevailed, the cheaply available cure has only been beef. What alternative does the BJP provide to such a proteinous food that is easily available to the poorest of the poor, who in caste terms happen to be SCs and STs?

Neither the BJP nor the intellectuals who hold the view that draught animals are sacred, seem to have realised the implications of their argument. Such a view, if extended to its logical end, can lead to a disaster. If they extend their argument that the cows and bulls should not be forced to pull the plough or bullock cart—as there is bound to be coercion and torture in the process—Indian agriculture will collapse. The post-Buddhist Brahminism went to the extent that "the plough with its iron point would injure the earth and the creatures living in it"; therefore, human beings should not resort to tilling (Irfan Habib, *Essays in Indian History*, 1995). Should we then stop using bulls in agrarian operations? Some members of the Sangh Parivar have gone to the extent of saying "that India should import the mad cows of Britain" in order to save them from slaughter in Britain. India has so many beggars, lepers and destitutes living on the pavements. The Sangh Parivar have never bothered about them, but are bothered about the mad cows getting slaughtered in Britain. Is it patriotism and humanism?

The food rights of people form part of their civil and democratic rights. No religious community can ban the food of another religious community until and unless a particular community turns cannibal. So also no caste can ban the food of another caste. The discourse that vegetarian food is morally superior has no validity for those who are historically habituated to eat meat and beef. Among many castes and communities in India, for example, a festival cannot be imagined without meat. Vegetarian food in such communities is treated as inferior food. If a guest is served with vegetarian food, it is considered a humiliation. Among many castes and communities there are jokes that ridicule vegetarianism. Indian society has been co-existing with all these practices and must be allowed to do so.

On the one hand, the BJP is trying to define SCs, BCs as Hindus; on the other, their food habits are not treated as part of Hindu ethos. It expects the SCs to give up their culture, get brahmanised by converting themselves into vegetarian Hindus. In spite of massive propaganda against meat by priests and pandits, the Dalit bahujan castes continue to eat meat. What does the BJP aim to do? Will it label all beef-eaters as non-Hindus? In which case, what about lamb meat-eaters or chicken-eaters? If it says that all meat, chicken, and beef-eaters are not Hindus, many Brahmins by that definition are also out of Hinduism—because the Brahmins who go abroad cannot escape beef, and we know many Brahmins who are addicted beef-eaters.

If beef is banned in India that will be the beginning of the end of our multi culturalism. Cultural plurality has been the essence of Indian society. Cultural plurality has not emerged with the Muslim invasion nor did it emerge with Christian colonisers. The very caste system synthesised multi culturality in India right from ancient days. The attempt to homogenise India's cultural and legal practices is a dangerous trend.

The notion of a Uniform Civil Code (UCC) is also based on homogenisation of marriage, divorce and other family related practices. Even here, the diversity is not confined to the Hindu, Muslim and Christian practices. Each caste has its own customary practice of marriage, divorce and property distribution. Homogenisation of such practices by hegemonising a particular religious or caste practice will only lead to social friction.

The BJP seems to think that including such cultural issues in its election manifesto will give it a moral authority to take legal steps by projecting the election victory as a referendum on such issues. Previous elections have shown that even with 31-35 per cent votes a party can come to power. On an issue like beef- eating, even if all the beef-eaters vote against the BJP, the BJP can come to power. How can such a mandate give moral authority to the BJP to ban beef? Even on an issue like the UCC, the same thing can happen.

The issues which counterpose one section of people against another, would find both supporters and opponents emotionally charged. It only generates a war of nerves and that may become an instrument for aggrandising votes but does not provide democratic space for articulating informed opinion. Such issues are not like economic issues. Economic issues allow a space of debate even in rural areas. If a party offers land to the landless, house to the homeless, education to the illiterate, there is a possibility of forcing even the rich to think about such issues. In other words, even if a confrontation develops among sections of people on such issues, the confrontation will contribute towards a positive transformation. How does stopping a section of people from eating what they have been eating for generations help the economic situation to improve?

Culture is a historical continuum of psychic likes and dislikes. Food habits form part of that cultural continuum. Political parties cannot set agendas attacking cultural habits of people. That itself forms the core of communalism. The BJP today says it would impose a ban on beef, tomorrow it may say that it would ban meat; then it would extend the logic and say that wearing trousers is anti-Hindu and impose a ban on trousers and bush-shirts. What does this mean? Where does India go from here? How can a nation progress with such agendas?

9

DEVELOPMENT POLICY AND SOCIAL CHANGE WITH REFERENCE TO SCHEDULED CASTES

G. Nancharaiah

The major disability of Scheduled Castes is poverty which they share with the disadvantaged sections of other castes. But their special disability, untouchability, perpetuates their poverty. Untouchability which was the by-product of caste system was not only a form of social discrimination but also a source of economic exploitation. Untouchables for centuries were not allowed to enter the villages during daytime or to use the public utilities such as roads, wells, tanks, etc. They were made to live on the outskirts of the villages and physically segregated from the mainstream of life. They were assigned occupations which were unclean and filthy and they were forced to remain in the same occupations.[1] They were discriminated in the product market and in the factor market on the ground of untouchability.[2]

The untouchables were denied the right to education. They were denied the right of owning land and wearing jewellery. They were also denied the right to bargain for a decent wage and they were obliged to accept whatever was paid to them. They had to perform a number of duties in the villages without any remuneration. Dr. Ambedkar observed that untouchability was more than a religious system. It was also an economic system worse than slavery. In slavery, the master at any rate had the responsibility to feed, clothe and house the slave and keep him in good condition.

Otherwise, the market rate of the slave would decline. But under untouchability, the maintenance of the untouchable was the responsibility of nobody. Untouchability is a system of unmitigated economic exploitation.[3] And there is enough evidence that it is rampant in rural India.[4]

The Scheduled Castes people are predominantly agricultural labourers and most of them are landless. They tie themselves to the landowners by a variety of complex relationships to ensure their survival. This relationship is reflected in terms of a much larger number of Scheduled Caste agricultural labourers employed as cowboys, permanent farm servants and attached labourers.[5]

In 1971, the Scheduled Castes constituted 14.83 per cent of the all India population. In Andhra Pradesh, they were 13.37 per cent. According to the 1981 Census the Scheduled Castes constitued 15.75 per cent of the all India population—17.34 per cent rural and 10.63 per cent urban population. Of the total Scheduled Castes population, 84 per cent lived in rural and 16 per cent in urban areas. In Andhra Pradesh the Scheduled Castes constituted 14.8 per cent of the total population, viz., 16.44 per cent of rural and 9.68 per cent of urban population. Of the total Scheduled Castes population 84 per cent lived in rural and 15.19 per cent in urban areas.[6] As per 1991 Census out of total population 74.27 per cent live in rural and 25.73 per cent live in urban areas at all India level while in case of the Scheduled Castes, 81.28 per cent of Scheduled Caste population live in rural areas and 19.72 per cent live in urban areas.[7]

In 1981, the Scheduled Castes constituted 15.75 per cent of the total population at the all India level, while it is 14.87 per cent in Andhra Pradesh. The percentage of SCs increased to 16.48 per cent in 1991 at all India level while it increased to 15.93 per cent in Andhra Pradesh. It is also to be noted that SC cultivators constitute 27.87 per cent of total SC main workers in 1991 while agricultural labourers constitute about 50 per cent. In 1991, in Andhra Pradesh, SC cultivators constituted 12.77 per cent of SC main workers while SC agricultural labourers constituted 72 per cent. Thus, 78 per cent of SC main workers depend on agriculture all over the country while 84 per cent of SC workers depend on agriculture in Andhra Pradesh and most of them as agricultural labourers.[8]

Table 1. All India Occupational Distribution

Category	*1981*	*1991*	*1981*	*1991*
	Percentage in total main workers of Scheduled Castes		*Percentage in total main workers of General population*	
Cultivators	28.17	25.44	41.58	38.75
Agricultural Labourers	48.22	49.06	24.94	26.15
Household Industry, Manufacturing, Processing, Servicing and Repairs	3.31	2.41	3.47	3.63
Other workers	20.30	23.09	30.01	31.47
Total	100.00	100.00	100.00	100.00

Source: Registrar General and Census Commissioner Part I-B (ii) 1981 xxxiii and Part B (i), 1981 a: xxxv, and Census of 1991 (Col. 2 was taken from data computed by Dr. Thangaraj).

Though there is a marginal decline in 1981 compared to 1971, more than 49 per cent of Scheduled Caste workers are agricultural labourers, against the all-India percentage of about 25, i.e. almost double the percentage of agricultural labourers in the general population. The share of agricultural labourers among the Scheduled Castes has risen to nearly 50 per cent while that of cultivators declined from about 28 per cent in 1981 to 25 per cent in 1991. The important reason for this is the skewed distribution of land. As per the 1981 agricultural census, holdings of more than 10 hectares constituted 2.4 per cent of the total operational holdings and controlled as much as 23 per cent of the total operated area, while those below 2 hectares constituted 74.5 per cent of total holdings but controlled only 26.3 per cent of the total operated area. The land distribution pattern remained almost the same in 1985-86 also. The top two per cent of holdings control 20 per cent of operated area while the bottom 76 per cent of holdings control only about 25 per cent of the operated area.[9]

The Scheduled Caste population constituted more than 16 per cent of total population in 1986 but their holdings totalled to only about 12 per cent of total operational holdings covering only 7.5 per cent of the total area operated. It is also to be noted that about 71 per cent of their holdings are marginal holdings while 57 per cent of holdings are marginal holdings in the case of the general population. The average size of the holding in the case of the Scheduled Castes is 0.81 hectares while it is one hectare in the case of the general population.[10]

This skewed distribution should be viewed together with the fact that land is concentrated mostly in the hands of the upper and dominant peasant castes to the exclusion of the Scheduled Castes.[11] In the case of Andhra Pradesh the Scheduled Castes constitute about 15 per cent of the total population but control less than 7 per cent of the total area operated.[12] As a result, they are heavily dependent on the landed gentry even for their bare existence.

In view of the fact that a larger percentage of the Scheduled Castes live in the rural areas and also since about 50 per cent of their workers are agricultural labourers, an attempt is made here to study the position of the Scheduled Caste agricultural labourers vis-a-vis the others and the changing composition of the Scheduled Caste agricultural labourers, particularly those working as permanent farm servants, in the context of the green revolution and various developmental measures undertaken by the Government, especially since 1971, at the village level.

This study examines at the micro-level, i.e. in two villages, (1) the position of the Scheduled Castes as agricultural labourers vis-a-vis the others and (2) the changing proportion of Scheduled Caste permanent farm servants (*palerulu*) among the total Scheduled Caste agricultural labourers and the important factors contributing to it in the context of the green revolution and various developmental measures initiated by the Government since 1971.

This study is confined to two delta villages, Kanchakoduru in Krishna district and Malakapalli in West Godavari district in Andhra Pradesh. These villages have been selected on the following grounds. They have a significant proportion of Scheduled Castes and have been exposed to the green revolution and various developmental measures initiated by the Government, like land reforms; and others relating to direct attack on poverty. In case of Kanchakoduru village the analysis covers up to 1982 and the position and changes in the composition of Scheduled Caste labourers could be presented upto 1982 only. This has been drawn from my work published in Social Action.[13] In case of the other village, Malakapalli the analysis covers upto 1994. This is based on the work of one of my research students.[14]

In Kanchakoduru village there are 248 households of which 105 i.e., 38 per cent, belong to the Scheduled Castes. Of these 105 households 60 are landless agricultural labourers, i.e., about 57 per cent while in the case of non-SCs it is only 23 per cent. In addition to these landless households there are other households particularly those owning less than 2.5 acres who derive the major share of their income from agricultural labour. Out of 45 landowning households, 39 or 87 per cent are having less than 2.5 acres while they are only 60 per cent in the case of other landowning households. Among the Scheduled Castes, 261 out of the total population of 431, are workers i.e., 62 per cent as against 51 per cent in the case of the others and 55 per cent in the general category. The male-female ratio among them is 10 : 9. This means that almost all the females of the Scheduled Caste community, who are in working age group, are participating in the workforce as against 40 per cent among the others.

It is found that in the case of Scheduled Caste workers, agricultural labourers constitute 77 per cent as against 61 per cent among the others and 68 per cent for the total. Only 16 per cent of the Scheduled Caste workers are cultivators, while they are 21 per cent in general and 25 per cent in the case of the others. In the case of transport and other services, there is no Scheduled Caste person. This can be attributed to untouchability which prevents Scheduled Castes from taking up occupations other than agriculture. It is also found that Scheduled Caste agricultural labour constitutes about 50 per cent of the total in this category while their population constitutes 38 per cent of the total.

Changing Composition of Scheduled Caste Agricultural Labourers

Palerulu: Palerulu or permanent farm servants are hired to perform field or domestic work. They are also known as *Kamatagadu* or *Noukaru* or *Jeetagadu* locally. Children are employed for grazing cattle. During the busy seasons one has to remain almost always in the field supervising or participating in work. Normally landlords with larger holdings employ permanent farm servants. The male adults and children alone are employed as *Paleru,* not female labourers probably because of the arduous nature of the work. Sometimes *Palerulu* may be sent by their masters to work as agricultural coolies in others fields. But their earnings go to their master. *Palerulu* do not have any control over their labour. They are practically bonded labourers during that period of agreement. This is a vestige of the former bonded system.

The wages of *Palerulu* who are provided food, are usually at a lower level than of those who do not have this facility. *Palerulu* are paid their wages, locally called as *Kattubadi,* per year in the form of paddy. In some cases one or two pairs of clothes are also given by their masters. Other perquisites like festival income, some grain to be left in the threshing floor for *Paleru,* interest free loans, etc., depend on the patron-client relationship. The employment is usually for one year.

Out of the 138 male main workers of Scheduled Castes in 1981-82, 80 are agricultural labourers and 42 of them, i.e. 57 per cent, worked as *Palerulu.* Most of them started as *Paleru* even before attaining the age of ten. This clearly indicates the miserable economic condition of their families. Twelve of them (29 per cent) gave it up before 1971-72 while about 60 per cent of them left it after 1971-72. Also in 1981-82 five persons were still working as permanent farm servants. Besides there were five children below 14 years of age and an elderly man of about 65 years working as *Palerulu.* He worked as *Palerulu* for more than 35 years and gave it up before 1971-72 due to physical weakness. Later, he again worked as *Palerulu.*

It is also to be noted that out of these 42 persons, 39 are heads of households and worked as *Palerulu* for almost 20-25 years. Most of them started as *Palerulu* when they were below 10 years of age.

Thus out of 105 Scheduled Caste households 39 heads of families, i.e. 37 per cent earned their livelihood working mainly as *Palerulu*. Even in 1982, out of 5 persons working as *Palerulu*, 3 were family heads. They were paid wages in the form of paddy at the rate of an average of 27 bags (75 kgs) per year in 1981-82 while it was 17 bags in 1971-72.

It is clear from the above discussion that before 1971, the proportion of permanent farm servants was very high and it declined during 1971-72 to 1981-82. Child labour among *Palerulu* was predominant. Almost all of them started working before the age of 10. Even in 1981-82 out of 10 farm hands 5, i.e. 50 per cent were below 14 years.

The main reason for the decline in number was that they did not want to live as slaves forever and that they wanted to lead independent lives. Additional reasons were: (*a*) Decline in the perquisites. The perquisites which assumed importance under the traditional agrarian system were declining with the commercialisation of agriculture, and (*b*) higher prices of outputs which in turn lead to a rise in money wages.

From the above analysis it follows that in 1981-82 although most of the *Palerulu* gave up that job and became casual labourers, they predominantly remained as agricultural labourers. However, inequalities in the distribution of land persist despite governmental intervention* child labour from SCs still exists. Almost all males and females of the Scheduled Castes under the working age-group joined the workforce as agricultural labourers.

Malakapalli village has 1,249 households out of which the Scheduled Caste households are 522. The Scheduled Caste population constitutes 41.8 per cent of the total population with the Scheduled Tribes accounting for another 1.2 per cent. Among the Scheduled Castes 58.97 per cent are workers and 41.03 per cent are non-workers. Out of total Scheduled Caste workers 79 per cent are agricultural labourers and only 11 per cent are cultivators. Among Scheduled Caste households 26 per cent are landless while only about 16 per cent are landless in the case of other castes. Two per

*In this village, in 1982, holdings below 5 acres constituted 88 per cent of the total but controlled only 52 per cent of the total land owned. On the other hand, holdings above 10 acres constituted only 4 per cent of the total holdings but controlled 26 per cent of the total land owned.

cent marginal farmers with another about two per cent being small farmers. There are no medium and large farms. All medium and large farmers belong to other castes who constitute about 42 per cent of the total population. The Scheduled Castes control only about 183 acres while others the remaining 2,100 acres. The required information has been collected from the village agricultural labourers by inquiring about their past history and their present position. A sample of 100 agricultural labour households (above 35 years old age group) from various castes is randomly selected in this village (see Table 2).

Table 2. Sizewise and Castewise Distribution of Ownership of Holdings in Malakapalli 1991 Census (percentages)

No. of Holdings		*Total*		*Scheduled Caste*		*Others*	
	Holdings Landless	*House-holds*	*Extent*	*House-holds*	*Extent*	*House-holds*	*Extent*
		42.12	—	76.16	—	16.43	—
05	1.26	20.09	175.46	17.70	115.80	21.91	56.66
34	2.46	14.65	321.22	4.09	32.54	22.61	288.68
47	4.93	12.09	517.37	1.86	29.66	19.80	487.71
Medium land holdings 94	7.40	4.88	363.01	0.19	5.50	8.43	357.51
41	9.87	2.64	276.71	—	—	4.64	276.71
Medium land holdings 88	12.35	1.53	203.83	—	—	2.67	203.83
36	18.52	1.44	267.75	—	—	2.53	267.75
53	24.70	0.40	110.80	—	—	0.70	110.80
Large land holdings 71	49.41	0.16	50.64	—	—	0.28	50.64
42 and above		—	—	—	—	—	—
Total		1249	2,286,79	43.00	183.50	57.00	2100.29

Including S.T. 15 Households.

Source: Mandal Hand Book of Statistics, Tallapudi Mandal, W.G. Dt.

Malakapalli village has a high proportion of Scheduled Castes to the total population in 1991. Out of 1249 total households, 526 households are landless and nearly 77 per cent of them belong to the Scheduled Castes while the rest are from other castes. The marginal farmers among the Scheduled Castes are only 21.77 per cent whereas in case of others it forms 44.56 per cent. In addition to this the cultivators are more concentrated (i.e. 20.17 per cent) among other castes, but only 8.11 per cent are among the Scheduled Castes and 14.45 per cent in general.

The occupational distribution of the village shows a predominance of agricultural labourers which constitute almost 55.25 per cent of the total workforce. Out of the 48.41 per cent total workforce, the Scheduled Castes comprise the highest percentage of 59 per cent, but it is only 41.69 per cent among other castes. Among the Scheduled Castes, agricultural labourers constitute 79.05 per cent as against 33.84 per cent among the other castes and 55.25 per cent in the total village. It is also found that 91.04 per cent of the Scheduled Castes female workers are agricultural labourers.

The total population of the sample of 100* agricultural labour households is 528 persons, comprising 49.25 per cent males and 50.75 per cent females. The total population of the Scheduled Castes is 366 (69.32 per cent) persons, of whom 174 (66.93 per cent) are males and 192 (71.64 per cent) are females. Whereas in case of other castes, the total population is 162 (30.68 per cent) persons, of whom 86 (33.07 per cent) are males and 76 (28.36 per cent) are females. Hence it is clear that the female population is more among the Scheduled Caste when compared to the other castes.

It is found that out of 30 labour households of other castes, 9 households have less than 2 acres of farm land and 3 households have 3 acres each. But in the case of the Scheduled Castes all 70 labour households are landless and are depending on agricultural labour for their livelihood.

Out of the total 528 sample population, literates constituted 211 (39.96 per cent) persons in the village. Among the Scheduled Castes, literacy rate is only 36 per cent while it is 49 per cent among other castes.

*A sample of 100 agricultural labourer households comprising 70 from Scheduled Castes and 30 from other castes has been selected using the random sampling method for studying the change in their position.

Out of the 100 household heads of the sample, 88 per cent started their lives as *palerulu.* Out of 70 Scheduled Caste households, 67 (95.27 per cent) worked as *palerulu* in 1964-65 or before. Among 30 household heads of other castes 21 (70 per cent) worked as *palerulu.* Out of 70 household heads of the Scheduled Castes 67 (95.72 per cent) worked as *palerulu* before or after 1964-65, nearly 21 (31.34 per cent) of them gave it up before 1974-75 and about 42 (62.68 per cent) of them left it after 1974-75. In 1993-94, four household heads were still working as *palerulu,* whereas in the case of other castes, out of 30 household heads 21 (70 per cent) labourers worked as *palerulu* before or after 1964-65. Sixteen (76.20 per cent) of them gave it up before 1974-75 and the remaining household heads left it after 1974-75. Only one household head was working as *palerulu* in 1993-94. This person entered the contract of attached labour to raise money for the wedding of his two daughters. It is also found that among Scheduled Castes about 5 children below 14 years were working as cattle boys which was not the case in other castes. Thus, the proportion of attached labourers was high before 1974-75 but declined significantly by 1993-94.

Debt clearance after marriage, labour migration to the urban areas, wage payments from kind to cash, the low level of wage rate of attached labourers compared to the casual wage rate, the differential treatment of farmers on the basis of social hierarchy, adverse working conditions, decline in perquisites, the increasing cost of cattle—these have been found to be important reasons for change in the composition of labourers, i.e. change of attached labourers into casual labourers.

From the above analysis of Malakapalli village, it follows that land concentration continues in the hands of the upper castes in 1991. Although the degree of attached labour declined substantially Scheduled Caste workers remained mainly as agricultural labourers and child labour continues in case of Scheduled Castes workers to some extent even in 1993-94. The Scheduled Caste farmers are mostly marginal farmers.

In the light of the above analysis, one can conclude that the process of change that has been initiated through land legislation, new technology and other developmental measures could not bring about any significant change in the socio-economic conditions of the Scheduled Castes. Their asset position in terms of land did not improve, although there was change in the composition of the agricultural labourers. They essentially remained agricultural labourers. It is also to be noted that studies on poverty established that the incidence of poverty is higher in these groups of agricultural labourers.

Under these circumstances, there is need for effective State intervention in the form of strict implementation of land legislation to reduce land inequalities as it is the main reason for poverty and social tension in rural India. There is also need for shifting the Scheduled Caste agricultural workers from farm to non-farm activities for which the State has to play a crucial role in extending educational facilities which alone can improve the skills of the workers.

REFERENCES

1. Govt. of Maharashtra, Dr. Babasaheb Ambedkar; *Writings and Speeches*, Vol. 5, 1989, p. 21.
2. Nancharaian, G. *Land and Caste*, Himalaya Publishing House, Bombay, 1988, pp. 93-94.
3. Govt. of Maharashtra, Dr. Ambedkar : *Writings and Speeches*, Vol. 9, 1989, pp. 1961-87.
4. Govt. of India, Report of the Commissioner for Scheduled Castes and Scheduled Tribes (twenty-eighth report) 1986-87, pp. 224-25.
5. Rao, Hanumantha, *Caste and Poverty: A Case Study of Scheduled Castes in a Delta Village*, Hyderabad, Swatantra Printers, 1977, p. 14.
6. Census of India, 1981, Series 1, India Part (*iii*) B (*ii*) Primary census Abstracts : Scheduled Castes, New Delhi, pp. xxiii – xxv.
7. Data compiled by Dr. Thangaraj from Census of India, 1991.
8. *Ibid.*
9. Thangaraj, "Accress to land for the Scheduled Castes and Tribes in India", Working Paper No. 12, p. 19.
10. *Ibid.*, 23.
11. Nancharaiah, G. *op. cit.*, p. 3.
12. Thangaraj, *op. cit.*, p. 20.

13. Nancharaiah, 'The changing position of the Scheduled Castes as agricultural labourers in the labour market', *Social Action*, Vol. 40, No. 2 April-June, 1990, pp. 172-183.

14. Venkata Rao G., *New Technology and its impact on agricultural labour Institutions: A study of a village in coastal Andhra*, 1995 (M. Phil. dissertation submitted to the University of Hyderabad).

10

DALITS AND HUMAN RIGHTS— A PART OF THE WHOLE BUT A PART APART

S.K. Thorat

I propose to highlight the nature and dimension of human rights problem of the Dalit community in India. Second to identify the possible reasons behind the human rights violations and finally to point out the limitations of the simplistic approach adopted by some organisations including the NHRC to handle this problem.

The Protection of Human Rights Act of 1993 defines human rights in these words:

> "Human Rights means the rights relating to life, equality and dignity of individual guaranteed by the constitution or embodied in the International Covenants and enforceable by the Courts of India".

Human Rights and Dalits

Do the Dalits in India avail themselves of these rights relating to life, liberty, equality and dignity of the individual as guaranteed by the Indian Constitution? As the following account would show despite completion of fifty years of independence the violation of human rights of Dalits continues on a large scale.

Civic Rights Violation

The Protection of Civil Rights, 1976 (earlier called Untouchability (offences Act of 1955) provides penalties for preventing a person, on the ground of untouchability, from entering a place of public worship and offering prayers or taking water from a sacred tank, well or spring. Enforcing any kind of social disability such as denying access to any shop, restaurant, hotel, public entertainment, or denying the use of any road, river, well, tank, water tap, bathing ghat, cremation ground, etc., attracts the provision of this Act.

Besides the Civil Rights Act the Parliament also enacted the Scheduled Castes and Scheduled Tribes (Prevention of Atrocities) Act, 1989 in order to prevent the commission of offence of atrocities against the members of SC/ST to provide Special Courts for trial of such offences. The need for this Act was felt because "under the circumstances, the existing laws like the protection of Civil Rights Act, 1955, and normal provisions of Indian Penal Code have been found to be inadequate to provide safeguard against the crisis against SC/ST (P.K. Gupta 1991)".

The term "atrocity" has not been defined in any law; however, it encompassed all I.P.C. offences in which SC/ST persons were victims.

Table 1 shows that despite the presence of CR Act during the years 1981 to 1985 the total number of cases registered was 19,378. The number of registered cases against the Scheduled Castes work out to 2531 in 1993, 1731 in 1994, and 1773 in 1995. The incidence of CR Cases was relatively higher in U.P., Tamil Nadu, Rajasthan, M.P., Maharashtra, Karnataka and Gujarat.

Many agreed that these numbers are "the tip of the iceberg". There are thousands and thousands of incidences which are not reported due to fear of the high caste people.

Table 2 shows that, between the five years period 1981 to 1986 about 91097 cases of atrocities were registered by the Scheduled Castes, and another 23,958 against the Scheduled Tribes. The number of atrocity cases registered by the Scheduled Castes was 14,938 in 1994 and 12,313 in 1995. Thus on an annual basis 13,000 to 14,000 cases were registered every year.

The break-up of the atrocities for the latest year 1995 shows that this includes 513 murder, 4,000 grievous hurt, 439 arson and

787 cases of rapes. The data June 1981 onward shows that annually about 500 Scheduled Caste persons are murdered, 4,000 are hurt, 400 to 900 are subject to arson and 10,000 faced other offences giving an average of 15,000 cases of atrocities annually.

With 513 murdered every year can we say that the Scheduled Castes enjoy the right to life? With 4,000 cases of arson annually, can we say that the Scheduled Castes' right to safe and secure life is guaranteed? With 700 to 800 cases of rape annually can we say that Dalit women have a safe, secure and dignified life? And finally with 3,000 cases of Civil Rights Violation annually can we say that the Scheduled Castes enjoy the same liberty and equality in social relation as the high caste people do?

The macro level or overall picture at times hides more than it reveals about the actual human rights violation of Dalits. The following two evidences bring the situation more clearly.

Evidence from Karnataka

The study is based on 52 villages drawn from 52 taluks with 941 samples. For Karnataka Dr. Mumtaz Khan (1995) concludes that: "Contrary to the expectations..., the practices of untouchability in several areas of human social interactions are very much alive in the rural areas".

The author further observed that: as high as 80 per cent respondents say that hotels are still barred for them; and if allowed they have to sit in last rows and use separate cups and saucers.

Table 1. Areas of Practice of Untouchability

Area	*Untouchability Practice per cent of respondent*
Hotels	80.5
Temples	77.2
Religious Procession	77.2
Tank Water	68.4
Tap Water	77.2
Social Mixing	70.2
Economic Activities	56.0
Political Activities	29.8

Seventy per cent say temples are barred for them, and an equal per cent say they are not allowed to participate in religious processions. Both the sources of water, i.e., tank and tap are prohibited for majority of them. Seventy per cent say that social mixing is not allowed

The only area where prohibition was minimum was political matter.

Andhra Pradesh Evidence

Dr. Venkateswarlu (1970) in a study of six villages during 1977 of 396 respondents came with the evidence that:

1. Most of the Harijans feel that temples are still bar to them.

2. Most of them feel that they are not to enter the house of the caste Hindu.

3. Marriage processions by Harijans are objected to on one pretext or another, by a large number of upper caste people.

4. Similarly, if a Harijan wants to draw water from a well or a tap in the caste Hindu locality the latter would object to it and sometimes physically obstruct.

5. Physical violence has been perpetrated against the Harijans. A majority of Harijan respondents reported that they were beaten, ranging from, very frequently, to, rarely, there were also cases of raids on Harijans' houses. Sometimes raids were followed by looting, kidnapping, insults, rapes, physical torture, threats and attempts to murder (pp. 109-13).

Violation of Political Rights

The SC/ST Commission's report does not mention the cases of violation of political rights. However some micro level studies provide some information on this issue. A study on Karnataka observed that: "Tensions in the political spheres of village life occur quite often due to high caste preventing the Harijan from participating in political activities, for not voting for a particular candidate. Dr. Venkateswarlu has given enough statistical support in favour of violation of political rights".

Economic Discrimination

Tensions in the economic field of village life occurs when the labourers demand higher wages, intend to change their traditional occupation to more income earning occupation or when they try to occupy the land allotted by the government.

Evidence is given where Harijan labourers are beaten for demanding higher wages.

Similarly when the Harijans wanted to switch over from traditional to some other occupation which meant partly breaking the traditional occupation, they were harassed by being abused or beaten. So there was restriction on the freedom of occupation.

A number of studies point out the discrimination of Dalits in land, and employment market. Minaksi Das observed discrimination in wage earning as well. The Dalit labourer tends to get lower wages as compared to a non-Dalit worker.

Discrimination in Education

A number of studies observed discrimination of Scheduled Caste in the school and college. Dr. Geeta Nambissan observed that "within the school it appears that Dalit students continue to experience social discrimination and thus can be seen both in official curriculum i.e. in the approved content of education and hidden curriculum of schooling. Scheduled Caste communities and the experience of untouchability rarely form part of school knowledge. Though untouchability and maintenance of social distance from certain communities still persists in most parts of India, such practices are rarely mentioned in school books or discussed in the classroom" (*PUCL Bulletin*, April 1995 edited by Dr. R.M. Pal and published by People's Union for Civil Liberties).

Thus children belonging to communities that belong to lowest caste social hierarchy continue to be discriminated against within the school and classroom. The personal experiences of Dalits educated in post-independent period mentioned instances of Dalit children being asked to sit separately from their classmates, of being refused drinking water and served in broken tea cups, made to sit separately. Teachers refuse to touch their slates or copies or resort to physical punishment for fear of pollution. Dr. A. Haque also observed identical problems of discrimination in schools.

Civil Rights Violation and Institutions

Mumtaz Khan examined the role of various authorities, such as the police and the judiciary. The prosecutors and Civil Rights Directorate as much depend on the goodwill, commitment and efficiency of these Civil Rights Act enforcement authorities. About the role of the police he observed that : 1. The vast majority of Dalits are not happy with the treatment meted out to them by the police. About 61 per cent say that treatment was relatively bad. 2. Victims faced multiple problems at the time of registration which include non-availability, refusal to register, attempt to compromise, threats and rude behaviour. 3. The reasons for delay were hatred, fear of caste Hindus and higher officers, and indifference. 4. The attitude of Muslim and Christian officers, are different from that of Hindu Officers. 5. The Scheduled Castes seem to have no faith in the structure and functions of the judiciary. The main reason which prompts the Scheduled Castes to lose faith in the Judiciary is the fact that cases ending in convictions do not even amount to one per cent.

Human Rights Violation, Economic Deprivation and the Caste Ideology

Dr. Ambedkar as early as in 1947 argued that there is a connection between individual liberty and the shape and form of economic structure and the connection between the two is real: "Ask those who are unemployed whether what are called Fundamental Rights are of any value to them. If a person who is unemployed is offered a choice between a job of some sort of wage with an interdict on joining a union and the exercise of his rights to freedom of speech, association, religion, etc., can there be any doubt as to what his choice will be? How can it be otherwise? The fear of starvation, the fear of losing a house, the fear of losing saving, if any, the fear of being compelled to take away children from the school, the fear of having to be a burden on public charity are factors too strong to permit a man to stand out for his fundamental rights. The unemployed are thus compelled to relinquish their Fundamental Rights for the sake of securing the privilege to work and subsist" (*State and Minorities*, 1947).

The dependence of Dalits for economic survival on the high castes provides a situation for both men and women to relinquish the fundamental rights. The Dalits in rural areas are far too behind other groups. In the late 1980's 63 per cent of Scheduled Caste households were wage labour households, but only 31 per cent of non-Dalits belonged to this category. Only a fraction of them own land and 73 per cent of those who did were marginal farmers with too little land to live on. The result has been a high incidence of poverty among the Scheduled Castes—50 per cent as compared to only 37 per cent among the general population in the late 1980s.

A number of studies indicate that civil rights violations and atrocities are committed over land dispute and wages. The important reason is thus the economic deprivation of the Scheduled Castes.

But the economic reason does not explain the whole story. The non-Dalit poor are not subject to the same violence as the Dalit poor are. A number of studies identify resentment against manifestation of awareness amongst the Scheduled Castes about their rights and privileges as enshrined in the Constitution and various legislations and executive measures. The empirical studies on Andhra Pradesh, Tamil Nadu, Maharashtra, Karnataka and Orissa, etc., clearly suggest that wherever Dalits have asserted their civil, political and economic rights, they have been subject to violence and atrocities as these acts of theirs go against the dominant caste ideology.

Annexure-I

Table 2. Incidence of Rural Labour Household

Social group	*% Rural labour HH*			*% Rural labour HH with land*			*% Rural labour HH without land*		
	1974-75	*1983*	*1987*	*1974-75*	*1983*	*1987*	*1974-75*	*1983*	*1987*
Scheduled Caste	NA	57.41	62.55	44.38	37.76	75.67	55.82	62.24	24.33
Scheduled Tribe	31.03	44.04	49.61	51.29	50.04	83.3	48.71	49.96	16.7
Non SC/ST	22.01	29.14	31.15	55.97	45.07	79.56	44.02	54.92	20.43

Source: Rural Labour Enquiry Report 1974, 1983, 1987.

Annexure-II

Table 3. Distribution of Households and Area Owned : 1981-82 All India

Size/Categories	*SC*		*Non SC/ST*	
	Household	*Area owned*	*Household*	*Area owned*
1. Landless	12.61	—	10.18	—
2. Marginal farmers	72.40	28.32	52.20	7.60
3. Small farmers	8.40	22.82	18.00	10.00
4. Semi-medium farmers	4.52	24.19	12.05	15.77
5. Medium farmers	1.80	19.19	7.00	51.73
6. Large farmers	0.28 (100)	7.69 (100)	1.32 (100)	13.98 (100)
7. Average size	0.62	1.93	2.12	—
8. Gini ratio	0.81	—	0.78	—

NSS Round 37,1982.

Table on land holdings.

Table 4. Number of Children (5-14 years) currently attending educational institution per 1000 children (all India)—1987-88

Social group	*Rural Female*	*Urban Female*
Scheduled Tribe	204	527
Scheduled Caste	255	523
Others	392	691

Table 5. Female Literacy Rates

Social group	*Literacy rate*		*Total*	*Rural*	*Urban*
	1971	*1981*	*1991*	*1991*	*1991*
Scheduled Caste	8.44	10.93	27.76	19.46	42.29
Scheduled Tribe	4.85	8.04	18.79	16.22	45.66
All communities excluding SCs and STs	22.25	29.0	39.29	30.62	64.05

Table 6. Percentage of 'Unemployed' (see 5 year the above) according to usual status currently weekly status and currently daily status

Percentage of Persons Unemployed

Schedule group	*Rural female*				*Urban female*			
	US—PS	*US excluding SS workers*	*cws*	*cds*	*US—PS*	*LS excluding*	*cws*	*cds*
Scheduled Tribe	0.18 1.22	0.08 —	1.21 1.23	2.57 (1972-78) 2.37 (1983-84)	0.46 2.00	0.46 —	0.83 1.67	1.94 2.75
Scheduled Caste	0.50 2.58	0.23 —	2.16 1.90	4.23 4.09 (1983-84)	0.97 3.95	0.71 —	1.15 2.07	2.10 3.27
Others	0.43 1.53	0.29 —	0.91 0.97	1.72 (1977-78) 0.97 (1983-84)	1.05 2.95	0.92 —	1.09 1.71	1.42 1.98

US—PS : Usual status

cws : Currently weekly status

cds : Currently daily status

Table 7. Number of poor among Scheduled Castes, Scheduled Tribes and the rest of the population (Millions)

Social group	*Rural*		*Percentage Change*	*Urban*		*Percentage Change*
	1977-78	*1983-84*		*1977-78*	*1983-84*	
Scheduled Castes	53.7	19.6	(–) 7.6	7.7	7.8	( ) 1.3
Scheduled Tribes	33.7	31.3	(–) 7.1	1.3	1.5	( ) 15.4
Rest of the Population	165.7	140.6	(–) 15.1	44.7	40.2	(–) 10.1
All India	253.1	221.5	(–) 12.5	53.7	49.5	(–) 7.8

Source: "Changes in Rural Poverty in India", C.H. Hanumantha Rao, *Mainstream*, January 11, 1986.

Table 8. Number of Persons Below Poverty Line
(Scheduled Castes, Scheduled Tribes vs All Population)

Category	*Areas*	*1977-78*	*1983-84*	*Percentage Change*
Scheduled Caste	Rural	64.6	53.1	– 17.8
	Urban	54.3	40.4	– 25.6
	Combined	63.2	50.9	– 19.5
Scheduled Tribe	Rural	72.4	58.4	– 19.3
	Urban	52.6	39.9	– 24.1
	Combined	71.4	57.1	– 20.0
All Population	Rural	51.2	40.4	– 21.1
	Urban	38.2	28.1	– 26.4
	Combined	48.3	37.4	– 22.6

Source: "Changes in Rural Poverty in India.", C.H. Hanumantha Rao, *Mainstream*, January 11, 1986.

11

RELIGIOUS AND SOCIAL PRACTICES AND HUMAN RIGHTS OF DALITS

Virendra Dayal

Since 1993, we vowed in the NHRC that we would take on the most difficult issues as openly and pointedly as we could. Hence we took serious note of the TADA and buried it; of the tragic situation of 400 million illiterates and have been pressing for implementation of Article 45, our nation cannot be strong unless illiteracy is totally removed. We placed on our agenda the plight of the girl child / woman and foeticide. Our canvas included civil and political and economic, social and cultural rights; most of all, relationship between justice and equity and human rights. This led us to the question of the Dalits and other vulnerable groups / sections of our society plus the need for systemic reforms: police/ jails / judiciary.

Indeed, once you see the world through the lens of justice and equity—a synonym for human rights—every aspect of governance and every area of study takes on a different complexion : Economics and economy; history and political science; the practice of democracy and what constitutes good governance—and indeed the issue of what is religion—a questioning of religion and of social practices permitted by it.

Hinduism has a lot to answer for, but I must confess, as a born Hindu, I find it much easier to identify with the Dalits than those who, in the name of my religion, would sanctify the humilation of others; they are not my coreligionists, any more than are those who would tear down a mosque, or make of some of us "Children of a Lesser God" (as it were). The issue is not to exonerate Hinduism, but to try to reach the *truth*: organised religion has perpetrated terrible crimes in more than one age, in more than one continent: Christianity—burning at the stake and the Spanish Inquisition; the Dutch Reformal Church justifying apartheid; the "demonization" of Jews that led to the Holocaust; the odious destruction of the Inca and Maya civilizations by the Conquistadores; the hideousness of the Crusades/Jihads of "Medieval" Europe. Even in Japan, Shintoism tolerated behaviour very much like untouchability and a group suffered hereditary difficulties. Yet, of course, as Indians, we must set our own house in order and the problem of Hinduism/Dalits must be resolved here, by ourselves, in and for our own country.

It is a great tragedy that we missed not only the Industrial Revolution but also the Age of Reason—the first crippled us technologically, the second crippled our capacity to apply to belief and religion the test of reason—so we entered this century doubly bereft—and we must now doubly cure ourselves. We must, therefore, speak the language of reason as pointed out by Dr. Pal. While science, technology, the revolution in Information Technology will help us, globalization will raise grave problems of equity and justice, even as it may destroy certain evils. We will no longer be able to humiliate each other behind the walls of national sovereignty; that day and age is over and Satellite TV will see to that; but even more so the age of isolation, intellectually, is over; obscurantism will be in for difficult times, as knowledge spreads in cyber-space; superstition will stand exposed, as readily in a remote village in Tamil Nadu as in New Delhi; charlatans and fake godmen would know what has hit them.

A new Age of Reason can and must dawn in India. Its great a pity that we did not get this debate going between some major religious figures of Hinduism/Islam and others; all need to know that their beliefs will have to face the test of reason which is utterly democratic. Swami Vivekananda was quite unique when he said that those whom the gods love, die young, unfortunately for the rest of us. We can, therefore, reasonably hope that, in our work, the compulsions of a changing planet and the newest revolution, in some ways more powerful and bloodless and irreversible than any that preceded it, the Revolution of Information Technology, will destroy shibboleths and shake our ancient country out of its sloth and cruelties. We need to see ourselves as others do.

We need to be honest, brutally honest, even in our education in calling our evils by the names they deserve; by starting a movement for Human Rights and Dalits Rights (as pointed out by Dr. Pal); by recognizing that, indeed, bad economics and bad economic planning can scuttle life itself (the most fundamental right as Dr. Kancha Ilaiah said yesterday) ; by understanding that Human Rights mean, in fact, to be human (as Dr. Gopal Guru observed). I would add that the Right to be human to fulfil our potential, to realize that no religion can be worthwhile when it makes some more equal than others in the eyes of God, and that none of us are children of a Lesser God.

12

NEED FOR A RENAISSANCE

V.S. Malimath

The NHRC has been entrusted with the function of reviewing the safeguards provided under the Constitution or any law for the protection of human rights and to make suitable recommendations and also to review the factors that inhibit the enjoyment of human rights and to recommend remedial measures. The NHRC has special responsibility towards the Dalits who are deprived of the core values of human rights, namely, freedom, equality, and dignity. This national Workshop on Human Rights organised by the DLET, in collaboration with the NHRC, is the first major initiative of the Commission to examine the problems of the Dalits with a view to finding out suitable remedial measures. We are thankful to Dr. Pal for taking the initiative and bringing the NHRC and DLET together. We are also thankful to the DLET for providing this platform to have a serious dialogue on the subject.

The general comment made at the workshop that the abolition of untouchability by Article 17 of the Constitution, special provisions for reservation contained in Articles 15 and 16, the Directive Principles of State Policy in Article 46 requiring the State to promote the educational and the economic interests of the Scheduled Castes and the Scheduled Tribes and to protect them from social injustice and all forms of exploitation and the laws made in that behalf, namely, the Protection of Civil Rights Act, 1976, and the SC/ST Prevention of Atrocities Act, 1989, have not resulted in substantial improvement of the position and status of the Dalits even after 50 years of Independence. They continue to suffer social degradation and economic and educational deprivation. It has, therefore, become necessary to take up the issue of Dalit uplift as a National Human Rights Movement.

Laws, however, strongly worded, cannot bring about a change in the attitude of the people towards the less fortunate brethren. It appears to me that the concepts of freedom, equality, and dignity, which find a place of pride in our Constitution, have not yet become ingrained in the hearts and minds of the people. The concept of superiority and inferiority is the antithesis of the core values of freedom, equality, and dignity. Man, over the centuries, has shown evidence of the lack of respect for these core values. Inequality is being practised all over the world under different labels, putting forward different philosophies in support of their respective claims. Over the centuries, the blacks have suffered inequality and indignity at the hands of the whites. Different religions have claimed superiority over the others, resulting in the claim by the followers of one religion as being superior to the followers of other religion. Inequality is writ large between the rich and the poor; those in power and those without; the adults and the children; men and women; and the physically strong and the weak.

Varnashrama, the philosophy of the Hindus, which treats the Dalits as low-class people, militates against the core values of human rights, namely, freedom, equality, and dignity. What is worse is that even among the Dalits, we have those belonging to the superior sects and those belonging to the weaker sects. In Karnataka, among the Dalits, there are two categories—one, known as the right-hand caste, and the other, the left-hand caste. The left-hand Dalit is treated as inferior to the right-hand Dalit. Thus, there is a facet of inequality and indignity being practised among the Dalits themselves.

All these illustrations point to the fact that there is something basically wrong with the people all over the world. Unless a radical change is brought about in our thinking and attitudes towards other people, whether they are the blacks, the poor, the powerless, the women, the children and the physically weak, the Dalits, and so on, we will not be able to realise the cherished human rights of freedom of equality and dignity. This requires a change of heart; this requires sensitization; this requires development of a human rights culture. I am, therefore, in favour of a movement not only at the national level, but the international level, to fight against all these evils which militate against freedom, equality, and dignity. Every section of society requires to be tackled. Every human being is required to change and to learn to respect the human rights of others.

So far as the Dalits are concerned, I would like to say that they should not be content with reservation of seats in the educational institutions and jobs in Government service. What they should really aim at is the general uplift of the Dalits as a whole. This can only be achieved by proper attention being paid to education and inculcating the spirit of pursuit of excellence. The more fortunate among the Dalits have not done enough for their fellow-beings. They must help the other Dalits by putting forward ideals to pursue and giving them encouragement and assistance to pursue their goals. Self-help is the best help. Let the Dalits organise themselves for their own uplift and march forward. They should, in the years to come, aim at matching the best brains in the country and occupy positions of pride and importance by dint of their own calibre and competence. While there should be a general national movement for the uplift of the Dalits, there should be an internal movement in the community itself for marching ahead.

We must all be partners in the great movement to bring about a renaissance where everyone enjoys freedom, equality, and dignity.

13

INCULCATING HUMAN RIGHTS CULTURE: TOWARDS A NEW NATIONAL MOVEMENT

Anand Kumar

This is a presentation to discuss the context, concept and orientation of a new national movement in India for inculcating a human rights culture. Such a movement deserves immediate attention of our society. It should be the basic activity for all the enlightened and liberated individuals and groups during the celebrations of 50 years of India's freedom from foreign rule. It may lead us to create a more effective reservation policy which addresses the challenge of eliminating caste and gender based discriminations in a more substantial way.

India should be proud of her successful national movement against foreign rule. But the nation must feel ashamed of her internal failures on the front of creating a just social order beyond the burdens of caste and gender deprivations in spite of 50 years of independence.

The Indian social system suffers from two traditional malaise whose continuity contributes towards extraordinary degrees of dehumanising of our nation and people. The power matrix in India is organized by the principles of caste, wealth and education. Anybody existing outside the orbits of the caste system (the untouchables) without wealth (landless labourers and other daily wage earners), and without formal education (illiterates) is externalised from the discourse of power.

He or she is compelled to exist with the status of "externalised" and in a setting informed by powerlessness as there are only these three recognised channels to the power structure in the Indian social order.

What are the consequences of such a power arrangement? It has led us to live with extremely unjust norms and customs in the context of caste and gender in spite of several five-year plans of change and progress even after 1947. According to Marc Galenter (1981), "since independence, India had undergone what might crudely be summarized as development at the uppermost levels and stagnation at the bottom".

In day to day life we are witnessing a high level of insensitivity towards the basic rights of the Scheduled Castes and Scheduled Tribes on the one hand, and that of all women on the other. The following two descriptions may be sufficient to underline the nature of our national crisis. According to a Government of India (Ministry of Social Welfare) document 1991, every hour two Dalits were assaulted; every day three Dalit women were raped; two Dalits were murdered; and two Dalits' houses were burnt somewhere in India. In another report by the Department of Woman and Child Development (Government of India), every 26 minutes one woman was molested ; every 50 minutes one act of eve-teasing took place; every 54 minutes one woman was raped; every 102 minutes one dowry death; and every 7 minutes one act of criminal offences against women took place in our country in 1991. Thus, it may not be unfair to conclude that freedom from foreign rule has not been meaningfully translated into liberation for Dalit and women from internal tyranny.

They live in fear. They are still deprived of freedom. But the issue cannot be resolved by blaming any particular clan, caste, religion, class, party or government as it is a societal crisis which has refused to be resolved by the prevailing model of nation building. It needs a new national orientation to influence all of us at many levels: (*a*) individual, (*b*) family, (*c*) community, (*d*) caste, (*e*) religion, (*f*) class, (*g*) party, (*h*) region, (*i*) state, (*j*) nation and (*k*) civilization. It asks for a cultural revolution where human rights of all citizens of India are recognized, nurtured, and protected with active cooperation of each other against the internal tyranny of traditions, structures, privileged groups and individuals.

After 50 years of national freedom, it is also necessary to recognize certain facts about a few popular myths in this context: (*a*) Urbanization and industrialization have not helped in radically changing the national scenario, (*b*) religious conversion has helped the concerned communities only in a marginal manner, (*c*) Reservations are useful for low degree of upward mobility for large communities with educational achievements and urban linkages. Out of more than 400 Dalit communities, the result of the present form of reservations is positive for only a few dozen large castes. (*d*) There is a low demand for education in many castes as they are relatively weak in economic terms. They are arrested in a vicious circle where lower economic capacity prevents them from taking advantage of the present form of education which in turn pushes them further away from the emerging opportunities. (*e*) The women, rural in general, and Dalit women in particular are in a triangular trap of (*i*) fuel, (*ii*) fodder and (*iii*) water which prevent them from devoting time to acquire power of literacy. Their families pull young girls of school going age out of school and put them in these essential domestic duties.

If Indian society needs to go beyond the spectrum of 'religious conversion' to 'reservation' in order to liberate itself from the twin deficiencies of gender injustice and caste deprivation, what is the way out? It is imperative that a woman-oriented strategy of national conscientization should be given a chance in our future policies, projects and popular mobilizations. The SC communities should be the focus of our new national drive against illiteracy, caste oppression, and violence against women as they are the last to receive the advantage of our post-colonial projects. It will bring us face to face with the most discriminated and powerless part of Indian population.

Let us not ignore that the Schedule Castes are a non-homogeneous spatially dispersed minority. They are victims of separation of the world of knowledge from the world of work. They are largely engaged in agricultural labour where the prevailing pattern of education has very limited relevance. Unless there is a hope of large scale of occupational diversification for the agriculture labourers, there is no chance for any new orientation among them to get attracted to the current literacy programmes for themselves or their children. This should not make us indifferent to the positive achievement in urban setting where laws enacted by the state have also contributed in some ways. Scheduled Castes manage breaking the knowledge barrier through their determination for a better tomorrow.

In overall terms, specialists have identified four basic variables in the context of educating the Scheduled Caste—

(*i*) Gender;

(*ii*) Region;

(*iii*) Ethnicity;

(*iv*) Religion.

If we take into account their individual role and communities effect, a comprehensive understanding of the difference in the progress of education between (*a*) general population and the Scheduled Caste, and (*b*) various castes within the Scheduled Castes is possible. Such an analysis suggests a strategy which will require three level initiatives:

(*i*) Family;

(*ii*) School;

(*iii*) Environment.

A new national movement may work for incentives for the whole family for joining the educational process by creating a micro level support system. It will also use creative ways within a decentralized national framework to improve the form and content of the prevailing school system. There, the object of schooling will be to bring together world of knowledge and world of work. In such an endeavour, village panchayats, and not the district will be the unit of initiatives. So that a newly empowered Panchayat may be used as the instrument of nation building through educational empowerment of the woman and the Dalit. Similarly a vast space for N.G.O. intervention (as youth and citizen's initiative for social reconstruction through a new national movement) may be possible in different communities and regions. It may interact with the growing networks of N.G.Os for gender justice, human rights, and preservation of environment.

The new national movement will have to develop a bi-focal approach:

(*i*) Intensification of the empowerment drive within the scheduled castes community as well as rural and urban women; and

(*ii*) Nurturing values, institutions and processes for a culture of human rights at the national level.

Such a bi-focal vision will prevent India from drifting away from the constitutional values and commitment for justice—social, political, and economic. It will be a wholistic approach which may restore a sense of purpose among the youth intelligentsia, political forces, power elite, and policy makers in these days of drastic drifts. Otherwise we will be overwhelmed by the consumerist forces and marketist logic of power where the survival of the powerless is of least concern.

Such a national movement need some revision and a few shifts in the prevailing strategies of Dalit emancipation and empowerment of women and the underprivileged sections of Indian society. The seven major shifts are the following:

1. From child as target to family as focus.
2. From caste-class nexus to caste-gender-class coordination.
3. From caste wars to nation building oriented human rights movements.
4. From general equality to citizenship rights.
5. From sectarian mobilization to community conscientization.

6. From parliamentary democracy to participatory democracy.
7. From state-centric campaign to civil society oriented strategies.

Such a shift is not difficult because we have reached a dead end in pursuing the other approaches including sanskritization, religious conversion, reservation, vote bank policies, immigration class based mobilization, etc. It is also possible as it has role and space for each concerned Indian man and woman to play an active role without colliding with each other. It has the potential of promoting active citizenship which may provide new energy to an otherwise exhausted nation in its search for a just social order. At least it will bring together two most powerless and marginalized categories of Indian people—the Dalit and the woman, in a new partnership along with millions of the enlightened others through a national movement for a culture of human rights.

14

DEVELOPMENTAL ISSUES IN HUMAN RIGHTS

—An examination of some specific issues concerning the Scheduled Castes and the Scheduled Tribes

R.V. Pillai

The plurality of Indian society is unparalleled. It has been the home of almost every major religion in the world; its nearly one billion people speak 18 major languages, besides many times that number of dialects. Our cultural diversity has produced a colourful mosaic of which we are legitimately proud. However, there is an equally conspicuous diversity of a different dimension; reflecting a social order characterised by inequalities and denial of opportunities, a social order that has stood in the way of a healthy universal respect for human rights and which has been a drag on our programmes of socio-economic development. Even after 50 years of Independence, these disparities and inequalities remain; awareness about them has been slow in growing; equally slow has been the sensitisation of functionaries involved in eliminating them.

It is a truism to say that social disparities based on a rigid caste structure have stood in the way of a free play of economic forces, emergence of an entrepreneurial class cutting across social divisions, mobility of labour and a more equal sharing of economic gains. Referring to the caste system, Jawaharlal Nehru wrote in his book entitled *Discovery of India*: "There can be no equality of status and opportunity within its framework, nor can there be political democracy, much less economic democracy." Dr. Ambedkar was of the firm view that "annihilation of caste" was the only solution to India's disunity and poverty. He stated: "The caste-system is not merely a division of labour. It is a division of labourers."

Awareness of the situation led the government immediately after Independence to resort to a strategy of planned economic development. It was felt that such a development would help break down the rigidities of the caste system and social hierarchies. However, the thrust of economic development has been such that the social services sector continued to lag behind, accentuating socio-economic disparities. The consequence has been that even after 45 years of planning, the government is striving to provide basic minimum services to the poor and the socially disadvantaged in order to equip them to reap the fruits of freedom, social justice and economic development. The increasing awareness that socio-economic development must be based on justice, equality of opportunity and respect for the dignity and worth of the human person also contributed to a heightened level of expectations and aspirations. During a recent seminar organised jointly by the Canadian Human Rights Commission and the National Human Rights Commission of India, I had the occasion to present a perception of the complaints of human rights violations which the NHRC has been receiving from the length and breadth of the country. I had submitted on that occasion that the complaints reflected, apart from individual grievances and concerns, upheavals in a society striving to transform itself from feudalism to modernism.

Developmental planning in India is a matter much discussed. However, in the context of Article 46 of the Constitution, I would like to highlight some of the aspects of an uneven socio-economic development to the disadvantage of the depressed classes and the attention they deserve in fostering a human rights culture.

A pre-requisite for socio-economic development is awareness; awareness of the present, and a vision of the future based on that awareness. The most essential factor contributing to this awareness is literacy; the ability to read, write and perceive; to comprehend developments beyond the community or the immediate neighbourhood; to discern and judge for oneself what is good and what is not. As Paulo Frieire, the Brazilian proponent of social activism stated: "Literacy per se, and even adult education at a fairly advanced stage, may not lead to a radical or qualitative change in the lives of individual learners. It may not lead to an end of the status of landlessness, assetlessness and bondage; but it can certainly be a tool of "critical consciousness" and in that sense can be an important tool to induce or stimulate change—social, economic, cultural and even political".

It is a sad commentary that after 50 years of Independence, the illiterate population of India has far exceeded the total population of the country at the time of Independence. This has been the consequence of undue emphasis on higher education and the meagre resources allocated to the education sector being consumed largely by universities and technical institutions. It is a cruel irony that while India is among the top nations in technical manpower, it also accommodates the largest number of illiterates. And the worst sufferers in this regard have been the disadvantaged communities. Myron Weiner observed: "Indian education has been largely an instrument for differentiation by separating children according to social class. For this reason, those who control the education system are remarkably indifferent to the low enrolment and high dropout among the lowest social classes. The result is one of the highest rates of child labour in the world, ...and a literacy rate that has fallen behind most of the third world."

According to the 1991 Census, while the literacy rate was 52.2 per cent for the whole population, it was 37.21 per cent among the Scheduled Castes. (Some of the State figures for literacy among the Scheduled Castes are: 26.85 per cent in Uttar Pradesh; 26.2 per cent in Rajasthan and 19.49 per cent in Bihar; the female literacy rates among the Scheduled Castes in these States are 10.69 per cent, 8.39 per cent and 7.07 per cent respectively.) The literacy level among the Scheduled Tribes was 29.6 per cent for the country as a whole. In Madhya Pradesh which accounts for nearly 23 per cent of the country's total Scheduled Tribe population, the literacy level among them was 21.54 per cent and in Andhra Pradesh 17.16 per cent. In the case of females, the literacy rates for the Scheduled Tribes population was 4.4 per cent in Rajasthan, 8.7 per cent in Andhra Pradesh, 10.2 per cent in Orissa and 10.7 per cent in Madhya Pradesh. According to the 1981 Census, there were 48 districts with tribal concentration where literacy of tribal females was less than 2 per cent.

The NHRC considers the issue of primary education up to the age of fourteen to be of such critical significance that it has taken a number of initiatives by way of addressing different agencies of the government. Further, the Chairperson of NHRC felt it necessary to write to the presidents of all political parties in January 1996 on our commitment to fulfil the promise of Article 45 of the Constitution. In his letter he observed that the grim reality of increasing number of illiterates enfeebled the country in every way, whether civil and political or economic, social and cultural. He added that this reality affected the dignity and self-esteem of countless Indians and exposed them to constant violations of their human rights. The Chairperson urged that definite steps be taken in Parliament to provide comprehensive legislative backing to the provisions of Article 45. It was further urged that such legislation be matched with necessary resources required for the purpose. It is a matter of gratification that the Common Minimum Programme of the present government (United Front Government in 1996) recognises this position and proposes to make the right to free and compulsory elementary education (as per Art 45 up to the age of 14) a Fundamental Right, as also to increase substantially the outlay for education with special attention to the requirements of truly universalising elementary education.

It must also be recognised that only an increased flow of funds into the education sector would not provide a total solution to this issue. What is equally important is the accessibility of children, particularly of the disadvantaged communities, to schools; the availability of physical infrastructure and manpower and material resources for the effective functioning of the schools. Also important is the level of commitment and motivation of parents, teachers as well as the children. Local communities and non-governmental organisations have a major role in this regard.

We need a national effort to galvanise the disadvantaged communities and groups to reap the benefit of a more determined effort that is being mounted now.

Giving land to the tiller was a promise made during the Independence movement and this promise is yet to become a reality in many parts of the country. In rural areas, the land owned by the top 1 per cent is estimated to be equal to the land owned by the bottom 55 per cent of the land owning families. The data of land distribution, consequent on the application of land ceiling laws, are often questioned. It is alleged that holdings have been divided and sub-divided among family members of different generations to circumvent land ceiling laws. In the absence of the ability to read and write, among tenants and share-croppers, land is often disguised as owner cultivated. A study conducted in 1989 estimated that a third of all cultivated land is held under concealed and informal tenancy. A report brought out by the Department of Rural Development in 1988 stated: "The rural rich maintain their position through use of muscle power and manipulation of administrative and judicial processes." According to the 1991 Census, 93 per cent of the Scheduled Tribe population and 81 per cent of the Scheduled Caste population live in rural areas and more than 90 per cent of the working population among Scheduled Tribes and 77 per cent of the working population among the Scheduled Castes were engaged in the primary sector. Prevalence of poverty among the disadvantaged in the rural areas as a consequence of landlessness and low wage income is well documented.

The annual report of the Ministry of Welfare for the year 1994-95 brings out the extent of poverty among the Scheduled Castes and the Scheduled Tribes. It was estimated that in 1983-84, 40.40 per cent of the total population of our country was below the poverty line. The percentage for the Scheduled Tribes during the year was 58.40 while for the Scheduled Castes it was 53. The 1987-88 Survey estimates put the percentages as 33.40 for the total population, 52.60 for the Scheduled Tribes and 44.7 for the Scheduled Castes. It may be noted that during the four-year period, a higher percentage of the total population came above the poverty line, than in the case of the Scheduled Tribes though marginally better in the case of the Scheduled Castes. In any case the incidence of poverty continues to be much higher among the SCs and STs, calling for more intense efforts to eradicate it.

The Special Component Plan and the Tribal Sub-Plans were introduced as additional support to the socio-economic development plans for these two groups. The government has itself admitted that despite sincere efforts, "There has not been very significant development in the education, entrepreneurial and other fields among the Scheduled Castes." A report of the Ministry of Welfare further states: "In many of the States, the exercise for the formulation of SCP (Special Component Plan) is of perfunctory nature." The question that arises in one's mind is whether apart from earmarking funds, there is a true appreciation of the developmental needs of these disadvantaged communities.

One is not off the mark in saying that in families with low income levels, the immediate victims are women and children. We need to ask the question whether in spite of special programmes, these more vulnerable segments among the socially disadvantaged are receiving the required level of attention. It may be recalled, in this connection, that on a complaint from a human rights activist, the NHRC enquired into the death of 125 tribal children in a district in Orissa as a result of malnutrition and lack of medical care, and ordered the payment of compensation to the affected families (Reported in the Commission's Second Annual Report). While we are exporting foodgrains, sections of the population continue to suffer from under nourishment. Among the many aspects of the situation is a proper lack of understanding that the coarse grains form the staple diet of some of the tribal communities. While there has been considerable emphasis on the development of improved varieties of rice and wheat, not much attention seems to have been paid to research on improving the production of coarse grains which form their staple diet.

The story of the most comprehensive poverty alleviation programme—the IRDP—has not been much different. It has suffered a great deal from want of attention to details of the **milieu** in which the poorest of the poor as well as the socially disadvantaged live, as also for want of essential forward and backward linkages. Milch animals being given to the Scheduled Caste families under this programme is a case in point. People who were assisted under this programme were not habituated to stall-feeding of animals, which, on being let out in the open, stray into farm lands of the upper castes leading to tension between communities. There has been very little enforcement of the Minimum Wages Act, with powerful landlords paying abnormally low daily wages. Even the government fixed rates under many of the income-support programmes for the rural poor are said to be well below the statutorily fixed minimum wages. The growing disparity in the income levels in the rural areas and the rising aspirations among the landless and the poor have found violent expressions in States particularly in Bihar and Andhra Pradesh. During its visits to these two States, the NHRC received representations highlighting the urgent need for effective land reforms as also a critical assessment of the developmental requirements of the depressed communities so that the widening gap between the rural rich and the poor do not lead to an aggravation of social tension and abuse of human rights.

Under Article 17 of our Constitution, 'Untouchability' stood abolished, and its practice became forbidden. In order to enforce the Constitutional provision, the Untouchability (Offences) Act, 1955 was passed by Parliament to make provisions for punishment for offences that amounted to observance of 'Untouchability' in any form. On realisation of the need to make the law stringent, the Act was amended and renamed as The Protection of Civil Rights Act, 1955 under which the practice of 'Untouchability' has been made an offence both cognizable and non-compoundable. However, convictions under this Act have been very few. Even where the cases ended in conviction, the punishment has been too formal. The following is a critical comment on the extent of punishment meted out in cases under this Act: "...In a rare instance where an offender was brought to Court, the Magistrate fined him two rupees. On appeal, the High Court raised the fine to a still inconsequential fifty rupees."

Under the Act, it is also incumbent upon the Central Government to present a report to the Parliament every year on the measures taken by it and the State Governments. The lack of efficacy of the law is reflected in a report presented to the Parliament by the Welfare Ministry: "*In view of the increasing trend of atrocities* on the Scheduled Castes and the Scheduled Tribes, the existing provisions under the Protection of Civil Rights Act had been found inadequate and *an additional legislation* called The Scheduled Castes and the Scheduled Tribes (Prevention of Atrocities) Act, 1989, to check and deter crimes against them by non-Scheduled Castes and non-Scheduled Tribes was passed and brought into force w.e.f. 30.1.1990."

The new Act enjoins upon the government to take a number of steps including the setting up of Special Courts, provision of legal aid and even the economic and social rehabilitation of victims of atrocities. Data available indicate that the conviction rate under these Acts has been very low (around 1 per cent). There are a number of socio-economic factors which contribute to the continued ineffective enforcement of the provisions of these statutes and a low rate of conviction. There is need for a close and critical examination of these factors and the instrumentalities involved to deal with the situation, more so at the State level.

A scheme was launched in March 1992 by the Government of India to eliminate the inhuman and degrading practice of manual handling of night soil. The scheme operates at two levels: one by the Ministry of Urban Affairs and Employment for the conversion of dry latrines into water-borne flush latrines in homesteads and provision of sewage facilities at the town/city level. The other scheme operated by the Ministry of Welfare provides for the rehabilitation of scavengers in alternative dignified occupations. considerable amount of money has been spent under this scheme, but very little seems to have been achieved on the ground. The government itself admits that the progress achieved "is extremely dismal barring a few States." (*Annual Report of the Ministry of Welfare*; 1994-95). Some of the States have not even completed the survey of scavengers. The district collectors are responsible for the overall implementation of the scheme. The level of awareness and commitment among them to implement the scheme faithfully or for that matter the level of social consciousness and societal support for this scheme for eradicating one of the most demeaning occupations is a matter of debate. Can we not have NGOs and other activists influencing State Governments and the district administrations in the completion of surveys and in drawing up meaningful rehabilitation programmes, and assisting beneficiaries to rehabilitate themselves in dignified occupations?

Substantial hydel and mineral wealth of our country lies in the tribal areas. The exploitation of this wealth through the damming of rivers and mining of the land has led not only to a large scale displacement of the tribal population but also to degradation of the environment. This process has been on the increase in recent years. A report of the Central Water Commission indicated that less than one-fourth of 32 dams of over 50 metres height constructed between 1951 and 1970 were in the tribal areas. However, between 1971 and 1990, out of the 85 additional dams of similar size completed or under construction, around 60 per cent were in tribal areas. Mining not only displaces the local population but also causes severe environmental damages such as pollution of surface water sources, damage to agricultural land through dumping of overburden, destruction of forest cover and air pollution. Displacement from original habitats often-times causes a breakdown of community organisation which is primarily based on land. Families get marginalised and morbidity level goes up. Cultural and religious practices which are aspects of the social dimensions of displacement are seriously affected. The land-for-land approach adopted for rehabilitation, more often than not, does not reflect a holistic perspective. In a letter to Baba Amte in August, 1984, Mrs. Indira Gandhi said, "I am most unhappy that development projects displace tribal people from their habitat especially as project authorities do not always take care to properly rehabilitate affected population."

Displacement of tribal population from their habitat is only one part of the story. There has been large scale movement of non-tribals into development project areas, as work contractors, shopkeepers, transporters, labourers, etc. Many of them over a period of time have got permanently settled in the project sites—and at times in places beyond—which are in the midst of vast tracts of tribal habitation. Reports of socio-economic exploitation of tribals by these settlers are legion.

The complaints the NHRC has been receiving in this regard, whether they be in relation to Sardar Sarovar Project or the Tehri Dam, are a clear indication of the continued lack of care in comprehensive planning for megaprojects and rehabilitation of affected tribal people. The Government of India has drafted a National Policy for Rehabilitation of persons displaced as a consequence of acquisition of land, addressing primarily the needs of the disadvantaged communities. Though the Draft was prepared in consultation with NGOs and some prominent activists, forums such as this need to deliberate on the character and content of the draft policy and examine how it respects the right to a life with dignity for the tribal people.

Basic to all the developmental efforts for the uplift of the SCs/STs is a respect for their human rights; respect for their right to equality and equal opportunity; a right to life with dignity; a right to enjoy the rights guaranteed by our Constitution. Statutes and schemes are important, but they become meaningless in the absence of a commitment to enforce or implement them. Projects and programmes for the uplift of the SCs and STs would remain on paper, or they would get derailed unless the agencies charged with the responsibility of implementing them are not only sensitized but also made effective. The role of human rights organisations and activists in the sensitisation of government functionaries is of great importance in this regard. This would also call for according to these functionaries a greater degree of importance and standing in the administrative hierarchy than they enjoy at present. Let the message spread that the ablest and the best are picked up for the very important task of social uplift and economic development of the poorest of the poor and the weakest of the weak.

Equally, there has to be a greater degree of accountability, a greater degree of public scrutiny of the acts of the functionaries at the cutting-edge level, punishing the guilty and rewarding those who perform. It is ultimately they who have to ensure that there are no roads and wells dividing communities in a village; there are no classrooms and playgrounds keeping the children apart; there are no complaints of discrimination or harassment in police station or primary health centre; there are no complaints of essential commodities disappearing from the ration shops meant for the weaker sections; or that there is a correct appreciation of the success and failures of policies and programmes for the uplift of the poor and the depressed.

15

AN APPRAISAL OF LAND REFORMS AND OTHER LEGISLATIVE MEASURES FOR THE UPLIFT OF SCs/STs

P.L. Mimroth

Social activists and thinkers are aware of the policy of protective discrimination contained in the specific constitutional provisions for safeguarding the interests of the SCs and STs : Under Article 17 (abolition of untochability), Article 23 (prohibition of forced labour), Article 45 (universalisation of primary education), Article 46 (promotion of educational and economic interests of SCs and STs), Articles 330 and 332 (proportionate reservation of seats in the Lok Sabha and the State assemblies) and Article 335 (appointment to services and posts in Union and State services), and numerous welfare and protective laws such as land reform acts, labour laws, Protection of Civil Rights Act 1955 and SCs and STs (Prevention of Atrocities) Act, 1989, tribal subplans and special component plans which have a direct bearing on these people. But it is a matter of great regret that even after the passage of 49 years of Independence, these constitutional safeguards and protective laws have not substantially raised the standard of life of the oppressed communities. On the contrary, Government policies on protection of the prices of agricultural commodities and schemes of subsidising inputs like power, fertilizer, pesticides and implements have given rise to a new affluent middle class of farmers from the upper classes and castes. This new peasant class does not hesitate to commit atrocities on the low peasantry and landless labourers belonging to the SC and ST communities.

During the 49 years of independence the policies of the government have strengthened the forces of feudalism and capitalism on the one hand and Hindu chauvinism and fundamentalism on the other. Age-old prejudices and denial of basic human rights to the exploited weaker sections in one form or another, still mark the performance and conduct of the high-caste dominated bureaucracy, where the representation of the SCs and STs is still very insignificant and ineffective.

In spite of the fact that 80 per cent of SCs and STs depend on land for employment, ensuring security of tenure, not to mention ownership, has not attracted the serious attention of any political party or successive Central and State Governments who claim to espouse the cause of these communities.

Land is a State subject. Several states have passed laws imposing ceilings on landholdings so that surplus land may be distributed among the landless. Possession of land gives power and prestige, besides providing an independent source of income. The upper castes own the land and the SCs and STs are denied the right to own land. The landlords had taken possession of what is called "Village Shamlat Land", "Grazing Land", "Waste Land", and land where the SCs and STs buried their dead before Hinduisation. Thousands of acres of land are in the possession of Brahmins for the ostensible purpose of maintenance of temples, deities, maths and shrines.

Uttar Pradesh, the most populous state in the country, passed a law under the title "Uttar Pradesh Zamindari and Land Reforms Act, 1951". Similarly, "Bihar Land Reforms (Fixation of Ceiling Areas and Acquisition of Surplus) Act, 1961", in Bihar, "Rajasthan Land Reforms Act, 1956", in Rajasthan, "The Himachal Pradesh Tenancy and Land Reforms Act", in Himachal Pradesh, among others have been enacted. But, unfortunately the laws have not been implemented faithfully with the result that most of the caste conflicts and atrocities on the disadvantaged sections take place owing to the non-implementation of the laws, including the reforms acts, the Minimum Wages Acts and those dealing with allotment of lands to the SCs and STs under different schemes. Conflicts have also taken place between those who own the land and those who want to own land or want to till the land allotted to them; between those who want to maintain their supremacy and the status quo and those who want a change.

The only state which has a fairly good record of land reforms including distribution of surplus land is the Marxist-ruled West Bengal. Kerala had passed a ceiling act as early as in 1969 under a United Left Front Government [Marxist-bed]. However, delay in its implementation and major loopholes in its provisions have led to large scale bogus transfers to obviate the land ceilings. In states like Bihar, it was traced to the inadequacies of abolition of zamindari system in the 1950s. It left big landlords and former zamindars with ownership and possession of vast areas of land. The Bihar law could not correct the earlier deficiencies due to large-scale *benami* transactions.

The Andhra Pradesh Land Reforms (Ceiling and Agricultural Holdings) Act, 1973 was enacted to fix a ceiling on agricultural holdings and was included in the ninth schedule of the Constitution. This Act which was to bring about an agrarian 'revolution' resulted only in the distribution of 2.46 lakh acres of dry, and uncultivable land out of 4.61 lakh acres of total land available and surplus.

Among the methods employed by the landlords to defeat land reforms are: (1) manipulation of records by bribing the revenue authorities. (2) benami transfers, and (3) obtaining order for the stay of implementation of the laws from the courts.

Since the powerful landlords dominate the legislatures and administration they have foreknowledge of the contents of legislation. The laws are also indifferently prepared with, for exploitation by, the powerful; unconscionable delay in the notifications of the laws leaves enough time for bogus and *benami* transfers in the names of relations, servants, and even non-existent persons. Some persons have even resorted to fake divorces to reduce the area of land for acquisition.

An effective way of undoing such *benami* transactions is to make them invalid with retrospective effect. The question arises, who will do it? Certainly not those in power for caste and class reasons.

No politician including those who claim to be messiahs of the Dalits, have applied their minds to find a solution to this basic problem. Dr. B.R. Ambedkar was an exception. Speaking in 1942 about the degraded condition of the Dalits he said:

> They are numerically small and economically poor. While this village system continues to exist in the present form, the untouchables will never achieve their independence, whether social or economic, and will never get over the inferiority complex which they have developed as a result of their state of social and economic dependence. The village system must therefore be broken. It is the only way that is open for the untouchables if they really wish to emancipate themselves from the strangle-hold which the Hindus have acquired over them through the village system. My suggestion is that you should insist upon a provision being made in the Constitution for the formation of new and independent villages exclusively of untouchables at public cost to be undertaken by the Government.

Unorganised farm workers and landless labourers have no protective laws to safeguard their interests and the few provisions that exist in favour of them are not enforced. The minimum wages Acts and other welfare measures enacted in some states do not benefit the SCs and STs. Many find employment as construction workers in neighbouring towns and are reduced to bonded labour. In some States the women are forced into prostitution to earn money for the family. Bonded labour and debt labour are age-old Hindu practices.

Bonded labour was abolished under Article 23 of the Constitution and a law specifically prohibiting bonded labour was enacted in 1976. There is no machinery to enforce the law and government could not provide any alternative source of livelihood to those who were liberated. This law has proved to be most ineffective.

Child Labour: India has the largest number of working children in the world. Millions of children, mostly belonging to the SCs and STs, are working long hours at nominal wages and in unhygienic surroundings in all sections of economy at the expense of their education, play, health and dignity and freedom. After five decades of independence, child labour prevails in all its ugly, inhuman forms. Various legislative enactments prohibiting child labour have totally failed to eradicate the evil. Dr. R.M. Pal, editor of *PUCL Bulletin* is perhaps the only activist in our country who maintains that Won-implementation of Article 45 of the constitution is a human rights violation, and that child labour can never be eradicated without implementing the provisions i.e. compulsory education to all children upto the age of fourteen.

Dalit Women: Dalit women suffer more from harassment, oppression and exploitation than their upper caste counterparts. The literacy rate among the SCs and STs women is very low. Infant mortality due to neglect and malnutrition is very high. A large number of Dalit women are inducted into prostitution. Procurers and pimps, mostly of the upper castes, hire victims from West Bengal, the tribal areas of U.P., central India and Nepal and sell them to the brothels of big cities. The Suppression of Immoral Traffic Act (SITA) is involved only when instances are brought to public notice by the newspapers. A fairly large number of women kidnapped and sold by the pimps and procurers belong to the SCs and STs.

The SC and ST woman is the first victim of caste conflicts. In order to terrorise the SC/STs, upper caste men, very often with the connivance of the police, humiliate and rape Dalit women. The police also falsely implicate them in criminal cases and rape them while in custody.

Witchcraft-related murders and humiliation of Dalit women in eastern India are very common.

During the last couple of months about 50 instances of horrible crimes like naked parading, physical assaults and rapes and other atrocities on helpless Dalit women took place in Rajasthan, Madhya Pradesh, U.P., Bihar and Orissa, despite the existence of protective laws such as SC and ST Prevention of Atrocities Act 1989 Section 3(*xi*) and (*xii*) which provide stringent and tough punishment and speedy trial to put checks on such heinous crimes against Dalit women.

Education: Dr. B.R. Ambedkar saw education as a human right and a fundamental right. Articles 45 and 46 of the Constitution provide for free and compulsory education to all children up to 14 years of age, and promotion of education and economic interests of SCs and STs were not made one of the fundamental rights enforceable by the courts. But now a Constitution Bench of the Supreme Court of India has declared primary education a fundamental right. For the first time children have been legally empowered to enforce their access to primary education. But as we all know this remains only on paper as no monitoring body or implementing machinery has been set up even in the light of admitted failure of politicians to abide by the 10-year limit from 1949 set in the Constitution for achieving this objective. In the name of modernisation and green revolution, vulnerable sections of SCs and STs are forced to migrate from rural to urban areas. Their children are deprived of educational avenues. A recent survey indicates great disparities and gaps (*a*) in literacy levels between (*i*) the males and females among the SCs and STs, (*ii*) the SCs and STs and non-SCs and STs in the population, (*iii*) the Rural and Urban SCs and STs and (*b*) in educational enrolment levels, from the primary to the postgraduate stages. The SCs and STs Commissioner's report further reveals the disparities between the (*i*) all India and state sectors, (*ii*) different states, and (*iii*) the different sections of the SCs and STs.

Despite the increasing visibility of SCs and STs in various educational and professional courses, they have not advanced in proportion to their population or as entire communities, resulting in the creation of forward and backward sections within each single community. It is also observed that the numerically large and dominant communities among the SCs and STs virtually monopolize educational opportunities and also compete among themselves, thus marginalising the smaller sections and those engaged in traditional occupations.

It has been observed that in professional colleges, many seats reserved for the SCs and STs are not filled on account of non-availability of eligible candidates or they are kept vacant because the authorities do not follow the instructions of the Central Government.

In some cases, the judiciary also has put obstacles in the advancement process of the SCs and STs, the most glaring example being the Supreme Court Judgement in *Tapan Kumar Roy Vs. Convenor,*

Engineering and Agricultural Medical Commission Entrance Test, Andhra University, AIR 1989 (May) AP 132 wherein it is held that Scheduled Castes and Scheduled Tribes status will be determined in relation to his state and not on an all-India basis. As a result of this Supreme Court decision, poor migrant labourers belonging to the SCs and STs residing in other states after escaping from famine, unemployment and social oppressions at their native places, are not entitled to avail themselves of facilities in the matter of education, recruitment or other economic development concessions at their new place of habitation.

Reservation in Public Services: Law-makers make the laws whereas the bureaucracy enforces them through the administration which is manned by upper caste people. The judiciary interprets the laws in such a way as to check the administration in executing policies. Education for long has been the monopoly of the Brahmins and other upper caste people in India. Access to education was denied to the lower caste people. They had no share in the administration. The legal profession from which judges are appointed also became the monopoly of Brahmins and other high castes, and Dalits have a very negligible representation in the legal profession and the judiciary. Both are the monopoly of the upper castes.

Reservation for SCs and STs in the public services was made under the Constitution in 1950. Reservation in the legislature was initially provided for ten years but for the services there was no time limit. Reservation provides opportunities for employment to only a fraction of the SC and ST population, but it affects a large number of people. The bureaucracy dominated by the upper caste is hostile towards the SCs and STs. They have no will to implement the reservation orders issued by the Government. The ruling party, too, has no political will to enforce the laws and rules framed by the government. Executive orders issued by the governments are challenged in the Courts on grounds of violation of the principle of equality (Articles 14, 15 and 16). Barring a very few judgements which were partially in favour of the SCs and STs, the rest militated against them. The judicial process has been used to delay implementation of the laws and deny the privileges and concessions granted to them under the Constitution. The Central Government while issuing orders regarding reservation in favour of the SCs and STs kept the armed forces, the largest employer, outside the purview of reservation. Posts in the departments of Science and Technology, the airlines, and the universities will become the exclusive preserve of the upper castes in the light of the Mandal Case Judgement (Indira Sawhney's) Case, which superceded all previous landmark cases like Rangachari's Case, the Akhil Bharat Shoshit Karamchari Sangh Case. Matters regarding promotion of SCs and STs in many offices and various State Governments like Rajasthan have been thrown out either by the Courts or by the authorities quoting Supreme Court judgements relating to reservation in promotion despite the constitutional amendment subsequent to the Mandal Case judgement. The Supreme Court has also recently diluted the reservation policy, especially the reservation in promotion, by delivering conflicting and vague judgements. The 50 per cent ceiling fixed for total reservation by the Supreme Court does not seem to be justified and reasonable in view of increasing social changes. Also without the carrying forward of vacancies, there is bound to be a heavy backlog of reserved vacancies. In fact, even today there is no adequate and fair representation of SCs and STs in the Civil Services and posts in all grades and categories in any of the Department.

The Prevention of Contract Labour Act prohibits employment of *safai karmacharis* and casual employees but this is increasingly becoming fashionable in Government offices and public sector undertakings like the Railways and the municipal bodies to employ them on daily wages mainly because termination of service is easy and the employer has no liability to pay terminal benefits, gratuity and pension.

Atrocities: The main root of atrocities on the Dalits over the centuries is the caste system. Caste is the bane of Indian society and the worst enemy of the Dalits.

It is difficult for the Hindus to abolish caste because it has a religious sanction behind it and gives them many social and economic advantages. It is not so in other religions. The Hindus have fouled the air all over and everybody is infested—Sikhs, Muslims and Christians. So in spite of abolition of untouchability and in spite of stringent laws like the Scheduled Caste and Scheduled Tribes (Prevention of Atrocities) Act 1989, atrocities on the Dalits have been ever on the increase.

The Protection of Civil Rights Act of 1955 provides for penalties for refusing admission to hospitals, educational institutions, hostels or temples; for refusing to sell goods or render services; for preventing the exercise of any right under Article 17; for demanding any unlawful compulsory labour relating to untouchability like scavenging, sweeping, removal of carcasses, flaying animals or removing the umbilical cord or any job similar. It also provides for the cancellation and suspension of licences, resumption or suspension of grants and imposition of collective fines. Every offence under the Act shall be cognizable and non-compoundable. It incorporates a number of statutory provisions intended to avoid complications and delays attendant on the proceedings under the Code of Criminal Procedure. The Act further lays down that, if an offence described in the Act is committed in relation to a member of the Scheduled Caste, "the Court shall presume, unless the contrary is proved, that such act was committed on the ground of untouchability". The benefit of probation is also not given to the offenders. The true intention and purpose of the Act is to eradicate the centuries-old obnoxious and oppressive practice of untouchability from Indian society.

Notwithstanding such a law there has been an increasing trend of atrocities on the Scheduled Caste/Tribes. Hence a new legislation, the Scheduled Castes and Scheduled Tribes (Prevention of Atrocities) Act, 1989, was enacted to check crimes against them by non-Scheduled Caste and non-Scheduled Tribe members. It came into effect from 31.1.1990. In this Act, Section 3 has specified the acts and omissions which constitute offences which were punishable. The new law empowers the State Governments to take suitable measures for effective implementation including the following:

1. Provision of adequate facilities including legal aid to the victims of atrocities.
2. Provision of travelling and maintenance expenses to witnesses and victims during investigation and trial of cases.
3. Provision of economic and social rehabilitation of the victims.
4. Provision for appointment of officers for initiating and supervising prosecution in implementation of the cases.
5. Special courts and special prosecutors for the purpose of speedy and proper trial of the cases.

Enactment of the law is only the first step. What is really important is its enforcement. It could have helped to check the atrocities, if those entrusted with its enforcement implemented it sincerely. But experience shows that like the land reform laws these laws also have not been implemented effectively and vigorously. The enforcement machinery dominated by upper caste people has lacked the will to pursue it. The SCs and STs are too weak to take advantage of such laws.

The police is the premier law enforcement machinery, but in most cases they adopt a hostile attitude towards poor Dalit complainants. The Commissioner for the SCs and STs observed in his report for 1985-86 that the high rate of acquittal in cases under the Protection of Civil Rights Acts was interalia due to: (1) delay in the disposal of the cases by the police during which the victims and the witnesses are influenced and forced to compromise by allurement, or intimidation by social, economic and political pressures; and (2) Faulty or slipshod investigation by the police.

Migration of the Dalits from villages and formation of new villages or settlements for them to acquire empowerment in all fields is the only solution to save the SCs and STs from atrocities but this cannot be done without government help and without a change in the power structure. The existing legal provisions and constitutional safeguards for the uplift of SCs and STs have led to prolixity and repetitiveness in legislation without bringing about any concrete change. Furthermore, there is hardly any political will to enforce and implement the land reform laws and other protective laws vigorously.

The time has come for the SCs and STs to stand up and struggle because the successive Central and State Governments have totally failed to bring about agrarian reforms or educating the Dalit masses and carrying out social reforms like the eradication of caste and untouchability and the restructuring of society based on justice, equality and fraternity. Their time and energy have been spent mostly on political battles. The upper classes should also change their mental outlook towards the Dalits in order to shed casteism if they are interested in establishing an egalitarian society in India.

16

CONCEPT OF A NATIONAL HUMAN RIGHTS MOVEMENT AND ANNIHILATION OF CASTE

R.R. Sivalingam

Liberation, liberation, liberation/Liberation for Parayas and Theeyas and Pulayas/Liberation for Paravas, Kuravas and Maravars/Let us work together with skill and no evil/Let us attain knowledge and education/in this our country/There is no poor no slavery/in this Indian nation/There is no depressed man/

When I lustily sang these words of poet Bharathi, on the 15th of August 1947 little did I dream that I will live to read the following news appearing in the *Hindu* of July 18, 1996 under the caption, "A Barbaric Episode" in a village called Barkikharwan in Bhojpur district:

> "The private armies a phenomenon for which Bihar has acquired a notoriety of sorts are at their usual game of barbaric killings yet again. Some 20 persons most of them women and children were massacred and over 40 huts torched in the Barakikharwan village in Bhojpur district a few days ago allegedly by a gang of the outlawed Ranbir Sena. Not even a three-year old girl was spared by the marauders who went on a butchering-spree, targeting the Dalits and other weaker sections who are known activists or sympathisers of the CPI (ML). Clearly the administration has been remiss in not preventing the

carnage because the Sena would appear to have made at least two attempts earlier this month which were thwarted by the villagers themselves. A heavily armed outfit with access to sophisticated weapons, Ranbir Sena is of the upper caste Rajput and Bhumihar landlords and has continued to be active despite the ban clamped on it by the Government officially. More recently on the eve of the Lok Sabha poll it sought to unleash terror among the oppressed sections and was found responsible for the attack on a marriage party that resulted in the killing of six supporters of the CPI (ML) and the Election Commission directed the Bihar Government to disarm the private armies.

A distinctive negative feature of Bihar's socio-political scene has been the presence of a plethora of private armies promoted by and owning allegiance to particular castes, as distinguished from extremist groups battling the vested interests. While the Ranbir Sena represented the upper castes, the Kurmis—a backward community—and the Dalits have their own but not-so-powerful militias to protect their interests and are active in certain areas."

Bharathi sang the song of human dignity for all more than a quarter century before India's independence and very much before the Universal Declaration of Human Rights on 10 December 1948. But the stirring words still remain a dream as is the Declaration of Human Rights along with the pompous proclamations of the Constitution of India. It is not to say that we have not tried but it remains a steadfast truth that the curse of caste still characterizes the stratified society of India today.

But in the second most populous country in the world 150 million people nearly equal to half of the population of USA are overburdened with deprivation not merely of Human Rights but of Humanity itself. Caste has refused to die in India. It has strong roots abroad too in strange lands through Indian migrants.

According to historians the code of Manu or the Manu Smriti is the source of dividing humanity into Chaturvarna around 6th century B.C. The obnoxiousness of caste and its inhuman features have been resisted from almost the inception of the caste system. For example, the biggest challenge to the caste came simultaneously in the 6th century BC through Buddhism. Buddhism was the most effective challenger of the caste system. The spread of Buddhism was indeed very remarkable, for not only did it spread throughout India from Patna to Kanyakumari, but also spread to various parts of the world—Japan, China, Thailand, Vietnam, Kampuchea and even to Russia, West Asia, etc. In India it lost its force and appeal because of Hindu revivalist movements particularly that of Shankara around 7th century AD. Within a millennium Buddhism faded out of India and the Hindu caste-system reasserted itself. But the resistance did not die.

It came in the form of Islam, when Muslim invasions subjugated India. Islam was born a millennium after Manu in the 5th century. It resulted in a frontal attack on the caste system. The Muslim converts provided core labour supply and the fighting soldiers to the Islamic power in India. It is felt that it is the degrading caste system which provided a large popular base for strengthening colonial powers in India. The people whose caste system rendered them degraded beings, became the bulwark of Islam. After the fall of Constantinople in the 15th century, Christianity came to India which continued the onslaught against the caste system begun by Buddhism and continued by Islam. But amazingly despite such mighty historical forces against caste it has refused to die. Numerous instances of violation of Human Rights of Dalit population (150 million) continues day in and day out. It has adopted various subtle means of survival. It survives within the fold of Islam too in the guise of mileages. There is a growing Dalit Christian movement. Among the Buddhists of Sri Lanka there is a strong streak of the caste system. Caste has demonstrated its capability to conquer its conquerors. How are we then going to face the current challenge of caste to the realisation of Universal Human Rights in all walks of life?

The inherent strength of the caste system lies in the crafty manipulation of the system. From the days of Manu the manipulators of the caste system and its staunch supporters remain the Brahmins who are undoubtedly the glorious beneficiaries of the caste system elevating themselves to a degree above humanity by calling themselves "pusuras". The system is also based on economic exploitation, social degradation and political domination. Economic exploitation begins with Manu himself. According to the code of Manu the interest prescribed for borrowing is based not only on the purpose of loans as it is today but also on the caste of the borrower. Brahmins were supposed to pay an interest of 2 per cent per month. Kshatriyas 3 per cent, Vaishiyas 4 per cent and Shudras 5 per cent. This clever method of retaining economic supremacy along with social supremacy and social and economic depresssion of Shudras, has continued and has taken multifarious forms. Socially certain demeaning or what was considered polluting labour, was reserved for the so-called low caste such as scavenging, leather work in some parts of India, midwifery, care of graveyard, burial of dead bodies, removal of carrions, etc.

These were socially ordained to be mandated labour for the bottom caste group through economic deprivation. They were forced to eat meat including dead animals. Having forced economic exploitation and social segregation they were labelled as untouchables and polluting. These socio-economic processes are very well documented and ably argued by the great Dalit liberator, Dr. Ambedkar.

Over a period of time this inequitous economic system and occupational segregation has so affected the psyche of both the deprived and the dominating caste groups that they have failed to see it as an evil and look upon the system as ordained by scriptures, religion or God. It is stated that the mental colonialism imposed by the Varnashram in Dharma is so strong that it refuses to quit India unlike the political colonialism of the Europeans. Despite great social reformers like Jotiba Phule, Dr. Ambedkar, Narayana Guru of Kerala and various other zealous reformers the caste oppression continues. The oppressed have not risen in a mass movement except for a sporadic retaliation here and there. They have demonstrated an incredible capacity for silent sufferings and a spirit of endurance of those gruesome oppressions. The religious endeavours, be they Buddhism, Christianity, Islam, Jainism or the Bhakti movements, have failed to extirpate the caste curse. What has the British rule done to the obnoxious caste system? Some are of the opinion that the British rule had been a liberative influence. Dr. Ambedkar had, however, a different opinion. In his address at the conference of the depressed classes in Nagpur in 1930 he said:

"In the first quarter of the nineteenth century when British rule became a reality five famines occurred that took the lives of about a million people. In the second twenty-five years there were two famines, and about four hundred thousand died. In the third twenty-five years there were six famines and the toll of death became five million. And in the last twenty-five years of that century what do we see? Eighteen famines! And the estimated death toll of from 15 million to 20 million. Gentlemen, what must be the cause of this? To put the cause in plain words is the government policy the British have followed. The aim has always remained to limit the growth of trade and industry in this country. This is not simply a logical fault; but the effort to rule India in such a way that it will always remain a customer of British state. It is due to this policy that India has been turned through ages into a poor country. In the process of establishing this poverty who have been the main victims?

"Gentlemen, you cannot sit singing the praises of the British bureaucracy for simply giving us improved roads, improved canals, railways, a stable administration and new ideals of geography or for stopping internal wars. There is scope for praising the maintenance of law and order. But, gentlemen, nobody including Dalits can live by eating law and order; they live on bread and we cannot forget this. I would be the first to agree that the praise given to the British would vanish once we turned our attention to the forcible extraction of profit by big capitalists and landlords. We cannot understand how you can expect the British government to liberate people from the exploitation of the capitalists and landlords.

"Let us think about this from only your limited perspective. Before the British came your condition was extremely miserable due to untouchability. Has the British government done anything to remove your untouchability? Before the British came you could not take water from village wells. Has the British government made any effort to give you that right? Before the British came you could not enter temples. Can you do that today? Before the coming of the British you could not be employed in police service. Does the British government give you employment now? Before the British came you had no permission to be in the army. Is this opportunity open to you now? Gentlemen, you cannot give a positive answer to any of these questions. Those who have ruled this country for such a long period could have done many good things. But there has definitely not been a single fundamental change in your situation. During the British period the faults of the social structure and the patches of the varna system have been kept as they were."

No doubt there was linking of the Indian economy with the world economy under the British through trade, plantation economy, factory production and production for export as distinct from subsistence agriculture. The British began the 'export' of Dalits also to distant plantations under the indentured labour system.

To quote Gail Omvedt: "Colonialism thus had a complex effect on the functioning of the caste system. It did not simply create 'classes' along with 'castes'. On the one hand new groups like a factory working class and plantation proletariat came into existence, and new professionals and some businessmen developed from high caste Brahmans and Banias. A 'peasantry' also acquired an accentuated existence, increasingly linked to production for the world market. But while at one level formally non-scriptive openings (such as education and entry into factory occupations) could mean that a very few from the lower castes could win their way into non- traditional occupations, by and large caste channelled workers to segmented labour markets: Brahmans continued to have near- monopoly control over administrative positions and professions; merchant castes (Banias, Jains, Chettiars) became moneylenders, merchants and businessmen; middle Shudra castes dominated factory occupations, while miners and plantation workers were drawn from the lowest groups. Caste hierarchy thus remained, with Brahmans at the top and the most mobile; with the middle 'peasant' castes impoverished and in many ways more attached to village (except for the very meagre openings in factories) than they had been before and with the lowest castes, especially Dalits, also mobile but so greatly impoverished and exploited as to find it very hard to benefit from such mobility".

Has the nationalist movement, dominated as it was by the caste conscious Brahmin-Bania elite, done anything to eliminate if not extirpate the social scourge of caste?

The period of reform movements began with Raja Rammohun Roy (in 1828) in the formation of Brahmo Samaj. The religious revivalist movement was represented by Arya Samaj, Sanatana Dharma, Ramakrishna Mission, etc. They were elitist and concerned with the resurgence of Hindutva and were very marginally interested in the status of the untouchables.

A Dalit response to the total lack of concern for them or a mere pretence of a concern was in the form of Dalit Associations and Movements such as:

1. The Satvani Movements in Madhya Pradesh,
2. The Shri Narayana Guru Dharma Paripalana Yogam of Kerala,
3. Jatava ... Maha Sabha of Agra,
4. The Adi-Dravida Mahajana Sabha,
5. Paraya Mahajana Sabha of Madras,
6. The Bhaiskrita Hitakari Sabha Maharashtra,
7. Mahar Conference, Maharashtra,
8. All Bengal Namasudra Association,
9. Bengal Depressed Classes Association,
10. The Adi-Andhra Movement,
11. Depressed Indian Association, Bombay,
12. The Valmikie Samaj of Punjab,
13. The self-respect movement in Tamil Nadu.

In spite of such a plethora of reformist movements with consciousness for Dalit liberation, it has not been possible to destroy this scourge. It is alive and kicking even today particularly in the rural areas. Great liberation leaders like Jothiba Phule, Periyar and Dr. Ambedkar have tried their utmost. Ambedkar's answer was to convert to Buddhism as he did in 1956. Jothiba Phule emphasised asset acquisition and a decentralised development model. Periyar emphasised on the acquisition of political power while directing his attacks on the symbols of Brahminism and the gods of Hinduism. He started an atheistic and rationalist movement.

According to Gail Omvedt, "caste struggle', like 'class struggle' could become revolutionary only when it could pose an alternative, a more advanced system, rather than being simply a negative protest or a competitive struggle for more economic or social-cultural rights within the framework of exploitation. But whether it could do so obviously depended upon the possibilities of the historical conjuncture. In the early era of transition when the caste system of exploitation was being constituted, the limitations of the anti-systemic role of religions like Buddhism and Jainism were that they could not be linked to a more productive historical system. The Buddhist Sangha, as many commentators have noted, embodied equalitarian and collective features from the tribal period, but only as a refuge from the world. Buddhism also tended to be linked with the more mercantile open kingdoms of the period. During the period of the medieval synthesis after the defeat of these 'heterodox' religions only a negative rebellion appears to have been possible, represented by the bhakti cults which embodied aspirations to equality but accepted a Hindu framework for this wordly social interaction. It was only from the time of British rule and the rise of a capitalist-industrial society that a more equalitarian and more productive society became a historical possibility and was posed as such in the ideologies of radical democracy and socialism. This period saw the rise of new working class struggles, the taking on of new forms in peasant struggles, but it also saw a new anti-caste revolt which was increasingly spearheaded by a Dalit liberation movement."

The self-respect movement pioneered by Periyar (E.V. Ramasamy Periyar) in the 1920s is one of the most vigorous anti-caste movements. Periyar started the anti-Brahmin crusade from within the Congress from 1920-26 and thereafter through the self-respect movement. Periyar while he was a prominent leader of the Congress in Tamil Nadu was invited to lead anti-caste protest demonstration in Waikam, Travancore State, then under the rule of the Travancore Rajah. He was imprisoned for leading a procession of untouchables protesting against the Brahminic caste restrictions of untouchability which was practised in one of the most inhuman forms in that state.

The Travancore Regime

In the State of Travancore the Dalit women were not allowed to cover their breasts and they had to campaign and agitate for their right to cover their breasts. This is detailed in a book *Breasts Cloth Controversy in Travancore*. The Eezhava women were not only forbidden to wear blouses but they were not even allowed to wear their saree to cover their breasts. They were not allowed to carry water pots on the hips but on the heads, so that they could not cover their breasts. Even more atrocious was the tax system. When an Eezhava youth attained puberty and sprouted moustache he had to pay "Hair Tax" and when young women attained puberty they had to pay "Breast Tax". Such was the degree of oppressions in the state of Travancore from where a very powerful anti-caste movement was led by Periyar giving the right to the Dalits to walk on the streets and also enter the temples.

The Reform Movement grew from petitions and demand to protests and processions involving mass actions by the depressed castes. Periyar soon exposed the weak-kneed response of the Congress leadership in fighting the evil of caste. Congress confined itself to passing ritualistic resolutions which were somehow diluted and dismissed by the crafty Brahmin leadership of the Congress.

Periyar was an admirer of Mahatma Gandhi. In spite of this he did not see eye to eye with him due to his support for the Varnashram Dharma. Dr. Ambedkar too differed with Gandhi for the same reason. It is said the Yerawada Pact between Gandhi and Ambedkar was the first ever serious attmept to raise the political status of the depressed classes. But subsequent events showed that everything the Congress did was nothing more than tokenism. The Congress was more interested in preserving the unity, strength and solidarity of the Hindu population than in the annihilation of caste.

Even though the movement of Periyar was largely successful in empowering the depressed classes and flowered into the South Indian Liberation Front and its later incarnation as the Justice Party, it was basically an anti-Brahmin movement more concerned with raising the political status of the non-Brahmin castes, the backward communities and the most backward communities and the extent to which the untouchables gained was by way of the falling crumbs from the tables of Naidus, Mudaliars, Vellalars and Reddiars.

Even during that period the feudal relationship among the castes, based on rural agriculture and land owning patterns, left the bottom rung of the ladder by and large intact.

In Thanjavur in the thirties the social reality of land ownership could not contribute to the liberation of Dalits. In Thanjavur itself temples and Mutts owned one-third of the cultivable land. These lands were in the occupation of caste Hindus like Vellalars, Kallars, Moopanars, etc. This was concealed landlordism. Sankara Mutt alone under the control of Brahmins owned 4000 acres. In Sirkali, Sithambaranatha Mudaliyar owned 40,000 acres, Ramanatha Mudaliyar owned 12,000 acres and Thiyagaraja Mudaliyar owned 12,000 acres, etc. With heavy concentration of agricultural land in the hands of caste Hindus the 21 per cent Dalits were totally dependent on the landlords and could not enjoy the rights of free labour.

The political palliatives offered by the Justice Party and then the Congress began with concessional fees at colleges and ended with the current reservationist controversies.

The proclamation of the implementation of Mandal Commission's recommendations for reservations let loose a fanatic opposition to those progressive measures by caste Hindu groups even resorting to inducing immature youth to set themselves ablaze in public places in an attempt to arouse nation-wide opposition to the Mandal Commission's reservation policy.

The national newspapers controlled by vested interests worked overtime to focus the nation's attention on anti-reservation protests. They lampooned V.P. Singh's announcement as resorting to cheap vote-catching devices and trotted out fancy arguments against it. That these human torches were inducted or forced was exposed by certain evidence but they were quietly suppressed by the newspapers. These instances go to prove that even in contemporary times there is very strenuous opposition among a very wide section of the caste Hindus to promoting social justice in favour of the scheduled castes/scheduled tribes.

If this is the overt state of the mind in society today, how can we succeed in annihilating caste? The continuing gruesome violence against the scheduled castes/scheduled tribes can be gleaned by the numerous reported incidents in the daily newspapers, leave alone the unreported incidents of violence. In Tsunder in Andhra Pradesh, in Keelavenmani and Kodiyankulam in Tamil Nadu, in Bihar and in Rajasthan inhuman murder, massacre and arson continue unabated. We can only conclude that despite the onslaughts of religious movement, reform movement, political palliatives and concessions caste has refused to die.

Human Rights

The latest to join in the crusade against the hydra-headed monster caste is the Human Rights movement. The United Nations was created to establish peace and abolish war on the eve of the end of the second world war. The proposal to form the UN (made at Dumberton Oaks in 1944) states that "with a view to the creation of conditions of stability and well being which are necessary for peaceful and friendly relations among nations, the organisation should *promote respect for human rights and fundamental freedoms*". In the very declaration of the purpose for the founding of the United Nations, concern for Human Rights and Fundamental Freedom had been emphasised. Hitler's treatment of Jews was one of the most convincing grounds for international protection of Human Rights. A country which can treat her own citizens in an outrageous manner can be a threat to human civilisation itself. India's treatment of its scheduled caste/scheduled tribes citizens, though not so grave as the treatment of Jews and its inability to check atrocities against a section of its citizens may well be a civilisational blot on free India.

It is strange that a world community which has been vociferous in its condemnation of Zionism, apartheid in South

Africa, racism and ethnic violence in Bosnia has never condemned the caste killings and human rights deprivations suffered by the scheduled castes / scheduled tribes in India.

Perhaps it is because the Universal Declaration of Human Rights approved by the United Nations General Assembly on 10 December 1948 very soon after India's independence, was not meant to be universal. It was not *universal* when it was declared in 1948 for there were then many countries under colonialism. Even in the recent Vienna Conference on Human Rights (1993) the Universality of the declaration was questioned. The Dalits of India have not come to accept the universality of Human Rights because for millennia they have been deprived of Human Rights and dignity.

While the UN charter talks of "promoting and encouraging respect for Human Rights and fundamental freedoms for all without distinction as to race, sex, language or religion" it fails to mention the world's oldest discrimination based on 'caste' and perpetuated by determining the social status of an individual at birth and never altering it, till death.

It is perhaps the reluctance of the UN in interfering with the internal problems of a member nation, that it has thus far kept out of even mentioning 'caste' in its mandate to promote Human Rights. But when overt discrimination affects 150 million people, a sizeable section of humanity, the UN cannot close its eyes to such blatant violations of Human Rights.

The Declaration and other international covenants have only moral political force and are not legally binding on states. In order to impose legal obligation the International covenant on civil and political rights and the International covenant on economic, social and cultural rights the optional protocal together bind the member states to fulfil their legal obligation to ensure guarantee and protect Human Rights for all.

In this context it will not be out of place to cite Article 26 of the Covenant on Civil and Political Rights: "All persons are equal before the law and are entitled without discrimination to the equal protection of the law. In this respect the law shall prohibit any discrimination and *guarantee* to all persons equal and effective protection against discrimination on any grounds such as race, colour, sex, language, religion, political or other opinion, national or social origin, property, birth or other status". This article is adequate enough to cover discrimination based on caste and India cannot be faulted for lacking in legislative and constitutional provisions, but it certainly has failed in its obligation to protect and guarantee.

The conspiratorial connivance in the continuity of the caste system by the powers that be, leads to the violation of a number of Articles in the UDHR.

It is important, therefore, that we conscientise and awaken the Dalits and Tribals of their guaranteed rights in the Universal Declaration as also in our Constitution.

We should extend and ensure not merely the enjoyment of explicitly stated Human Rights but also extinguish social privileges enjoyed by the small caste hierarchy. The monopoly of temple priesthood and the exercise of religious and family rituals must be removed from being the exclusive privileges of the Brahmin community.

In order to eliminate the caste system though it is absolutely essential to conscientise, mobilise, energise and empower the Dalits and Tribals, at the same time the unconditional support and campaign of the so-called upper caste also becomes obligatory in discarding the caste system.

In the schools, universities and in all fora of education it should be made evident and explicit that the caste system is the anti-thesis of Universal Human Rights. In rural areas any form of caste oppression should be monitored and immediately removed. Development funds should not be made available to caste groups who indulge in attacks on Dalits and Tribals.

In instances where wanton caste oppression is being established by judicial enquiry the civic rights of such offenders should be suspended for a period of five years. A youth brigade against caste must be created which should continuously monitor violations of Human Rights and bring it to the appropriate forum for immediate remedy. Finally it is suggested that only a mass movement against caste among all sections of the people which would eventually establish a casteless society in India, can destroy this millennial immorality. Human Rights movement in India provides certain opportunities which were not available to the earlier forces that launched their onslaught against the vicious caste system.

When religious movements demand the elimination of caste it involved conversion and total opposition to existing religious order as for example, the Buddhist movement being directly opposed to Hinduism and its caste system. Therefore counter religious measures cropped up thereby defeating the anti-caste movements.

When reformist movements began their attacks on caste they were uncoordinated, confused and not sustained. They even led to competitiveness among social reformers making suspect their own genuineness.

The legal protection given in our constitution has also become ineffective because those in power and those who exercise judicial authority are themselves upholding the caste system as it was evidenced in the implementation of the recommendations of the Mandal Commission. We do hope that a Human Rights movement, being universal and humane in its approach and entrusted with the responsibility of promoting and protecting Human Rights, can launch a secular, non-political, human crusade with international support against the curse of caste. Let us hope such a relentless crusade against the antiquated caste system will become manifest from now onwards.

REFERENCES

1. Gail Omvedt: *Dalits and the Democratic Revolution*.
2. Auctoby Morechan: *Human Rights : International Relation*:
3. Social Action—Vol. 43 No. 4 : A Quarterly review of Social Trends.
4. Dr. K. Kesavan : *Suyamariathai Iyakkamum Podu Udamayum*.

5. P. Kambar Manickan and Mohan Larbeer : *Dalit Viduthailai Iyal.*
6. Sundaram Manickam : *The Nandan Syndrome.*
7. Human Rights and Third World : *Economic and Political Weekly.*
8. *The Hindu.*
9. *Thamizhagathil Dalit Ina Makkal.*
10. Dr. P. Kannaian and Brindavan C. Moses—*Labour Education and Aid Society : Liberation of Panchami Land.*

17

RELIGIOUS AND SOCIAL PROTECTION OF SC/STs

Bhau Lokhande

The constitution of India enshrines equal rights to all its citizens and the same rights have been embodied in Universal Declaration of Human Rights. Section 12 of the Protection of Human Rights Act 1993 provides: to promote research in the field of Human Rights, to spread human rights literacy among various sections of society and promote awareness of the safeguards available for the protection of these rights through publications, the media workshops and other available means.

Unfortunately in India untouchability has been the biggest threat to human rights. Therefore, the architect of the Indian constitution Dr. B.R. Ambedkar abolished the curse of untouchability, vide Article 17, which declares, "Untouchability is abolished and its practice in any form is forbidden. The enforcement of any disability arising out of untouchability shall be an offence punishable in accordance with law".

While defining untouchability Dr. Ambedkar said that untouchability is a kind of disease of the Hindus. It is not a mental disease, nor any tumour, nor a rheumatic pain or kind of disabilities which can be removed, but it is a mental twist. Every Hindu believes that to observe untouchability is the right thing.

Besides all must realise that untouchability is founded on religion. Manu very definitely prescribes untouchability. He said that the untouchables should live outside the village. They shall have only earthen pots, they shall not have clean clothes, that they shall beg for food and so on. For thousands of years by the teaching of this dirty law Hindus got inculcated in their minds the doctrine that untouchability is a most sacred thing. Thus the religious books imposed the sanctity of sacredness on the minds of people and made them fanatics. In this context Dr. Ambedkar states, "The social significance of a religion with a book lies in the fact that it controls the minds of the people by giving them the impression that the religion contained in the book is true. It gives the religion authority over people and includes obedience in them".[1]

It is in this context that the Mahars of Maharashtra requested the Secretary of the State for India in 1910 for restoration of previleges which their forefathers had enjoyed in the past. They said,,"As British subjects, we cannot, we should not submit to ordinances which are entirely foreign to British ideas of public justice and public honour. We are sick of the bondage which the barbarism of Hindu customs impose upon us; we long to enjoy the perfect freedom which the British nation and British Government desire to offer impartially to all those who are connected with them as British Subjects. We would therefore appeal to the Imperial Government to move on our behalf. We have long submitted to the Jagannath of caste, we have for ages been crushed under its ponderous wheels. But we can now no longer submit to the tyranny. Our Hindu rulers did not recognize our manhood, and treated us worse than their cattle; and shall not that nation which emancipated the Negro at infinite self-sacrifice, and enlightened and elevated the poorer people of its own commonwealth condescend to give us a helping hand".[2]

The same sort of emotional challenge was made by Dr. Ambedkar at the first Round Table Conference in London in 1930. He asked pointedly, "Before the British, we were in a loathsome condition due to our untouchability. Has the British Government done anything to remove it? Before the British we were denied entry into the police force. Does the British Government admit us in the force? Before the British we were not allowed to serve in the military. Is that career now open to us? The British have done some good we cheerfully acknowledge. But there is certainly no fundamental change in our position. Indeed so far as we are concerned the British Government has accepted the social arrangements as it found them and has preserved them faithfully".[3]

The discriminatory attitude of Hindus does not allow them to accept the principle of equality because they have developed a stake in the system of inequality. Social, religious and economic advantages accrue from the practice of untouchability. It is therefore very difficult to abolish untouchability. In this connection Dr. Ambedkar said, "Those who believe that untouchability will soon vanish do not seem to have paid attention to the economic advantages which it gives to the Hindus. An untouchable cannot do anything to get rid of his untouchability. It does not arise out of any personal fault on his part. Untouchability is an attitude of the Hindu, for untouchability to vanish it is the Hindu who must change".[4]

While speaking on the Scheduled Castes and Scheduled Tribes Commissioner's report Dr. Ambedkar stated, "I do not think that untouchability will vanish. They (Hindus) believe 'yes'. I think 'No'. As I had said because it has a mental twist. It will take years and years. At some time, there is no reason why we should not strongly agitate for seeing whether untouchability goes or not, that the social, economic, political and constitutional rights of the Scheduled Caste are fully protected. To that extent efforts must necessarily be directed".[5]

Let us note what Mahatma Gandhi says in this context; and since it is the opinion of the Father of the Nation one cannot dismiss it as an exceptional case. In *Harijan* dated 6.3.1937 Gandhiji wrote, "What I mean is, one born a scavanger must earn his livelihood by being a scavanger, and then do whatever else he likes. For a scavènger is as worthy of his hire as a lawyer or your president. That according to me is Hinduism. There is no better communism on earth. Varnashram Dharma acts even as the law of gravitation. The law of Varna is the antithesis of competition which kills".

Untouchability is an aspect of social psychology. While giving the correct diagnosis of caste mentality Dr. Ambedkar states, "The caste system has two aspects. In one of its aspects, it divides men into separate communities in a graded order, one above the other in social status. Each caste takes its pride and its consolation in the fact that in the scale of castes it is above some other caste. Castes from graded system of sovereignties, high and low, which are jealous of their status and which know that if a general dissolution came, some of them stood to lose more of their prestige and power than others do".[6]

This is the actual position of the religious and social status of human beings in Hindu society. No religion except Hinduism gives religious sanction to discrimination between man and man. And religions other than Hinduism do not know the word untouchability and such a word is not found even in their dictionary. Negroes were treated as slaves but they were not untouchables or unseeables. Jews also were treated inhumanly but they also were not untouchables. Above all no religious book, whatever it may be, approves of and award sanctity to human discrimination.

The Indian constitution abolished untouchability and discrimination. But the so-called religious and sacred books are preaching the same poison. Until and unless the religion discards all sorts of inequality and opts for equality, fraternity and liberty how can one hope for genuine human rights. It is therefore necessary that the religious books must be revised leaving out the objectionable parts of discrimination. When the constitution of India can be amended several times why cannot the so-called religious books which contain objectionable laws and stories be amended?

If we are really sincere in our efforts then the Shankaracharya should come forward to accept this challenge and declare that the objectionable parts of the religious books including Purush Sukta of Rigveda and the killing of Shambuka by Rama and of Karna and Eklavya should be discarded and dropped. The story of Shabari is not sufficient to pacify the minds of people. They are not ready to accept the death of Shambuka for committing the mistake of making penance.

To escape from the disease people got converted to Islam, Christianity, Sikhism and Buddhism also. But this disease had polluted the minds of the converted people also. The caste Hindu mind claims that their Shastras are superior to the existing law. We will have to shed this complex and accept the superiority of law over the scriptures. Then only can we expect and hope for some good results in India.

I would like to conclude with the suggestion that the religious books containing retrograde laws and stories preaching and upholding inequality should be banned. Either the religious heads should do it voluntarily or they should be compelled to do so by public opinion or by judicial measures.

If this is done India can enjoy human rights in the real sense and the world can recognise it as a human rights champion. Otherwise India has no right to speak about human rights and world peace.

REFERENCES

1. Writings and Speeches, Vol. V, Dr. B.R. Ambedkar, p. 182.
2. J.N. Farquhar, *Modern Religious Movement in India*, pp. 368-69.
3. Round Table Conference Proceedings, 1930-32, London, pp. 123-29.
4. What Congress and Gandhi have done to the Untouchables, Dr. B.R. Ambedkar, p. 19.
5. Thus spoke Ambedkar, Bhagwan, Das pp. 94-95.
6. Annihilation of Caste, W. and S. Vol. I., Dr. B.R. Ambedkar, p. 72.

18

A NOTE ON CONSTITUTIONAL SAFEGUARDS AND LEGISLATIVE MEASURES FOR THE UPLIFT OF SCHEDULED CASTES

R.D. Maurya

Looking at the socio-economic composition of India's population, one striking feature that unfolds itself is a large measure of disparity in the social status and the ownership of productive assets as well as in the distribution of income among the various sections of the society. The commonly used expression 'weaker sections' refers to that section of the country's population which has been placed in a comparatively unfavourable condition in terms of social positions, assets and income distribution and comprises in the urban areas the urban poor such as slum dwellers and in the rural areas the rural poor namely landless labourers, small and marginal farmers, rural artisans, Scheduled Castes, Scheduled Tribes, religious minorities and other backward classes.

For centuries social injustices based on caste, creed, religion, class, etc., have been the bane of the Indian society. Of them caste with its ideology of graded inequality and with its package of social disabilities imposed on lower castes has played a major role in weakening our social fabric. It is also responsible for keeping a major chunk of population socially and educationally deprived and economically backward for many millennium. Over a period of time, we have developed a system of social stratification in which society is divided into two conflicting groups of people—the advantaged and disadvantaged. The former group had the monopoly of economic, political and social power and the later denied their rights in all these spheres of life. The hierarchical system of socio-economic power structure of traditional Indian society has placed the higher castes groups in commanding position of dominance and forced the lower castes groups in submissive silence. Even after independence this trend continued and whatever socio-economic transformation took place on limited scale due to the forces of modernization and the policy of reservation within the framework of positive discrimination have failed in breaking the monopoly of upper castes and classes. So that even today the Scheduled Castes, Scheduled Tribes and other backward classes remain most vulnerable sections of our society. Lack of the ownership of means of production and social discrimination are the main causes for acute poverty and exploitation of the Scheduled Castes, Scheduled Tribes and other weaker sections of society.

According to the 1981 Census, 46.6 per cent of all workers were cultivators and 24.9 per cent were agricultural labourers. Among Scheduled Caste workers, 28.2 per cent were cultivators and 48.2 per cent were agricultural labourers. According to annual report (1990-91) of the Ministry of Welfare, Government of India most of the Scheduled Castes still suffer from social discrimination and economic deprivation. The stigma of untouchability continues to occupy a central place in all their sufferings. About 78 per cent Scheduled Castes people are estimated to be below poverty line. Most bonded labourers in the country are from the Scheduled Castes, Scheduled Tribes and other backward classes.* The percentage of literacy among Scheduled Castes women is only 10.93 as against 24.93 among other women (excluding the Scheduled Castes and Scheduled Tribes). The Report of the Commissioner for Scheduled Castes and Scheduled Tribes for the year 1987-88, makes a shocking revelation about the fast deteriorating condition of the people in the lower strata of our society known as Scheduled Castes

*The percentage of literacy among the Scheduled Castes is just 21.38 as against All India average of 41.70 per cent.

and Scheduled Tribes. It sounds a note of caution for the government by pointing out that the entire economic system of our country has been moving in such a way that inequality has increased instead of decreasing and continues to increase.

In this paper an attempt has been made to analyse the situation of weaker section development without the support of constitutional safeguards and other protective measures. Although the theme of this paper is futuristic in nature, however with the help of empirical support the issues related to the development of weaker sections would be discussed in proper prospective.

Historically speaking the principle of positive discrimination and constitutional safeguards had been evolved in specific context of Dalit liberation struggle during the freedom struggle of India. D.N. Sandanshiv, an eminent jurist observes that in 1947 "Hindus got India, Muslims got Pakistan and the Scheduled Castes and Scheduled Tribes got reservations" (1986 : 3). The complementary provisions necessary to reconstruct an egalitarian social order are absent in the constitution. They are relegated to the Directive Principles of State Policy.

The President, by promulgating ordinances in 1950, identified the SCs and STs. But this was not the case for the backward classes other than the SCs and STs, though the constitution uses the term "backward classes" or "weaker sections". While discussing the Draft Article 10(3), several members in the Constituent Assembly pointed out that the term 'backward' was vague, loose and indefinite. However, Article 340 provides that the President may by order appoint a commission to investigate the condition of socially and educationally backward classes within the territory of India.

The specific constitutional provisions intended to safeguard the interests of the Scheduled Castes are on the abolition of untouchability and prohibition on its practice in any form (Article 17); prohibition of 'begar' or forced or bonded labour (Article 23); consideration of the claims of the Scheduled Castes and the Scheduled Tribes in appointments to services and posts in connection with the affairs of the union or a state (Article 335); and reservation of seats in proportion to their numbers for the

Scheduled Castes and the Scheduled Tribes in the Lok Sabha (Article 330) and in the Vidhan Sabhas (Article 332).

There are also provisions which reinforce the status of the Scheduled Castes as protected weaker section. They include the departures from the antidiscriminatory and formal equality provisions of the constitution, empowering the State to make any provision for the advancement of any socially and educationally backward class of citizens [Article 15 (4)] and for the reservation of appointments or posts in favour of any backward class of citizens which in the opinion of the state is not adequately represented [Article 16 (4)]. They also include the directive in Article 46 that the state shall promote with special care the educational and economic interests of the weaker sections of the people, and in particular, of the Scheduled Castes and Scheduled Tribes, and shall protect them from social injustice and all forms of exploitation. For analytical purposes the measures undertaken in pursuance of the various constitutional provisions for the Scheduled Castes and Scheduled Tribes may be treated under three broad categories, namely, protective, developmental and preferential. Abolition of untouchability and the disabilities arising out of its practice in any form, and prohibition of bonded labour come under the first category. Various educational schemes such as post-matric scholarships and girls hostels under central sector, and prematric stipends, reimbursement of tuition fee, book banks, and hostels under the state sector, special component plans of the centre and states for Scheduled Castes and Tribal sub-plan for Scheduled Tribes, special central assistance, and the Scheduled Castes and Scheduled Tribes Development Corporations are of the second category. Legislative, educational and employment reservations are of the third category. Of these, the effective implementation of the measures of the first two categories is a precondition for actualising the measures of the third category (Radhakrishnan : 1991).

The policy of reservation and other protective and promotional measures for the development of weaker sections have been under implementation for the last five decades. However, the implementation of these measures hitherto has not been too effective to achieve their desired objectives.

According to the Twenty-eighth Report 1986-87 of the Commissioner for Scheduled Castes and Scheduled Tribes the implementation of reservation quota for SC's and ST's have not been satisfactory particularly in groups A and B services of Central Government as shown in the following table:

Group of Posts	*Scheduled Castes*		*Scheduled Tribes*		*Increase*	
	1/1/1990	*1/1/87*	*1/1/77*	*1/1/87*	*SC*	*ST*
A	4.16	8.23	0.77	2.05	4.07	1.28
B	6.07	10.40	0.77	1.92	4.33	1.15
C	11.84	14.46	2.78	4.23	2.26	1.45
D	19.07	20.09	4.35	5.84	1.02	1.49

The representation of Scheduled Castes and Scheduled Tribes in educational profession in general and higher education in particular is negligible at all levels. The following table shows the level of representation in 41 State Universities.

Teaching Posts (41 Universities)

Category	*Total*	*SC*	*Percentage*	*ST*	*Percentage*
Professors	2,133	13	0.61	1	0.05
Readers/ Associate Professors	3,261	34	1.04	5	0.15
Lecturers	5,341	169	3.16	32	0.60
Research Associate etc.	674	71	10.53	2	0.30

Source: 28 report 1986-87 of The Commissioner for SC, STs.

The situation in central universities is even worse. One has to go a long way to achieve the stipulated percentage of reservation that is 15 per cent for Scheduled Castes and 7.5 per cent for Scheduled Tribes, provided by the constitution in various services. The top positions in decision making bodies of administration, judiciary, industry, trade and business and educational institutions are still out to reach to the weaker sections of society. For example, of the country's 18 High Courts, 12 are without a single Scheduled

Castes judge and in as many as 14 no tribal sit in judgement. The Backward Classes more popularly known as the OBC's are not better placed having secured representation among the judges in only six high courts. At present out of a total sanctioned posts of 512 High Court judges, there are only 12 Scheduled Castes and seven Scheduled Tribes judges, according to the latest available figures.

The Scheduled Castes and Scheduled Tribes judges, as of January 1, 1996 had a dismal share of 3.7 per cent of the total strength of the High Court judges. If reservation should have been implemented as per constitutional requirement their representation in High Courts would have been 22.5 per cent. Allahabad High Court which has the highest member of 70 judges, has not even a single Scheduled Tribes judge. Bombay High Court, the second largest with 54 judges also has the same position, (*Indian Express,* April 11, 1993).

In view of the above facts one could draw a conclusion that in spite of constitutional safeguards the socio-economic condition of the weaker section is deteriorating; and in the absence of these protective measures they will be further marginalised, and whatever little elite formation has taken place among these sections of society will also dry out. Past experiences show that if there is little ambiguity in guidelines regarding the implementation of job reservations and lack of standardised procedures of recruitment one finds that weaker sections do not get any entry in jobs. For example, there is poor representation of Scheduled Castes and Scheduled Tribes in central universities teaching faculties particularly at the level of Professors and Readers because there is no reservation available for Schedule Caste and Scheduled Tribe in these jobs. It is shocking that even after 50 years of independence without the support of reservation not even a single Scheduled Caste person could become a professor in any central universities though, we have produced hundreds of I.A.S. and I.P.S. from Scheduled Castes and Scheduled Tribes community due to the provision of reservation.

A question which has been deliberately or inadvertently overlooked by many, however, is the root of the evil which is the caste system. A major argument of the anti-reservationists is that the reservation of jobs for the backward castes will perpetuate the caste system. Does this mean that if there is no reservation, the caste system will wither away? (Tharvan : 1990).

In recent years the socio-economic climate of the country has been hostile towards the weaker section of society. It is a dangerous trend for the unity and integrity of the nation. The upper castes and classes do not want to snare their prosperity and monopoly of power with the deprived sections of the society. Steep rise in the cases of atrocities against the weaker sections and social tensions is result of this repressive social psychic.

In the given situation we have to go a long way to achieve the prescribed percentage of reservation i.e. 15 per cent of Scheduled Castes and 7.5 per cent for Scheduled Tribes. The political and administrative power structure is still dominated by upper castes. However, reservation in services and legislation has given a limited access in power structure to SCs. Extension of reservation to SCs in Panchayat bodies at all levels in proportion to their population has further expanded the horizontal base of power structure in rural areas. Inequality is increasing in our country at a fast rate. In this milieu, the socio-economic condition of the Scheduled Castes and other weaker sections of society is bound to deteriorate at a still faster pace. The specific directions in the constitution for termination of inhuman traditions and inequitous practices have not been followed. Sufficient conditions for achieving the goal of social development and justice have not been created in the system. Hence a very large number of Scheduled Castes continue to be socially, economically, and educationally backward and are languishing at the bottom of the social and economic pyramid. In rural areas in 1987-88 the percentage of Scheduled Castes population below the poverty line was 44.7 as compared to the All India percentage of 33.4. Most Scheduled Castes do not own land or other productive assets. In 1982 the Scheduled Castes owned only about 8 per cent of the total land owned in rural areas in the country as a whole though their households accounted for about 20 per cent of the total rural households.

This low access to land, the principal resource and the main source of power, domination, oppression, and exploitation in rural India have several implications.

The present status of deprived communities such as Scheduled Castes could be understood better in the context of the overall economic and social development. The vulnerable groups like Scheduled Castes have benefited as well as suffered from the advantages and disadvantages generated by the economic structure. Of course, being on the periphery they are more disadvantaged than those who are at the Centre, i.e., the upper caste and class Hindus.

The present policy of liberalization and privatization will further alienate the deprived groups from the mainstream of the economy. In the process of restructuring the economy the resources have been transferred in favour of the privileged class of the society and the poorer strata of society have been left at the mercy of market forces which happen to be inherently hostile towards low income groups with almost double digit inflation. If State withdraws from its welfare roles and commitment of social justice towards Scheduled Castes as enshrined in the preamble of Indian Constitution, the socio-economic condition of Scheduled Castes will be further marginalized.

19

HUMAN RIGHTS VIOLATIONS: REMEDIAL MEASURES

N.L. Sao

The Preamble to the Universal Declaration of Human Rights (UDHR) serves as the foundation and philosophy of human rights. It states, "If man is not to be compelled to have recourse, as a last resort, to rebellion against tyranny and oppression, then human rights should be protected by the rule of law". The Preamble clearly implies that man as the last resort rebels against oppression in the absence of the rule of law. Rebellions always cause social chaos. Therefore maintaining social harmony and peace, which are prerequisites for a nation's progress and prosperity, are proclaimed by the U.N. General Assembly in the UDHR as a common standard of achievement for all people and all nations. There are now a host of international conventions including those for prevention and punishment of genocide and elimination of all forms of racial and gender-based discriminations besides torture. Today what a government does to its own people is not only its own concern but is also the concern of the UNO, the UNHRC and other international bodies. In fact the work of our NHRC which was set up in 1993 by the Government of India, will also be watched by the UN bodies.

Article 4 of the United Nations Convention Against Torture and Other Cruel, Inhuman or Degrading Treatment or Punishment, enjoins on every signatory nation to "ensure that all acts of torture are offences under its criminal law" and to make these offences punishable by appropriate penalties. Article 8 makes acts of torture extraditable offences.

The Preamble to the Constitution of India defines the objective of the Constitution as: to secure justice, liberty, equality and fraternity to all the Indian citizens. In the chapter on Fundamental Rights, the Indian Constitution guarantees human rights to every citizen. It also adequately empowers the Central and State Governments to eliminate human rights violations in the country. The Indian Constitution provides for socio-economic, educational, cultural, political and service safeguards for the SC/STs (Dalits). Unfortunately, these constitutional safeguards have not improved the socio-economic condition of the SCs/STs nor have they reduced the incidence of atrocities perpetrated on the SCs/STs. Article 17 of the Constitution has abolished "untouchability" and its practice in any form. It was followed by the Protection of Civil Rights Act, 1955. Since atrocities did not stop, the Scheduled Castes and Scheduled Tribes (Prevention of Atrocities) Act, 1989 was enacted.

The special officer mentioned in Article 338 (1) was designated as early as 1950 by the first President of India, Dr. Rajendra Prasad. The duty of the special officer as specified in Article 338 (2) is to investigate all matters relating to the safeguards provided for the SCs and STs under the Constitution and report to the President on the working of those safeguards. Because of the persistent demand by SCs/ST members of Parliament the Special Officer under Article 338 was replaced by a multi-member Commission with increased functions and powers and the National Commission for the SCs/STs became a statutory body in June 1990. The commission does not have powers to give verdicts or issue directions. It can only give its findings and recommendations.

Despite all the constitutional safeguards and the machinery provided for their enforcement, the number of cases of atrocities against the SCs/STs has been increasing every year. Does it mean that the constitutional rights have become a mere paper declaration? No, on the contrary, it is a great step forward from the previous law of the land based on inequality as defined in the *Manusmriti*. In spite of the historical distortions of the Hindu society that have divided people, the Indian Constitution has provided the tools in the hands of the people to assert themselves against the onslaught of the organised few. People can approach the courts for redressal of their grievances—including violations of human rights. If the atrocities are committed on the Dalits despite the constitutional safeguards, the only logical conclusion one can draw is that the government has failed to implement the provisions of the law. The failure of constitutional safeguards to deter the torturers—mostly the high caste Hindus—raises the pertinent question: how can the NHRC reduce the incidence of atrocities against the Dalits, if not stop them altogether?

That the Central Government is aware of the frequent violations of human rights in the country is borne out by the agenda which was circulated to chief ministers of the states on the eve of the conference on human rights held on September 13, 1992 in New Delhi, Besides dealing with the necessity of setting up an NHRC, the agenda included such items as custodial crimes, atrocities against vulnerable sections of society, prison reforms, training in human rights issues, etc. Doubts about the motives of the Central Government in proposing a Human Rights Commission arose mainly from two considerations. In the first place, it is widely believed, for good reasons, that the proposal emanated from foreign funding agencies and donor countries. A large number of donor countries are particular that financial aid should be given only to those countries which have regard for human rights and democratic principles. However, the value of NHRC is not lessened even if the Commission is the result of the pressure, direct or indirect, of international democratic opinion.

Technological development has turned the world into a global village. Communication takes place at hyper speed. Human rights abuses are conveyed to all parts of the world in no time, and international bodies get involved. For example, at the Bangkok Asia-Pacific Precom conference in February 1993, (prior to the Vienna Conference in June 1993), the following resolution was passed: "Take appropriate steps to eradicate the practice of untouchability which is a crime against humanity by the year 2000, failing which sanctions will be imposed". Following this Dr. Manfred Nowak's report was adopted and published at the end of the plenary session of the Vienna NGO-Forum which reads: "The working group urges the United Nations to take appropriate steps to eradicate the practice of untouchability, which it considers a crime against humanity and discrimination on the basis of caste, religion and other factors by the year 2000. To this end, the Working Group recommends the appointment of a Special Rapporteur to carry out a study of the situation of the untouchables in South Asia, in particular of bonded labour, child servitude and child prostitution. In addition, a special committee is called for in order to initiate the process of declaring the untouchables as an indigenous people of South Asia to whom all the UN resolutions on indigenous peoples should be applicable".

When human rights violations take place against the Dalits, the focus is the victims for the only purpose of publicity in the media. The torturers are forgotten. The victims are economically and socially very vulnerable. Human rights activists, NGOs and the associations of Dalit employees must prepare them mentally, socially and politically to resist the torturers by democratic means. The Scheduled Castes and Scheduled Tribes (Prevention of Atrocities) Act, 1989 must be made use of against the torturers. The token economic assistance given to victims is inadequate.

Instead of dismissing the torturer as a sadist, or a maniac, he must be humanised by giving training in human rights and also punished promptly. Atrocities committed against individuals can be tackled in this way. But what about hundreds of armed high caste Hindus attacking Dalits? This is a national issue and the state must step in effectively. Time and again successive governments have failed to tackle large scale atrocities against the Dalits. The guilty are seldom punished. The cases against them drag in the courts for years and people forget about them. Hence the need for separate courts, as justice delayed is justice denied.

The high percentage of illiteracy make the Dalits vulnerable to oppression. The legacy of *Manusmriti* is still continuing. Successive governments have failed to enforce Article 45 of the Constitution because there is no political will. It is only because they want to follow Manu's code and not the Indian Constitution. The present Government should include this Article in the Chapter on Fundamental Rights.

There should be equitable development of all regions in the country. Then only distress migration to cities which results in slums can be stopped. The high rate of growth of population puts undue pressure on the process of development. Family planning programmes should be accorded high priority and zero population growth in ten years should be the target. Similarly basic needs of the people, like drinking water should be provided for all. For example, the majority of Dalit women have to spend several hours a day to fetch water for family needs. The UNO adopted a village in Myanmar for the purpose of water supply. All the households were supplied tap water for 24 hours. It was observed that the income of every family increased. To supply tap water to all the households in ten years should be the target for the government.

Some more measures which will go a long way in empowering not only the Dalits but the NHRC and Courts should be taken. Human rights education should be imparted in schools and colleges. A separate, independent ministry, headed by a cabinet rank minister for overseeing atrocities committed on the Dalits should be created. For the purpose of speedy disposal of such cases separate courts must be set up in each district to deal with such offences. For conducting cases in these courts, special public prosecutors are necessary at the district level court and an Advocate General at the High Court. The UNO should also set up an international court for conducting cases of human rights violations. The judges of this International Court should attend the special courts set up in India. The NHRC should have more power under the present Act, and should enjoy the status of a statutory body.

Controlling posts, like those of principal of college/school, managing director of a company, etc., must be brought under the policy of reservation by passing a special bill in the Lok Sabha and including it in the IXth Schedule of the Constitution. Intercaste and inter-state marriages be encouraged by the Central Government and by all State governments by giving them rewards and other facilities.

NGOs can play an important role in eliminating human rights violations. They should monitor and report human rights violations and pursue them in different forums. The NHRC and the National Commission for the SCs/STs should accept complaints from NGOs and promptly act on them. But for this to be effective, the Indian NGOs themselves must denounce the caste system and then take up the issue of human rights violations against the SCs/STs.

Even if all the measures mentioned above succeed, unless the mind-set of the upper caste people changes, atrocities will not be stopped. Integration of society may help to some extent in changing the mind-set. To achieve this goal every state institution (economic, scientific, educational, civil, etc.) must become multi-caste. It can be achieved by enforcing reservation on a caste basis. Only 10 per cent of all available jobs come under state institutions. The remaining 90 per cent jobs, which are in the private sector are out of the purview of reservation. Hence the SCs/STs, have no access to them. Merit is never a criterion for selecting a person for a job in India. Only high caste persons, therefore, are selected for jobs in the private sector, because of their economic/social status. As the jobs in the private sector are the preserve of high caste Hindus, strong opposition from this section is expected to reservation of jobs for the SCs/STs in the private sector. This was evident earlier in the opposition to the implementation of the Mandal Commission report. However, in spite of opposition from high caste Hindus, all private sector jobs must be subjected to reservation. For this purpose, the parliament must enact an appropriate law.

To sum up, atrocities against the Dalits are committed by high caste Hindus. How to tame and humanise the belligerent section of high caste Hindu society and make it civilised and humane is the challenge before the NGOs, the NHRC, and the serious people of our society.

Finally, let us be warned that if the Dalits are deprived of the right to be human, our country may face chaos, and may even be plunged in a civil war for which the perpetrators of violence will be solely responsible.

20

RELIGIOUS AND SOCIAL PROTECTION OF THE SCHEDULED CASTES AND SCHEDULED TRIBES

K. Kuppuswamy

When we talk of religious and social protection of the Scheduled Castes and Scheduled Tribes we mean that these sections of our society require to be guarded against and defended from the atrocities and onslaughts by the caste Hindus in the religious and social sphere.

Since the economic condition of a class or community would play a major role in ensuring its proper status in society the down-trodden people require protection in the economic realm also. Marxism conceives economic inequality and exploitation as the major cause of all social ills. The uneconomic nature of the hereditary occupation of the Dalits may be construed as mainly responsible for their distressing condition and inferior social status. Hence they would certainly require protection and advancement in the realm of economic prosperity also.

To understand the magnitude and realize the seriousness of the malady several studies were undertaken by government agencies and well meaning non-governmental organizations interested in social service. The facts gathered are analysed and their nature studied before remedies are formulated. Problems prevailing in different states and regions are different in character and dimension and call for dissimilar treatment and solution.

From the days of the British administration several measures have been introduced to protect the basic rights of the untouchables to enable them to live as human beings. Yet such protective measures have not greatly ameliorated their condition. Even after independence they continue to suffer and are being tormented by the upper class Hindus. The depressed classes should not solely depend on the well meaning measures of the ruling circle and the words of support and good intentioned actions of the Hindu leaders. Their efforts have not improved matters even to a limited extent. We should realize that our protection and salvation rests in our hands only and we should fortify ourselves against the offensive and ward off our adversaries.

Several legislative measures have been introduced and passed by the government since independence. Article 46 of the Constitution states: "The state shall promote with special care the educational and economic interests of the weaker sections of the people and in particular, of the Scheduled Castes and Scheduled Tribes and shall protect them from social injustice and all forms of exploitation". Article 17 of the Constitution prohibits untouchability. Enactments like protection of Civil Rights Act 1955 and Scheduled Castes and Scheduled Tribes (Prevention of Atrocities) Act 1989 seek to give protection to the Scheduled Castes and Scheduled Tribes.

Yet commission of crimes against the depressed class does not show any semblance of mitigation; on the contrary they are on the increase and the problems of the Scheduled Castes and Scheduled Tribes have multiplied and become intolerable.

During the previous centuries the situation was bad. The untouchables were denied every human right and were made to live a miserable life. Things improved a little during the British rule but the native Hindu classes gained the upper hand and the initial momentum lost its push.

At a Depressed Class Workmen's Conference Dr. Ambedkar said: "My heart breaks to see the pitiable sight of your faces and to hear your sad voices. You have been groaning from time immemorial and yet you are not ashamed to hug your helplessness as an inevitability. Why did you not perish in the prenatal stage, instead? Why do you worsen and sadden the picture of the sorrows, poverty, slavery and burdens of the world with your deplorable, despicable miserable life? You had better die and relieve this world, if you cannot rise to new life and if you cannot rejuvenate yourselves. As a matter of fact it is your birthright to get food, shelter and clothing in this land in equal proportion with every individual, high or low. If you believe in living a respectable life, you believe in self help which is the best help. You must abolish your slavery yourselves. Do not depend for its abolition upon God or a superhuman. Your salvation lies in political power and not in making pilgrimages and observance of fasts... It is the duty of the Legislature to provide you food, clothes, shelter, education, medicine and all the means of earning a livelihood. The work of law-making and of its execution is to be performed with your consent, help and will. In short, law is the abode of all worldly happiness. You capture the power of law making... We must shape our course for ourselves and by ourselves".

With these words of Dr. Ambedkar as the pointer for sustained action we should aim at achieving religious and social protection for the Scheduled Castes and Scheduled Tribes.

Let us take the religious aspect of the problem. Dr. Ambedkar considered Hinduism as the biggest enemy which promoted caste system and was responsible for rendering a class of people as untouchable. The social ideas of Manu and the Sastras are the main villains of the piece. He pleaded that to remove caste, we must remove Sastras. Mahakavi Bharathiyar has also attacked two Sastras in the same spirit and in this context I think it would be appropriate to quote him: "If Sastra renders different kinds of justice, one for the Sudra and another for the Brahmin, then it is not Sastra but conspiracy. There is no other Brahmin worth the name than Nandanar. If your character is unblemished, easily you achieve nobility".

It was the Brahmanism proper in the Hinduism that perpetrated untouchability and excluded a class from all religious privileges. Untouchables became outcastes and were banished from villages to exclusive slums.

Untouchables were prohibited from entering the temples. During the period shortly before and around independence Congress leaders and others organized temple entry movement. But the results were not enduring. Even today many temples in Tamil Nadu, Kerala and other places in the north are out of bounds to Scheduled Castes and Scheduled Tribes. Even the traditional rights enjoyed by the untouchable from time immemorial in the matter of beating of the drums by Paraihs during car festival at Kanchipuram and knocking at the door to arouse the deity from slumber in the dawn at Tirupati by a cobbler have been denied and sought to be taken over by caste Hindus. We have umpteem instances where Adi Dravidas who were traditionally having the rights to participate in village festivals being denied those rights nowadays with the result that communal skirmishes take place leading to atrocities like murder, rape and arson in Harijan colonies.

Shri Pratvadi Bhayankaram Annangarachari of Kanchipuram, a great Vaishnavite scholar offered equal seat in a religious assembly to one of his Harijan friends and a Muslim Judge along with orthodox Brahmins on his 80th birthday. Nobody seems to have protested. Are all the other Brahmins and caste Hindus ready to observe equality with Harijans on all occasions under all circumstances? Such questions remain questions ever.

When the foundation was laid for the Ram Temple at Rama Janam Bhoomi at Ayodhya it was said that it was a Harijan who was made to lay the first brick for the foundation of the temple. Does this symbolic act mean that the leopard has changed its spots and the Hindu movement has suddenly become enamoured of the Dalit cause ? I leave the answer to your surmise.

Instances such as Saivaite Nandanar's salvation and Vaishnavite Tiruppaanazhwar taken on the shoulders of a Brahmin priest for worship of Sri Ranganatha indicate that untouchables had been considered the favourites of the Hindu gods on several occasions in the past. Yet, the practice of excluding

Harijans from religious events and denial of religious rights to them have continued unabated through the ages.

Even in the case of Christianity despicable unsocial practices are observed. Even today certain religious rights at the Churches are being denied to them in some places by higher caste Christians and some priests. In several places in Tamil Nadu the Scheduled Castes colony is separated from the main village wholly inhabited by the Christian community.

In K.K. Pudur village in Chengalpattu District the Scheduled Caste people wanted the festive car carrying the idol to come to Scheduled Caste colony also. The high caste Christians refused to oblige and change the route. There was confusion and altercation but violence was prevented.

The Scheduled Castes and Scheduled Tribes claim equal rights in religious matters as an issue of equality and prestige. But everything is being done to deny such equality and prestige by the Hindu and Christian high caste people.

Such denial of rights to and degradation of the depressed classes could not be tolerated by Dr. Ambedkar and out of total dejection and despondency he rejected Hinduism and embraced Buddhism along with thousands of Dalits for ensuring the dignity and justice for the Scheduled Castes and Scheduled Tribes. The pity is that there is no commanding leader after Dr. Ambedkar to continue the crusade.

Bringing about equality and justice in the matter of religion can not be achieved by legislation and governmental action alone. That would call for a change of heart on the part of the community as a whole and a change of attitude towards religion. Class conscious elements in the Scheduled Castes and Scheduled Tribes and other backward looking progressive elements in the upper classes should realize the need for a simultaneous attack against untouchability and caste system. Only then the religious protection of the Scheduled Castes and Scheduled Tribes could be validly ensured. In the absence of reforms there would be conversion to other faiths.

In the social sphere, protection of the Scheduled Caste and Scheduled Tribes consists in the abolition of the caste system lock, stock and barrel. Caste is a social stigma. It is a cancer eating away the vitals of the nation.

To Quote Ambedkar: "Caste in the hands of the orthodox has been a powerful weapon for prosecuting the reformers. Caste is the monster that crosses your path. You cannot have political reform. You cannot have economic reform unless you kill this monster."

In spite of all that is said and done for the abolition of caste system in India, it is socially institutionalized in such a way that in politics, party tickets are distributed on caste considerations, elections are held as well as portfolios distributed on caste considerations. It is a mismatch between caste and democracy. Casteism has crippled the social process for change.

In this context I would like to point out that to ensure protection and enhance the prestige of the Scheduled Caste and Scheduled Tribe classes the next President of India should be chosen from those classes. On the religious level the President visit important temples all over the country and special treatment and customary courtesies are extended to the President as we observe in the case of Tirupati.Temple. Since such religious respect will be shown to the Scheduled Caste and Scheduled Tribe President the prestige of these communities who were so far shown step motherly treatment in religious matters, will acquire proper status.

To contain atrocities on the Dalits on a social level it is imperative that the law and order machinery is properly tuned to the purpose. It is in this context I recall a suggestion from our late lamented Periyar E.V.R.

He demanded that recruitment of personnel to the police force should entirely be reserved for the Scheduled Caste and Scheduled Tribe candidates only. Caste Hindu policemen could not act fairly and effectively against the interests of their own classes. The government should give serious consideration to such a proposal in the interests of protection of the social rights of the Scheduled Castes and Scheduled Tribes.

Dealing with the economic deprivation of Dalit labour Dr. Ambedkar explained the position: "In an agricultural country agriculture can be the main source of livelihood. But this source of earning a living is generally not open to untouchables. This is so, for a variety of reasons. In the first place, purchase of land is beyond their means. Secondly, even if an untouchable has the money he has no opportunity to do so. In most parts the Hindus would resent an untouchable coming forward to purchase land thereby trying to become equal Hindus. Such an act of daring on the part of an untouchable would not only be frowned upon but might easily invite punishment. In some parts they are disabled by law from purchasing land. For instance in Punjab there is a law called Land Alienation Act which specifies the communities which can purchase land and untouchables are excluded from the list. The result is that in most parts the untouchables are forced to be landless labourers. As labourers they cannot demand reasonable wages. They have no bargaining power. They must submit to the rate fixed or suffer violence".

Dr. Ambedkar advocated total nationalization of agriculture and collective farming of land in India which would go a long way in protecting the Dalits from the economic onslaught by the caste Hindu landlords. Dr. Ambedkar strongly suggested industrialisation of India also to enable absorption of rural landless labour into economic avocation.

21

DALIT WOMEN AND HUMAN RIGHTS: SOME NEGLECTED ISSUES

Vimal Thorat

During recent years the problem of the woman has received considerable attention. The problems of Dalit women, however, has not received the attention it deserves. There are specific reasons for this neglect. The mainstream view on this issue is that the problems confronting Dalit women are identical with that of general women. So there is no necessity to make special efforts for them. On the other hand, Dalit women feel that, although there is a great similarity in the problems of Dalit women (DW) and non-Dalit women (NDW), there are important differences in the nature of their problems.

In this study my main purpose is (*a*) to highlight the specific problems of Dalit women concerning human rights violation; (*b*) to understand the reasons behind the violation of human rights; and (*c*) to pose some issues for the Human Rights Commission.

Dalit Women and Human Rights Violation

The protection of Human Rights Act of 1993 defines the "human rights" as "human rights means the right to life, liberty, equality and dignity of individual guaranteed by the constitution or embodied in the international covenant and enforceable by Government of India."

As regards Human Rights of Women the National Human Rights Commission Annual Report of 1994-95 says the following: "Various laws having to do with the Status of women continue to be of deep interest to the Commission." It refers to the various Acts such as Dowry prohibition, the Sati prevention, the Indian Penal Code, and Code of Criminal Procedures and some amendment of Child Marriage Restraint Act.

It further observed that: "though the U.N. Convention on Elimination of all forms of Discrimination Against Women (CEDAW) was adopted by General Assembly in 1977, India ratified it in June 1993. The provisions of CEDAW would now have to be implemented by way of internal laws and administrative regulation. The commission recommends vigorous implementation of the country's obligation under this convention (page 20)".

The Act as well as the programmes of the National Human Rights Commission does not make any reference to the specific human rights issue of Dalit women. It also tends to treat the human right problems of Dalit women on par with non-Dalit women.

Civic Rights

Untouchability is abolished and its practice in any form is forbidden under Article 17 of the constitution. Parliament set to work on a statute to spell out the practical details and application of the principles embodied in the fundamental rights. The result was the Untouchability (Offence) Act of 1955. The Act was amended in November 1976 and named as "Protection of Civil Rights Act, 1955" it provides "penalties for preventing a person, on the ground of untouchability from entering a place of public working and offering prayer or taking water from a sacred tank, well or spring. Enforcing any kind of social disabilities such as denying access to shop, restaurant, hotel, public hospital or educational institution or any place of public entertainment or denying the use of any road, river, well, tank, water tap, bathing ghat, cremation ground, etc. attracts the provisions of this Act" (Pages 217 Scheduled Caste and Scheduled Tribe Commissioner's Report).

The total number of cases registered under the PCR Act during the years 1981-85 was 19,378. Their yearwise number was 4085 (1981), 4087 (1982), 3949 (1983), 3925 (1984) and 3322 (1985). The number of cases was 2531 in 1993 and 1731 in 1994. The number of cases were relatively higher in Karnataka, Maharashtra, Tamil Nadu and U.P. both in 1993 and 1994.

The number of cases of atrocities involving murder, dacoity, robbery, arson, rape work out to 90,097 (i.e. about a lakh) during 1981-86. In the year 1994 about 15,000 cases were registered. Thus an average of 15,000 incidences of atrocities occurred annually during 1981 and 1994.

If we take together the PCR and IPS cases in 1994 the number works out to 33848 cases of human rights violation in which women are also involved in one form or other.

Sexual Violence

Although we do not have a break-up of PCR and IPC cases separately for Dalit men and women, the Scheduled Caste and Scheduled Tribe Commissioner's report however, provides information on sexual violence against Dalit women. Sexual violence may be a general problem from which women in general suffer; in the case of Dalit women, it is far more intense and widespread. Because of lower social attitude towards Dalit women and their economic dependence, they become victims of the high caste sexual violence, on a scale far greater than that of the non-dalit women. Between 1981 and 1986 about 4000 Dalit women became victims of rape. In 1993 and 1994 this figure rose to 798 and 992 respectively. This means annually about seven hundred Dalit women fall prey to the sexual assault by high caste people. Since 1981 such cases have increased between 1981 and 1986 as well as during 1993 and 1994 in the country. The cases were relatively higher in U.P., M.P., Rajasthan and Bihar.

Victims of Social and Religious Practices like Devadasi and Joginis

The 28th report of the Commissioner for Scheduled Caste and Scheduled Tribe reported that by February, 1986 there were about 10,000 Joginis belong to Scheduled Castes in Nizamabad district of

Andhra Pradesh. The prevalence of this system has been observed in large parts of Andhra Pradesh. The survey conducted by District Collector and Scheduled Caste Finance Corporation revealed the prevalence of 15850 cases and 80 per cent of the Joginis belong to Scheduled Castes.

Under this social and religious system the unfortunate village girls are married to a village god by their parents. These girls are then sexually exploited by the upper caste landlords and rich men of the village who have initiated the process of "Divine marriage". This socially "Sanctioned" prostitution has been prevalent in large areas of Telengana, which adjoins Karnataka where similar practice of Devdasi exists. The Devdasi system also exists in parts of western Maharashtra (Kolhapur, Solapur and Dharwad).

The system of Jogins is worse than that of Devadasis, who are dedicated to a god and look after a temple. Unlike a Devadasi who lives in a temple, a Jogin lives in a Jhuggi, with her parents, where the landlord visits her. They take no responsibility of the children begotten of the union and the female children have no option but to become Joginis. These girls cannot marry again, cannot step out of their village and are no better than bonded labourers. This sanctioned prostitution has been in existence for a long time.

Human Rights Violation in Economic, Political and Educational Field

Beside the civic right violation and sexual exploitation, Dalit women also suffer from political, economic and the educational rights. Unfortunately enough studies are not available on the Human Rights violation of Dalit women in these areas. Nevertheless the limited evidences indicate that the Dalit women suffer from discrimination and unequal treatment in the field of economic activities and in education. Some of the studies point out the economic discrimination in employment of women belonging to Scheduled Caste in general and sweeper community and others involved in so called unclean occupations. There are evidences that Dalit women do not find jobs inside the houses of high castes. They are rarely employed as a maid servant due to the practice of untouchability. Similarly quite a few studies point out the practice of discrimination in the schools (Geeta Nambisson, 1996). In the area of politics women do not enjoy full freedom. Thus they are deprived of their political rights.

Human Rights Violation and Economic Deprivation

There is a close link between economic deprivation and violation of Human Rights of Dalit women. The Dalit women are perhaps the most economically deprived section of Indian society. A careful look at their economic situation reveals this point clearly. The workforce structure of DW is such that they rarely own any land. Most of them work as agricultural labourers. In 1991 about 71 per cent DW workers in rural areas were agricultural labourers. Only 19 per cent of them owned land. As against this the proportion of agricultural labour among NDW was 43 per cent. But NDW's proportion as a cultivator was about 42 per cent. Even in urban areas about 58 per cent DW are employed as agricultural labours. This proportion was only 5 per cent in the case of NDW. Another important economic problem of DW is lack of employment throughout the year. Agricultural work is seasonal. We generally find that both in rural and urban areas the percentage of unemployed among the Scheduled Caste female is higher than the unemployment rate of non-Scheduled Caste and Scheduled Tribe woman. For example, according to a recent National Sample Survey the unemployment rate of Dalit woman (on current daily basis) was 4 per cent. This was only 0.97 per cent for non-Scheduled Caste female.

Similarly, in urban areas the unemployment rate for the Dalit women was 3.27 per cent. This was only 1.98 per cent for non-Dalit women. This suggests that not only the large majority of Dalit women are agricultural labourers, but the rate of unemployment among them was also quite high.

Besides this a large number of Dalit women are engaged in unclean occupation which is considered to be inferior in nature. Because of their association with these occupations, these women face discrimination in social relation and also in employment.

The lack of educational development is another important problem from which the DW suffer. In 1991 the literacy rate among Dalit women was indeed quite low in the rural areas. In rural areas only 19.46 per cent Dalit women were literate. By comparison the rate for general population was 30.62 per cent. Similar disparities existed in 1991 for urban areas also. In fact in urban areas the literacy rate among Dalit female is the lowest.

The lack of income generating assets and heavy dependence on wage employment of Dalit women on the high caste landlord provide a situation for the latter to exploit them sexually and otherwise. Thus the economic situation of Dalit women compel them to surrender their civic, political and economic rights.

Human Rights Violation and Hindu Social System

Human rights violation of the Dalit women has a close interconnection between the status of women in general and the Dalit women in particular as prescribed in the Hindu social order.

The explanation for the different and discriminatory attitude of high caste male towards Dalit women is also to be found in the social and religious system of Hindus. As is well known, in the overall social framework of Hindu society women are not supposed to be free and all the sources of material development are blocked. Dalit women have no right to education, no right to acquire religious knowledge, no right to acquire property. In fact in the overall social scheme of the Hindu system the Dalit woman is located at the bottom.

Issues before Human Rights Commission

The question of Human Rights of Dalit women poses a challenge to the Human Rights Commission. At the moment the NHRC has no agenda for Dalit women. So NHRC should make a beginning in this respect on the following lines:

1. There are specific disabilities from which Dalit women suffer. The NHRC should bring out periodical reports on the human rights situation of DW in India. 2. It should bring out reports on the social and religious institutions perpetuating socially sanctioned prostitutions such as Devdasis and Joginis in Andhra Pradesh and Maharashtra and also in other states and make efforts to stop this system both legally and otherwise by introducing law and other measures. 3. Bringing out reports on the social and economic situation of Dalit women which leads to the violation of human rights and suggests social and economic measures to promote the atmosphere in which Dalit woman could enjoy human rights. 4. Give representation and participation in NHRC and other Commissions for Women.

22

HORRENDOUS PRACTICES IN THE NAME OF HINDUISM

Nirmala Arulprakash

The main purpose of human rights is to protect the weak and the vulnerable people who cannot always protect themselves. Human rights play a dominant role in today's world. Everyday life is based on what we call 'human rights' which include the right to live freely and to think and talk freely and to be treated fairly and with dignity by others.

The Africans (Blacks) in South Africa* and Namibia*, the Aboriginals in Australia, the Blacks in United State of America and similar sections of people in other parts of the world are denied their due rights and privileges. They have struggled for centuries to establish their rights and are successful to a certain extent to assert their claim to equality of rights with other human beings.

Similarly, a kind of degradation and segregation was in practice in India; more grave compared to other forms of discrimination, namely the disease of untouchability which entered into the very vitals of the Indian society. It is an evil off-shoot of the practice of caste system of the Hindu-fold. It is strange that Hindus with their sublime philosophy and benign outlook were party to such an intolerable dwarfing of manhood. It

*End of the apartheid regime at the hards of Dr. Nelson Mandela's peaceful revolution has wrought a metamorphosis in the two countries.

is not only a blot on Hindu religion, but has created intolerance, sectionalism and fissiparous tendencies. Many evils we find today in our society are traceable to this heinous monstrosity. The untouchables were forced to a life of servitude as a downtrodden community.

In the Hindu hierarchy, the division of labour turned into caste system. The Brahmins who recite Vedas and do rituals, the Kshatriyas or warriors, the Vyasyas or business class and the Shudras or labourers, who do different kinds of labour. The 'Panchamas' or the fifth class were segregated from the rest of the village or society. They were made to live separately and were treated as 'untouchables' and even as 'unseeables'. Under this social discrimination, men and women were subjected to severe humiliation. They were deprived of basic needs. They were forbidden to walk, talk or move freely. Even their shadow was considered polluting. The untouchables were forced to such a debased position that even animals were treated better than these people. Not only were they economically, socially, and religiously ignored but were forcibly deprived of dignity. Above all, they were subjected to torture and atrocities. Always laborious and hard working they were condemned to servitude without any return. They were neither paid for their hard work nor treated as human beings.

Their dwellings were in complete seclusion, in 'cheris' or shalltos. Even at present the same condition prevails, except for a few fortunate among them who are educated. In the cities, the Dalits find it difficult to rent houses unless they conceal their caste. So they try to pass off as of castes and they live a life saying that they belong to 'Pillai' (Nair) caste or other backward community. This kind of 'Sanskritisation' prevails even in the cities.

The 'Dalits' are mentioned as 'Scheduled Castes' as defined in para 26 of the Part I of the first schedule of the Government of India Act 1935. G.O. No. 850, Public Services dt., 18.05.1947. In Tamil Nadu, they are termed as 'Adi Dravidas'. The people of this community are spread over all the districts of Tamil Nadu from North Arcot to Tirunelvelly and in extreme South of Travancore.[1]

1. Thruston, *Castes and Tribes of Southern India*, Madras, 1909, p. 88.

Their occupations vary from ploughing (agriculture), weaving, mat and basket making, laying of roads and buildings houses, etc. Historical research reveals that this community was a large settled race and that they were the original inhabitants of Tamil Nadu. Moreover, the people of this community were Pre-Dravidians.

Atrocities against the Dalits are on the increase. The Untouchability Offences Act 1955, the Protection of Civil Rights Act 1967 and Article 17 of the constitution which abolishes untouchability, are all meant to eradicate untouchability. But they remain on paper alone and are practically not followed. The cruel practice of untouchability continues even today in the villages.

The position of Dalit women are more deplorable, compared to their male counterparts. A Dalit woman is doubly oppressed. Firstly, from a sense of insecurity, since she is dependent on the man and secondly castewise. Illiteracy, lack of awareness and poverty make her helpless, voiceless and completely oppressed. Dalit women are more prone to the social evil of untouchability. They are deprived of their basic survival needs and vulnerable to rape and other forms of sexual abuse. Specially rural Dalit women become the first and worst victims of rape and other atrocities. The police, who should prevent such crimes are also parties to inhuman crimes. From a small ten years old girl to sixty years old woman, none is spared. Despite the adoption of legislation against most of these crimes, oppression and violence are the lot of Dalit women.

Annamalainagar police station in Chidambaram was the talk of the day during 1992, when Padmini, a Dalit woman was raped by five policemen in the very presence of her husband who was locked up in the police station. He was later beaten to death.

In another incident, Prakash Mary of Ramavaram village in Madras had been forcibly taken on February 21, 1995 to the police station along with her daughter Poongothai for investigation of a petly crime. While Poongothai was let off Prakash Mary had been raped by ten policemen. She had watched the brutal violence from outside, helplessly. Similarly, Vijaya of Senji was taken to Ananthapuram police station near Villupuram in the name of investigation and was gangraped by the police.[2]

2. Junior Vikatan Publication of Ananda Vikatan, Madras.

Several cases go unnoticed since women never open their mouths and speak out. It was the Padmini case in Chidambaram which brought to light the atrocities committed on them.

In the name of religion, women are forced to follow horrendous practices. For example, they dance naked in the villages, which is said to be a form of worship. And in some villages, Dalit women are trapped in prostitution in the name of some religious practices. In Sirupanaiyur, a village at Villupuram District, Mariamma, a Dalit girl was recently married to the local god. A girl once married to god, cannot marry anyone. So she has to lead the life of a concubine. She can also bear children if she wishes. Thus, without a status in the society, she is made to live a life of degradation. This is due to ignorance and illiteracy.

All Dalits are not dark-skinned nor are they only dark. There are upper caste persons who are also dark in complexion. Most Indians are colour conscious and view features as indices of status in life. This should be vehemently opposed. The Tamil proverb 'dark Brahmins and fair paraiyans are improper' is a misguided concept. Since the Dalits are generally hard working doing manual labour in the fields and are exposed to sun they tend to be dark skinned. Further as they are deprived of basic needs and were forced to eke out a subsistent existence and live in inhospitable and unsanitary conditions they are backward. In urban areas, they are relatively better placed. This is because they are allowed to mix with upper caste persons and are also educated.

Benami transactions are possible because of the illiteracy of the Dalits besides their being victims of all kinds of exploitation. They are cheated by the landlords who take their thumb impression on loan applications and other documents to buy cattle or claim subsidies with the intended beneficiaries left high and dry.

Even in death the Dalits are not spared. If the body has to be carried to the graveyard through areas inhabited by the upper castes there will be trouble. The upper castes object to it so that the Dalit mourners have to make a detour covering miles and miles or be prepared for a fight with the upper castes. Even in the graveyard their dead have to be cremated separately. It is nothing short of apartheid. These atrocities show that the cause of untouchability is a riddle to grave disability and denial of human rights and dignity.

Does a dead body have caste? Are the dead among the upper castes immune from decomposition? Is it only a Dalit's body that strells and stinks? In God's creation all human beings are equal. So, if one does not treat another as an equal fellow being, he is either insane or inhuman.

The right of the Dalits to a life with dignity is denied by specific forms of violence and deprivation. They suffer open discrimination and suppression and social boycott in not only villages but more subtly in the public services. New methods are adopted to discriminate against them and deny them their due. They are not given places in government service which are effective. Even when injustice is done to a Dalit, the Dalit official is unable to intervene in his or her behalf. Animosity and hostility towards the Dalits assume enormous and diverse forms and manifestations. The Dalits are not able to secure their rightful place of honour in the social set-up. They are not able to secure a proportional share of economic development and social welfare programmes for the weaker sections. Above all, they have no access to power in the political hierarchy.

Hence, the sense of insecurity and economic helplessness is deepening in the minds of the Dalits. This feeling of 'Minority insecurity' threatens to cut at the very roots of the processes of national integration, which is a danger to democracy. With the spread of education, the youth is restive and frustrated. It is therefore, high time the issue of uplift of the Dalits is seriously considered for expeditious action.

According to the Report of the Ministry of Welfare, Government of India for the year 1992-93, the crimes committed against the Scheduled Castes and Scheduled Tribes registered in 1991 is as follows:

Raping of Dalit women	:	1067
No. of Dalits murdered	:	731
Arson incidents	:	645
Dalits, grievously hurt	:	1890
Other offences against Dalits	:	17029
Total no. of criminal cases		21362[3]

3. Report of the Ministry of Welfare, Govt. of India, 1992-93, New Delhi.

In other words, "every hour two Dalits were assaulted, every day three Dalits' women are raped, two Dalits are murdered and two Dalits houses are burnt".

This is only the tip of the iceberg. The figures refer only to the registered cases on the basis of complaints by persons who are bold to seek police protection at the risk of their lives. Unreported cases will be much higher comparatively. The Dalits refrain from reporting offences committed against them out of fear of dominant upper caste persons in the villages.

In Tamil Nadu, with a total population of 5,58,58,946, the Scheduled Castes comprise 19 per cent, that is 1,07,12,266; while the Scheduled Tribes number 5,74,194 which is 1 per cent.[4] But this 20 per cent of the population of the State is facing oppression. In spite of the laws prohibiting untouchability it is practiced with impunity. Babasaheb Dr. Ambedkar said, "For a general mass of the Hindus, the untouchable remains an untouchable, even though he becomes a Christian". The statement by the great leader is a living testimony to the reality of the social situation in India.

To escape from the lot, a large number of Dalits embrace Buddhism, Christianity, and Islam, though they very well know the fact that they would lose the benefits of reservation by conversion. Also it will be too late when they realise that in almost all the religions they are treated as Dalits, no less, no more. Unless untouchability is removed from the hearts of the people, the law will be ineffective. The Universal Declaration of Human Rights was proclaimed by the General Assembly U.N.O. on December 10, 1948. It has a number of Articles. But the first two Articles emphasise that, "all human beings without distinction are born free and equal in dignity and rights" and set out the basic principles of equality and non-discrimination in the enjoyment of human rights and fundamental freedoms.

These concepts of human rights apply to the entire world. As such, the basic principles of equality and freedom are the quintessentials of human life.

4. Adi-Dravidas and Tribal Welfare Office, Chennai-5 Pamphlet.

What we need is a change of heart. For changing the heart, the mind should be moved. And for social change, a sensible approach is required. Sense here means sixth sense because one person treating another human being as inferior is nothing but a senseless or brutal act. A man without the sixth sense treats fellow-men like an animal. So, men without sixth sense cannot be human. Hence, social change can take place only when both the mind and heart are attuned in action. If a man really has sense, he would come out of his old religious customs and taboos and accept his fellow human beings as his equal. If not, the discriminated intellectuals who are already alert have to sharpen their intellect further, for in an upsurge or revolution and bring about social change for ushering an egalitarian society.

Some Suggestions

1. Research Intelligence Cells should be set up to evaluate the conditions of the Dalits.
2. Economic uplift of the rural Dalits, through farming petty trades.
3. In addition to separate hostels, reservation of accommodation in the general hostels should be provided. Standards of separate hostels should be improved.
4. Women Welfare Cells to be set up to create an awareness for Dalit women and make them self-supporting.
5. Watchdog Committees to be set up at all levels to completely eradicate and wipe out untouchability.

23

DALIT MOVEMENT IN MAHARASHTRA

M.F. Jilthe

It may be conceded that democracy has today come to fruition with the global adoption of Human Rights though much remains to be desired. What is called Human Rights today is not really a new concept though it made its entry into politics and social life in the seventies of this century.

It was Lord Buddha who visualised this 2500 years ago which is evident from his philosophy which may be epitomized as *Bahujan Hitay Bahujan Sukhay,* i.e. greatest good of the greatest number. In his Sangh there were the monks of all shades and character who shed their differences after joining the sangh. Thus it is Gautama Buddha who brought into material form the concept of egalitarian society in which people lived in harmony, allowing themselves as much liberty as was needed for their spiritual development of which the ultimate beneficiary was the society at large. Discarding the theory of personal God he placed man at the centre of the universe. Otherworldliness was left to the speculation of other religions. Thus Buddha respected every living being and emphasized worth rather than birth as a measure of man.

This was diametrically opposed to the hierarchical set-up of the Hindu society where caste considerations were uppermost and worth was relegated into the background.

These long lost rights were not striven for until we come to the nineteenth century when Mahatma Phule went into the root cause of sufferings of the downtrodden people which was the craftiness and hypocrisy of the Brahmins in keeping the masses in ignorance and fostering in them the myth that Brahmins were the gods of the earth and obedience to them was the obedience to the Supreme Being. For centuries the masses languished in these superstitious beliefs, quite resigned to their fate and led a life worse than that of the animal. It was Mahatma Jotiba Phule, a farmer's son, who gave a clarion call to these people to rise against the tyranny of the Brahmins and throw away the authority of the Hindu Shastras and Puranas. He believed that only education could bring about the emancipation of these people and pull them out of it. This was the first conscious effort made towards liberation of the Dalits and the downtrodden people from the age old thraldom of the Brahmins and the caste-Hindus. He appealed to the barbers not to shave the heads of the widows who were chiefly Brahmins and they fully cooperated with him. He also made an appeal to the masses that they should not engage Brahmin priests at the marriage ceremony and asked them to officiate themselves on these occasions.

Mahatma Phule laid down the foundation of modern Maharashtra and was one of the great mentors of Dr. Ambedkar. Both of them saw man as man capable of playing a role in this world, perhaps a great role as the situation demanded.

Let us recall two incidents from the life of Dr. Ambedkar. The first is the satyagraha launched at the Chavadar Tank at Mahad in Kolaba district of the then Bombay Presidency. The Satyagraha was aimed at assesting the rights of Dalits to fetch drinking water from a particular tank. He strove to establish Dalits' identity as human beings.

This quest for recognition as human beings became the central theme in the high drama of his life and the shattering climax for others came when he became the chief architect of the Indian Constitution.

The second incident in this drama is the public bonfire of Manusmriti and all that it signified. It was time, Dr. Ambedkar announced, to begin a new era in which all people could breath freely.

In embracing Buddhism Dr. Ambedkar showed to the world that Buddha's light shines eternally and that this world could be a happier place to live in.

Dr. Ambedkar wanted that his converts should not have even small traces of Hinduism left in them and gave twenty-two pledges to them as an antidote. The new converts in obedience to his call discarded Hindu gods and goddesses as one of the reasons attributed to the atrocities committed against the Dalits is this.

If a counter-revolution by the upper castes has started in Maharashtra it is due to the awakening brought about by Dr. Ambedkar among the Dalits. The long battle for renaming Marathwada University after Dr. Ambedkar is clearly a result of this. It was the fight for the values that Dr. Ambedkar stood for Dalits has won the battle, but this is not all.

In recent times Maharashtra was rocked by the riddles of Rama and Krishna and there were rallies and counter-rallies. The mammoth rally of the Dalits at Mumbai was a historical one and was successful in displaying the monolithic strength of unity.

Demolition of Babri Masjid on 6th December 1992 was a sequel to this for the date was carefully chosen. It coincides with the Mahaparinirvana day of the great leader and one can easily see the strategy behind this.

Attacks on Dalits do take place in Maharashtra and during the regime of the Shivasena BJP government the frequency has increased. The government had scrapped Shri Krishna Commission which was entrusted with the task of investigating into the Bombay communal riots in 1992-93. In another incident the government unsuccessfully tried to impose blue uniform on Dalit students so that they could be easily discriminated against. These days Aurangabad in Maharashtra is shaken by an incident in which the Deputy Mayor assumed office after performing a purificatory rite because his predecessor belonged to a low caste. The Dalit leaders and workers strongly agitated against this and the agitation still continues.

There has been a great agitation raging in Maharashtra and it is over the death of a Dalit doctor who was allegedly burnt to death by the police.

The voice of the Dalits in Maharashtra can never be silenced. It is the voice of Dr. Ambedkar which reverberates through them and no power in the world can stifle it. But masses never actually participate in politics. They can only be roused into action. The direction must come from the leaders and intellectuals. And what can be a better guide than Dr. Ambedkar's advice to his followers: "educate to agitate and organise"?

24

RELIGIOUS AND SOCIAL PRACTICES AND HUMAN RIGHTS OF DALITS

N.G. Meshram

A large number of cases of atrocities on Dalits are registered in Madhya Pradesh, Rajasthan, Uttar Pradesh, Bihar and Gujarat, according to the data made available to the Lok Sabha on December 8, 1994 (*The Times of India*, dt. 13.8.1995). More recently, the attacks on Dalits in the southern districts of Tamil Nadu are the most barbaric and reprehensible. The police in league with caste Hindus ransacked Dalit houses, burnt their property, assaulted those in sight and poisoned the water sources of the Dalits. The entire population of Dalits was made to starve and denied water for several days (*The Times of India*, dated 28.9.1995).

A Dalit bridegroom was badly assaulted by caste Hindus in Raipur. His only crime was that he was mounted on a horse in a wedding procession. Dalits are compelled to pick up grains for food from the cow dung. Dalit women have to keep their breasts uncovered in some parts of South India. A Dalit cannot cohabit with his wife unless a Brahmin (*Namboodhri*) cohabits with her first in some parts of Kerala. Dalits are not allowed to choose names for their children, in some parts of India.

In all organs of the government, may it be judiciary, legislature or executive, with a few exceptions, communal feelings are rampant. A modern Hindu Brahmin by caste or so-called high caste, educated in civilised countries of Europe and America, read heaps of books of human rights, oriented in Western culture, but has no courage to befriend the Dalit and treat him as an equal in society. Fear of excommunication and punishment lurks on the horizon. A Dalit turning against the currents is sure to meet the anger of caste Hindus.

Why do the Brahmins and caste Hindus behave in this inhuman way with Dalits?

Dr. Babasaheb Ambedkar wrote: "If you ask a Hindu, why he behaves in this savage manner? Why he feels outraged by the efforts of Dalits for a clean and respectable life? His answer will be a simple one. He will say—'What you call the reform by the Dalits is not a reform. It is an outrage of our Dharma'. If you ask him further where this Dharma of his is laid down? His answer will again be a very simple one. He will reply—'Our Dharma is contained in our Shastras'. A Hindu in suppressing what, in the view of an unbiased man, is a just revolt of the Dalits against a fundamentally wrong system by violence, pilage, arson and loot, to a modern man appears to be acting quite irreligiously, or, to use the term familiar to Hindus, he is practicing of Adharma. But, the Hindu will never admit it. The Hindus believe that it is the untouchables (Dalits) who are breaking the Dharma. Hindus' act of lawlessness (Adharma), is guided by his sacred duty to restore Dharma. This is an answer, the truth of which cannot be denied by those who are familiar with the psychology of Hindus. But, this raises a further question, as to which Shastras have prescribed and what rule of social relationship do they contain. The principal source of Dharma, it is agreed by all the Hindus, are the Vedas, the Smrities and the customs. But the Vedas do not profess to be formal treaties on Dharma. They do not contain positive precepts (Vidhis) on matters of Dharma in a connected form. They contain only disconnected statements of certain topics concerned with Dharma. Smrities are formal treaties on Dharma. They contain enactment as to the Dharma. They form the law of the Dharma in the real sense of the term. Disputes as to what is Dharma and what is Adharma can be decided only by reference to the text of the law as given in the Smrities. The Smrities are the real source of what Hindus call Dharma. The Smrities are called Dharmashastras (scriptures) which prescribe the rules of the Dharma. There are a number of Smrities. Some are authoritative. Manu Smriti, Yajnavalakya Smriti and Narada Smriti are the standard and authoritative Smrities. Of this, Manu Smriti stands (first) pre-eminently as the source of all Dharma. Indepth study of Manu Smriti is necessary to understand the whole Hindu Dharma which is nothing but the evil design by man against man. It is a creation of the Brahmin to sustain his comfort and power. If any one attacks Manu Smriti is sure to invite trouble under the comprehension of Hindu that the great Adharma has been done. To restore Dharma, Hindus are ready to wage war and are prepared to inflict any degree of punishment which may appear to the world as inhuman, cruel and atrocious"

Religions, other than the religion of Aryans, have been generally good. The religions of foreign lands, viz. Christianity, Islam and Judaism came to India with their philosophies of benevolence unknown to the Hindus. Buddhism, the Dharma of this soil rose against the Adharma which Hindus called Dharma, while other foreign religions remained passive for obvious reasons. The moment these religions came under the influence of Hinduism, they also started behaving with Dalits as the Hindus did. 'Divide and Rule', the original principle of the Hindus, was adopted by the other religions. As the Varnas and castes were created in Hinduism, so also they were created by other religions.

Islam came to be divided into four tribes viz. Sheikh, Saiyed, Moghal and Pathan. Mahomedans themselves recognised two main social divisions—(1) Ashram or Sharog and (2) Ajlaf. Ashraf means 'noble' and includes descendants of foreigners and converts of high caste Hindus. All others including occupational groups and converts of lower ranks are known by the contemptuous term 'Ajlaf', wretches or mean people. They are also called *kamina* or Iter, base or *Rasil*, a corruption of *Rizal*, worthless. In some places, a third class is added, called *Arzal*, which is the lowest of all, with whom no other Mohomedan would associate. This third group is forbidden to enter into a mosque or to use the public burial ground. Within these groups, there are castes, with social precedence of exactly the same nature, as one finds in Hindus. Thus, there can be no matter of doubt that the Muslim society in India is afflicted by the same social evils, which afflict the Hindu society. Indeed the Muslims have all the social evils of the Hindus. (Dr. Ambedkar, *Thoughts on Pakistan*, pp. 225-226).

The practice of Christianity in India has not been different from the practice of Hinduism. St. Thomas, one of the first apostles of Christ came to India and established churches in Kerala. The first Christians were drawn from the rank of upper caste Hindus. They are called 'Syrian Christians'. They kept the good news brought by St. Thomas with themselves to avoid its being polluted by the lower castes. They did not make efforts to propagate it. During the sixteenth century, Roman Catholic Missionaries came from Portugal, under the leadership of Francis Xavier. On his arrival in Oct. 1542, the Lord's prayer and the Ten Commandments were preached in Tamil Nadu and Goa. People belonging to different castes from the south-west coast of India, were drawn to Christianity. Roberto de Nobili arrived in Madurai in 1606. He rejected the methods of missionary work of Francis Xavier, of converting any one. He hated the people of Portugal in Goa, being "unclean" people, eating beef and drinking liquor. He confined his mission of conversion among the upper caste Hindus. He called himself high caste raja (King) and claimed to be of Royal race from Rome. He declared himself along with his colleagues as 'new brahmins'. These new brahmins believed that the original Veda is lost and Roberto de Nobili declared that he has found it and that he is teaching from that. He followed all customs of Hindus, accepted caste and practised untouchability. Consequently, many upper caste Hindus became Christians. He introduced separate priests for upper and lower caste Christians. Hence, the church was divided into the church of Brahmin Christians and the church of Pariah (Dalit) Christians.

A Luthern missionary, Christiab Frederick Schwartz, trained in the University of Halle, came to India, and worked among the poor in a secular way. Protestant missionaries like Zienenbalg and Plutchau from Germany landed in south India in 1706. They began teaching gospel to Dalits and insisted on Dalit children to sit along with the missionaries. They opened both the church and the school for Dalits for the first time in this land. For three centuries, the Protestant missionaries worked for Dalits. However, the Protestant policy on caste was not very different from that of the Roman Catholics. (Dr. James Massey, *Indigenous People* 317, and *Towards Dalit Hermeneutics*, 39-43).

Missionaries were quick to perceive the hierarchical nature of Indian society. Perceiving the hindrance of caste to the mission, they adopted the object of converting high caste persons thinking that this would have an automatic effect of their domination and that the low castes would convert. The missionaries were in favour of upper castes and biased against the Dalits, for fear that their entry into the church would lead to 'baptised heathens' and would become a deterrent for the upper castes embracing Christianity. One missionary remarked that he would baptise one Brahmin rather than a thousand Chamars. There was opposition to Dalit conversion from upper caste christians also. National Christian Council (NCC) in 1920 felt that it did not want to be called a religion of the untouchables. He banned mass conversions. Thus, the liberation movements of the Dalits was blocked. Dalit converts were deprived of their agriculture work. Later, British rule also deprived the Dalits of the benefits introduced in the 1935 constitution (Dr. James Massey, *Outside the Camp*, 38).

However, the upper castes did not become Christians in the real sense. They became beneficiaries of educational and medical enterprises. Christian Missionaries opened schools and colleges for the upper castes more than for the Dalits. In Bombay, this phenomenon is clearly visible. Lord Jesus was born, loved and crucified for the Dalits the world over, but the practice of his missionaries is exactly opposite of what he stood for. This is the effect of the powerful influence of Hindus.

Sikhism and Zoroastrianism have very strong religious scriptures but are very weak in practice. They are completely assimilated in the Hindu practice. They have no courage to rebel against the evil practices of the society for reasons best known to them.

Buddhism did not suffer from territorial boundaries unlike the U.N. under Article 2 (7) of its Charter viz. non-interference in the domestic affairs of any sovereign nation. It travelled far and wide for the protection and restoration of human rights and fundamental freedom of the people the world over. In fact, Buddhism has been the custodian of human rights, much before U.N. It was the first religion to eliminate caste prejudicers and hereditory distinctions among human beings. Compassion and persuasion were the methods for conversion followed by the Buddha and his community of priests. The Dalits were the first to find solace and protection in this religion. Gautama Buddha provided the very antidote for the removal of craving of the human mind which is the root of all evil and suffering of ordinary people and of the kings which led to war and violation of human rights. Craving stands for desires which are not attainable.

Buddhism, too, came under the powerful influence of Hinduism. It came to be divided into two major sects viz. Hinayana (Theravada) and Mahayana. There remained no difference between Hinduism and the Mahayana sect of Buddhism. The societies practising Hinayana sect of Buddhism also have come under Hindu influence where caste hierarchy is being practised.

Hence, the cumulative effects of all the major religions upon the Dalits have been very alarming. Dalits have become unfriendly to all the religions. No religious practices can ensure protection of human rights of Dalits. These religions pay more attention to worship of God and rituals, than the human society of Dalits. Advancement of the Dalits is not on the agenda of the religious and social practices.

One civilisation claims superiority over another. European civilization claimed to have the right to rule over other civilisations. Thus the suppression and subjugation element came into existence. As a result, human rights abuse became rampant. People of one civilisation became the victims of another civilisation. To console their subjects, these civilisations (religions) devised the art of preaching. The object of preaching had an ulterior motive i.e. there should not be revolt against the evil design, which brought power and comfort to them. Hindus evolved the element of Dharma and Adharma for preaching. Islam believed that science exists within it and there is no need of advancement of science and belief in science.

Dalits were a flourishing civilisation, once upon a time. They are now subjugated. They are worse than slaves and serfs. The theory of John Locke is that human rights are the natural rights of all human beings. No law and no government can take them away. Right to life, right to liberty and right to property are the basic human rights in the opinion of Locke.

If we really want to make India a strong and economically powerful country, we should not neglect the Dalits. Negligence of the Dalits, the downtrodden people of our society, will keep the country stagnant.

The Organisation of African Unity (OAU) at Dakar had demanded reparations from the U.S.A. and Europe for the impoverishment of the African continent by colonisation and practice of slavery. Germany paid billions of dollars to Isreal as reparation for the holocaust. Washington is still paying compensation to its citizens of Japanese origin who were illegally detained in concentration camps during the Second World War. Iraq is being forced by the UNO to pay reparations to the people of Kuwait, Israel, Saudi Arabia for the loss of life, limb and property during the recent Gulf War. The case of the Dalits is not different. The case of Dalits is much older and it needs world attention. Once a flourishing civilisation the Dalits are now deprived of their nation's fundamental human rights. Deliberate attempts are being made to keep Dalits and their motherland from advancement. May wisdom prevail so that they do not demand reparations from those who are the cause of their backwardness and deprivation of human rights.

25

SOCIAL POLICY AND SOCIETAL CHANGES

Katti Padma Rao

The Scheduled Castes and Scheduled Tribes can be broadly termed Dalits. Though there are Scheduled Castes, Scheduled Tribes, Backward Communities and minorities among the Dalits those social sections having constitutional reservations are called Dalits.

After independence the freedom of the Scheduled Castes and Scheduled Tribes has been in statutes only. Thus, independence was only for the upper castes. But the social, cultural, economic and political blockade by the upper castes against the Scheduled Castes and Scheduled Tribes has been going on unabated. A congenial atmosphere in which the Scheduled Castes and Scheduled Tribes can live as respectable human beings, keep up their personal dignity, lead their lives with self-respect and protect their lives without fear of annihilation, has not so far been created in the country.

It has become a challenging task for the Scheduled Castes and Scheduled Tribes to achieve even the rights to live on their own soil. To preserve the rags put on by his wife to save his thatchy hut from becoming object of arson, to protect his child, have become a life and death problem for the Dalits. Faced with the situation in a society which has been alienating the Dalits have waged relentless struggle to create an alternative social system. The Dalit is not the owner of land tilled by him, of the plant transplanted by him, of the basket woven by him, and of the cloth embroidered by him. In one word, he is alienated from his own creations. Further, he is denied the use of his own creations.

The commune culture brought up and developed by the Dalits through ages has been broken up. Their human rights have been under attacks. This has been leading to the evolution of a new way of life illuminated by philosophical and cultural heritage.

Though the Indian constitution is known as an armoury of human rights, the weapons in it have become useless for the Dalits to defend themselves against oppression.

They are not sharp enough for the Dalits to destroy the enemy. The locks on the armoury of human rights are not being unlocked when the blood of the Dalits is flowing in the streets. "Rights are not granted. If granted they will be taken away. Granting a right always destroys the achievement by human action". Dividing and destroying are nothing but acts of domination of one race over the other.

The evolution in the Indian subcontinent has been always internal. The super imposed ruling sections could not plunder the soul of the Indian society. The reason being that the soul was simply beyond their reach. It runs through the Indian aboriginals (the Scheduled Castes and Scheduled Tribes) invisibly, i.e., the matriarchal culture. The impact of the patriarchal ruling sections could not shatter their matriarchal base.

Even though the Dalit learnt the 'word', handled the productive instrument and entered the industrial establishment he has been very natural in his activities and his approach has always been one of humanism, sympathy and compassion. That is the reason why he has got the greatest concern for human rights.

It has now fallen to his lot to reconstruct human society in which the human rights are safe. It can be said that Hindu imperialism has been the root cause of all the humiliations and indignities heaped upon the Dalits. Without discussing the basis of this Hindu imperialism it will be a futile exercise and tantamount to discussing the superstructure leaving out its base.

The main pillar of Hindu imperialism is its inequality, i.e., dividing human beings into intrinsically inferior and superior. The castes are the bricks in Hindu pyramids and its light house is superiority complex. And its lifeline is to live without doing any human labour.

The struggle for human rights is in its essence a struggle for a living system in a non-Hindu manner. Though the non-Hindu religious systems could not give necessary strength to the Dalits to overthrow the state system they have the necessary thinking faculty to question the religious systems.

The Dalits are now aware of another important fact that as the state and the wealth of the nation are in the grip of the upper strata, they are able to impose their domination on the Dalits and suppress human rights.

Inspired, awakend and illuminated by the social revolutionary thoughts of Mahatma Jyothi Rao Phule, Dr. B.R. Ambedkar, Periyar, Narayana Guru and other social thinkers, the Dalits have realised that only political power can preserve and safeguard their human rights. For the realisation of this object, it has become absolutely essential to develop an alternative thesis and a movement against the evils of Hinduism.

The movement for development of an alternate philosophy and its constructive programme as against Hinduism in India is the real human rights movement. The Scheduled Castes and Scheduled Tribes are builders of such a movement. This is the beginning but not the end of the struggle for human rights.

26

HUMAN RIGHTS IN A CASTE SOCIETY

Sashmi Nayak

The concepts and processes of human rights have diverse dimensions. It would, therefore, be difficult to compress the various dimensions into a brief paper. Historians, philosophers, jurists and activists have waxed eloquent on this subject from time immemorial. However, one is likely to miss the tree for the wood in speaking about human rights.

I would concentrate on perception of human rights from a Dalit and that, too, a woman's point of view. It may appear to be a lopsided point of view, but it is an important viewpoint, the reason being human rights—even rights as one understands them have not only a caste aspect, but also a gender bias. Both caste as an institution at the national level and gender with its international social dimensions have a lot to do with the instruments, institutions as well as operations that permeate enforcement of human rights. Moreover, human rights have their deep roots in the philosophical, constitutional and legal development of various societies in the world, all of which have serious and significant social as well as gender implications.

The provisions of human rights, termed as Fundamental Rights and Directive Principles, of State Policy contained in the Indian Constitution, are negated by the social and cultural rights deeply embedded in the caste system of this country. The country with more than 5000 sub-castes is divided, as if into smaller number of republics, each bound within its caste framework into a sectarian lot. The Western principles of liberalism as well as egalitarianism could not demolish the caste system, which stand as a monolithic monster and justifies every type of violation of human rights in the country. Some of these features may be analysed along historical, geographical, political, economic, legal as well as racial lines.

Historical: With the invasion of the Aryans the history and civilisation of the indigenous people of this country stood distorted. The various scriptures written by the Aryans distort the indigenous ideas of rights and responsibilities. The local natives were described as Asuras and demons and their subjection, extortion and extermination was justified. Victory and enslavement were won by force or fraud and killings were based on the principle of might being right. Although the killings were upheld as valid and normal, they were resorted to selectively. In fact, the process of colonization took a long time—many centuries.

Political: The historical forces gave a code of conduct based on the Aryan system of values. The Vedas and Puranas gave way to *Manusmriti,* which was the high point that divided the population into racial and ethnic groups. The *Manusmriti* managed to perpetuate human slavery and adopted a double standard of co-option and exclusion. While suppressing the original inhabitants, it managed to keep them as serfs. It also could entrap through an elaborate code of conduct, both the human mind as well as human society. It stigmatized the locals as 'excluded', 'untouchables' and 'unseeables' and treated them as part of the cattle and vegetation. Racial purity was intended to be maintained by endogamous marriages and social rejections. This gave rise to the description of the indigenous population as the 'other' or 'outsider' and a system of hierarchy was established in society, which resulted in what Ambedkar says, in the ascending scale of reverence and descending order of contempt.

Religious: The position of the untouchables or the Dalits or Bahujans, was based on a concocted philosophy and a diabolical theology. The doctrine of Karma and the theory of transmigration of soul was cunningly formulated to perpetuate inequality from birth to death and even afterwards. The mindset of the orthodox was put into a trap without any escape route for individual human beings. The concept of human rights was non-existent and its practice could never be dreamt of in such a socio-religious order. The entire contraption was perfected with such philosophical verbiage that, while confounding the human mind it never let him get out of it. The human psyche became a victim of contradiction and caste and religious acts were sacrosanct, beyond the limits of the civil society and State made laws.

The above doctrinnaire approach to life and beyond gave rise to a set of political and economic institutions in the country. While there was internal colonialism within the nation, state inside a geographical territory, there were sub-nations within the nations and sub-humans within the human society. Just as the Shastras justified violation of human rights and wanton killings in wars or otherwise, the political and economic doctrines justified expropriation and domination. Wars were justified by theological arguments. The advice of Lord Krishna to Arjuna that he should wage war and even kill his cousin Duryodhana and his guru Dronacharya, was justified on the ground that it was not killing of brothers or relations as such but killing opponents who were already dead. Thus crime was justified on false notions of good and evil and right and wrong. Similarly, the case of Eklavya or the incident of 'Jatugriha Daha' where the 'outcastes' could be dispensed with showed rank manipulation of the shastras and the perversion of human values.

This approach led to economic exploitation where caste and capital have supported each other and grown together making it difficult for the lower caste persons to penetrate, much less benefit, from development plans. In other words, the 'outsider' is an outsider not only from the social, political and cultural arena, but also economic and wealth benefits. In fact wealth could accrue only to a limited group of people of certain high caste clans. Thus inequality and injustice became entrained into the system. This is how today we see a forest dweller, who was a master of the land but now is landless and the so-called untouchable, assetless who lives only on manual labour wages. The concept and philosophy of human rights would be anathema; to such a society it is a dream which could never be realized. Since the illegal and extralegal system is supported by the spiritual and theological foundations, the constitutional and legal systems remain only in paper. Here is a case, where caste people practice apartheid and enjoy moral autonomy with impunity, and thus could not stand the scrutiny of any discerning rational human mind.

The most intriguing feature of the human rights violation in India is that the oppressor is invisible. There is no direct evidence of one or the other individual or caste that can be spotted and caught in the act of commission of the crime. There is however a pattern in the entire system which perpetrates crime, but the criminal cannot be identified and punished. This is because this violence has social approval and human rights violations have become part and have got the sanction of the political culture. In fact the violations are based on caste and religious prejudices, organisational resources and institutional support and can never be prevented; at best they can only be alleviated. This imbroglio is explained by the failure of innumerable social reformers and many enlightened rulers in the past. The press, the police and even the judiciary acquiesce in the crimes.

The violation of human rights in our country seems to have a pattern and is perhaps leading to a holocaust. The eminent historian of the German holocaust, Raul Hilberg, summed up the gradual development of holocaust in three stages. The first step began with Christianity's Ghettoisation of the Jews after failing to convert them. The second step involved the process of seeing the Jews as economic threat when the Jews emerged from the ghettos, but their assimilation in the mainstream failed. The third step consisted of the "final solution", which was arrived at by the "scientific theory" about the Jews as racially inferior, and were a menace to the purity of Aryan blood. The Nazis when they arrived at this point in history did not discard the past. They built on it. They did not lay the foundation, but they completed the superstructure. In fact they were ready administratively and psychologically to eliminate the Jews—millions of them were killed systematically and "scientifically".

A similar historical pattern seems to be emerging in the Indian scene today. The Dalits, instead of following the dominant society like a sheep, thanks to their growing awareness about their own situation and efforts of an elite section, seems to be asserting today. This workshop itself is a sign of it. The orthodox elites of this country are not able to integrate them, because of a basic fallacy in the fundamentalist doctrine in which they are trapped. They, in fact, need to be liberated and not the Dalits or at best both need to be emancipated. Since social and economic integration is becoming difficult because of the antithetical socio-economic interests, failure of land reforms, the on-going reckless economic liberalisation policy, the Dalits would always appear to be parasites in the Indian society and economy. They need separate and systematic treatment, but outside the caste hierarchy. They would soon appear to become a burden on the economic development of the country as globalisation proceeds, which will result in the further pauperization of the poor. In fact, they would appear as a threat to the economy of the country and naturally the third step will be the "scientific solution", which may have to be resorted to by this dominant section.

It will be of interest to note in this connection as to how and why the "final solution" was resorted to by the Nazis. The solution had the backing of the intellectuals in Germany. Today 'Hindutwa' has the backing of many scholars and the upper middle class elites of this country. They also stand by Indian history and culture, its philosophy and religious leaders, whose ideologies seem to be gaining in popularity. Take the case of our own Lord Jagannath's Puri Seer who justified Sati, and bars women from reciting the Vedas. The occasional spurt in violence or demolition of a mosque or a temple is a symptom of this deep rooted prejudice. The theory of cultural nationalism is akin to the Nazi approach of threat to the German society supposedly created by the Jews.

The Nazi doctrine was formulated by Joseph Arther Gonineau (1816-1862) an eminent German thinker of his time in his publication, "Inequality of Human Race". Similarly Sir Framer Galtun, the British scientist invented eugenics. He derived from the Darwinian theory of Survival of the Fittest and argued that society should discourage breeding by those who are unfit either physically, mentally and socially in Germany. The theory of eugenics was carried by the Nazis to its logical conclusion. This was a welcome solution to the problem of racism. The scientific community manufactured gas chambers for eliminating the Jews. In this background I was surprised to see a publication of CSIR entitled "Make it Cloud Nine" by a scientist, who indirectly feels that the SCs / STs are intellectually inferior and incapable of improvement due to their low genetic stock. The ground perhaps is getting ready to justify a sort of mercy killing to purify the so called blot on the Indian communities in days to come. The theories of inheritance of merit or intelligence, to the utter disregard of environment forces, seems to be engaging the attention of these scientists. The interpretation of Hindutwa in a different context by the Supreme Court has been a shot in the arm of the orthodox elites and also seems to be a pointer in the direction of social polarisation. It is therefore time the National Human Rights Commission took stock of the situation and initiated a movement for building counter theories through seminars, workshops and publications so as to neutralise or arrest the fast deteriorating situation. The only difference between the Nazi solution and the Indian solution will be that, while in Germany the police and the Army did the "Work" with the people assisting them; in India some people will commit genocide with others assisting them from the scene of action. The police inaction or wilful absence or non-registration of complaints when atrocities are committed against the Dalits is a case in point. The fact that atrocities are on the increase and that there is a pattern in them would predict doom for the Dalits, unless prevention is attempted in all seriousness.

27

UPLIFT OF SC/STs: LEGISLATIVE MEASURES HAVE FAILED

Madhuri Pal

The concept of human rights is wide. That does not, however, automatically lead us to the conclusion, as some well-known columnists attempt from time to time, that western concept of human rights or democracy is not relevant for India.

There can be no two opinions about the desirability of a democratic way of life—the question of Occidental or Oriental is not relevant at all. There could be, and at times need be, difference of opinion regarding forms of government—for example, parliamentary form of government based on the party system, or direct democracy as opposed to representative government, something like what is practised in Switzerland; but there cannot be any controversy about, or difference of opionion, on democracy. Similarly, there cannot be two opinions on the fact that an individual's human dignity must be respected, or that all human beings are born free and equal, and so on. It is, therefore, only proper that in a discussion of human rights, we take into account the provisions of the *Universal Declaration of Human Rights, 1948* as a common standard of achievement for all peoples and all nations. Furthermore, the fact that the United Nations has given legal form by way of adopting two Covenants, *The International Covenant on Economic, Social and Cultural Rights,* and *The International Covenant on Civil and Political Rights,* means that human rights include civil and political rights, and also economic, social and cultural rights.

It is in this context that we may examine our record, with specific reference to Scheduled Castes and Scheduled Tribes. Article 1 of the *Universal Declaration* states: "All human beings are born free and equal in dignity and rights. They are endowed with reason and conscience and should act towards one another in a spirit of brotherhood." Article 2 states that there should be no distinction and discrimination with regard to race, sex, colour, religion, etc. Article 4 provides for prohibition of slavery. Article 26 provides for right to education, and free education up to the elementary stage.

Our Constitution adheres to the *Universal Declaration* and has made provisions for safeguard and uplift of SC/STs, as also for others, in the following Articles: Article 17—abolition of untouchability; Article 23—prohibition of forced labour; Article 45—free and compulsory primary education; Article 46—promotion of educational and economic interest of SC/STs; Article 335—appointment to services and posts in Union and State services. In addition, our Constitution has also provided for proportional reservation of seats in Lok Sabha and State Assemblies in Articles 330 and 332.

Furthermore, we have also a number of laws for the welfare and protection of SC/STs. For example, we have law reforms Acts, labour laws, Protection of Civil Rights Act 1955, Prevention of Atrocities Act 1989. There are also laws such as Tribal Sub-Plans and Special Components Plans.

Why have these special provisions and laws been made? Obviously, our constitution makers and subsequent law-makers were conscious of the fact that some aspects of the caste system are not consistent with human rights. They must have taken into account, for example, what is stated in the *A New Dictionary of Sociology*: "A pure caste system is rooted in the religious order and may be thought of as a hierarchy of hereditary, endogamous, occupational groups with positions fixed and mobility barred by ritual distance between each caste" (Mitchell 1979).

A study of the *Universal Declaration* and our Constitution indicates that India has taken all constitutional measures to uphold the rights of SC/STs and to uplift them. We have to examine, however, whether the measures that our successive governments have taken have produced the desired results.

It is true that our society, under the impact of democratic values and democratic form of government, has been changing. For instance, though untouchability may not have disappeared completely, it does not appear to be practised widely in cities. But if newspaper reports are any indication, and even according to government statistics, atrocities on SC/STs have considerably increased. And that, in spite of the fact that the 1989 Act relating to prevention of atrocities on SC/STs is very severe, and offences under this Act are cognizable and non-compoundable; and also the fact that "the Court shall presume unless the contrary is proved that such act was committed on the ground of untouchability, the benefit of protection is not given to offenders."

According to Amnesty International's report, *India: Torture, Rape and Deaths in Custody 1992*, "Dalits and Adivasis are the poorest and most vulnerable groups of people in India." "...Dalits and Adivasis are frequently tortured for political reasons, to deter them or punish them for involvement in organised resistance to economic exploitation. Often Adivasis and Dalit villages have been raided, and their inhabitants tortured and raped, by police acting in collusion with local ruling groups, such as landowners."

Let me give a very recent instance of how laws made to safeguard tribals' right to their land are being flouted. Hundreds of tribals in Rayagada district of Orissa have been ousted from their small plots of land. *Benami* transactions, with the connivance of government officials, have become common. And such exploitation, in spite of the fact that a legislation, the "Orissa Scheduled Areas Transfer of Immovable Property Regulation Act 1956" is in operation. Under this Act no land in Scheduled Areas can be sold without obtaining prior permission from the authorities. If newspaper reports are to be believed, the Act has been thrown to the winds. Similarly, a few months ago there were reports in the newspapers that the then Kerala Government was actively considering to amend the law in Kerala which provides that land belonging to Scheduled Castes in certain areas cannot be sold. This was being contemplated in the light of the fact that a number of government officials bought (benami) land belonging to

Scheduled Caste people. [Recently, the Kerala government passed The Kerala Scheduled Tribes (Restriction on Transfer of Lands and Restoration of Alienated Lands) Amendment Bill 1996. The bill is against the best interests of the tribals—M.P.]

Even according to government statistics, caste-related evils have been on the increase. It is said that untouchability is disappearing—one may not be sure, though. However, are caste identities disappearing? Let me quote a comment made by the *Economic and Political Weekly* of May 1995, under the heading, "A Ritual Affirming Faith in Caste"—and that from a quarter least expected:

> "Forward Block leader Chitta Basu received an invitation from Somnath Chatterjee, CPI(M) leader in connection with the latter's two grandsons' 'thread' ceremony. This casual revelation, however, raises questions about the communist character of the host party itself. These days, of course, a communist does not have to abjure religion or theistic faith. But the thread ceremony is not a matter of theological faith, but a ritual affirming faith in varna and caste. The CPI(M), which these days has made Swami Vivekananda, the fiery denouncer of the varna and caste system, one of its chief mascots, has someone as one of its chief spokespersons—Chatterjee is the leader of the CPI(M) in the Lok Sabha—who still practises the rituals and flaunted the symbols of caste hierarchy. How Marxist is this Marxist Communist Party?"

28

THE CONCEPT OF NATIONAL HUMAN RIGHTS MOVEMENT AND UPLIFT OF SCs/STs

G.S. Bhargava

The human or civil rights movement in the country, like other public organizations such as trade unions, kisan sabhas and women's associations, began as a part of the freedom struggle. Although Gandhiji had been intensely alive to social evils like the practice of untouchability and had carried a veritable one-man crusade against it as well as for amelioration of the living conditions of Harijans (people of God) as he called the Scheduled Castes—he had toured the length and breadth of the country raising Rs. 3 crore (Rs. 30 million which at that time was a veritable fortune) for Harijan welfare fund and made it a point to live in Harijan *bustees* when he was not at his ashram at Sewagram—he did not perceive them as a denial or violation of human rights. He had brought to bear on it a paternalistic and ethical dimension and, although Harijan welfare was one of the fourteen points of his constructive programme and although he had made it obligatory for Congress members to participate in the constructive programme, especially for eligibility for elective posts, there was no organic link between the uplift of the SCs and political action like civil disobedience and legislative activity. The reason was that he did not want the movement for freedom from colonial rule to be sidetracked or diluted by simultaneous action on the social front. At one time, M.N. Roy also thought that trade unions, kisan sabhas and other organizations geared to sectoral interests as well as nationalists of different hues should function under the umbrella of the Indian National Congress. That was in the 1930s when Roy had unsuccessfully contested the Congress presidential election.

The basic difference in the approaches of Gandhiji and Dr. B.R. Ambedkar had been on this issue. Dr. Ambedkar had perceived the elimination of societal injustice to the SCs as an inseparable part of the political struggle for independence. He was deeply apprehensive that if there was transfer of power by the British to Indians without institutionalized efforts for mitigation, if not removal, of the social disabilities of the Scheduled Castes, the Hindu upper castes would monopolize power and perpetuate the plight of the SCs. That was why he agitated for and got from the British a proposal for separate electorates for the SCs in the then British Prime Minister, Ramsay MacDonald's [1]"Communal Award". On Gandhiji's pet scheme of decentralization of authority by establishment of panchayati raj institutions also Ambedkar had reservations for the same reason. He said it in so many words in his speech in the Constituent Assembly when he reacted negatively to Congress members' demand that the political system of free India should be based on Gandhiji's concept of 'gram swaraj' and not the British Westminster system. He was afraid that in the proposed panchayati raj the dominant upper castes would keep the SCs oppressed. Until a credible system of constitutional safeguards was worked out for the SCs, he wanted the freedom struggle to be relegated to the back burner. He had also used it as a lever to win concessions for the SCs from the Congress leadership. The Poona Pact was an instance in point.

Describing the conclusion of the Poona Pact, the circumstances in which it was concluded and its impact on the Hindu upper caste perspective on the SCs, Michael Brecher said:" Under the terms of the Poona Pact, the Untouchables abandoned separate electorates. To safeguard their interests, however, they were guaranteed a number of reserved seats from those assigned to the Hindu community in the British 'commual award'; in fact, twice as many as originally assured the Untouchables by that award. In short, the facade of an integrated Hindu community was maintained along with the substance of reserved seats—for a period of ten years... Gandhi called off the fast (unto death which had ultimately induced Dr. Ambedkar, at the instance of Hindu leaders, to give up the demand for separate electorates and sign the Poona Pact) and the crisis ended. *The most astonishing result of Gandhi's 'epic fast' was the widespread sympathy it evoked in favour of fifty million Untouchables. By focusing attention on the Harijans...the Mahatma set in motion a massive attack on this unmitigated evil of Hindu society. Temples of worship, hitherto held sacrosanct by caste Hindus, were thrown open to Untouchables all over the country. The right to use the village water supply, considered unthinkable in the past, was now granted to the Harijans as a pledge of faith in the Mahatma. The cause of the Untouchables took on the character of a holy crusade.* Unfortunately, the initial enthusiasm was soon dissipated...It is a slow process, for these are rooted in more than three thousand years of Hindu culture, but progress is being made". (emphasis added)

Brecher's account of the events focuses on several issues which are relevant to this paper. First and foremost, although the impact on the Hindu community of Gandhiji's fast unto death has not been sustained in later years—not necessarily by coercive actions like fasts and hunger strikes—its immediate effect acknowledged by foreign observers also shows that is the most effective way of countering societal injustice to the SCs. True, education of the people about the pernicious nature of abuse of human rights of the SCs may not by itself suffice. But without sensitization of both the victims and perpetrators of the human rights abuse, legislation, however full-proof in formulation and even if faithfully implemented, will not serve the expected purpose. At the same time, perhaps to lend an emotional edge to the problem, Gandhiji had put too much emphasis on allowing the Hindus into the temples. It is, no doubt, true that only the orthodox and the traditionalists with faith in rituals visit the temples and securing access for the Harijans to them is meant to convert the hardened sections of the community. But such is the ambivalence of the practitioners of discrimination against the SCs that letting the Harijans into the temples did not automatically imply recognition of their social equality.

Secondly, because of the Muslim League practice of sectarianism and the British Government's strategy of dividing and subdividing the victims of its colonial rule, projection of 'an integrated Hindu community' became politically imperative. That had put the problem of the disabilities of the SCs in a wrong—non-social—perspective, if not a patriotic mould. To this day, the BJP thinks social justice for the SCs will weaken the Hindu community vis-a-vis the Muslims. It also draws the line between extending statutory safeguards for the SC/STs and other depressed sections and similar concessions for Dalit Christians and Dalit Muslims because they are outside the Hindu community.

To go back to the genesis of the civil liberties movement, it became virtually non-functional after independence because Nehru and other national leaders were then manning the administration and brought to bear on civil liberties an outlook shaped by administrative responsibility. The ill-conceived violent agitation called 'people's war' by the Communists who had started a 'guerrilla war' in parts of the country with weapons smuggled from China and Burma had also provoked abridgment of human rights enshrined in the Constitution. Thus, leaders of the stature of C. Rajagopalachari and Sardar Patel who were home ministers in the early years of independence had made no bones about preventing Communists from 'misusing' the fledgling democratic system to subvert it. The Socialists who had by and large inherited the mantle of sustaining the civil liberties movement were not, naturally, keen to champion their arch-enemies, the Communists, although former followers of M.N. Roy, like N.M. Joshi and Maniben Kara kept the movement alive.

It took nearly thirty years for the civil liberties movement to regain centre stage and be back on the national agenda. The stimulus was again political. When Mrs. Indira Gandhi imposed an artificial emergency on the country to tide over a political crisis of a purely personal nature and to establish a dynasty, Jayaprakash Narayan who headed the resistance to it also launched the civil liberties movement again as part of the resistance to abridgment of rule of law and suspension of fundamental rights guaranteed under the Constitution. At least in the latter case the relevance of the civil rights movement to the struggle against the emergency is greater than the situation during the days of the freedom struggle when foreign rule per se was seen as antithetical to civil liberties even when some kind of constitutional government was in office and more importantly the commitment of the national leadership to preserve and promote civil liberties had been taken for granted. Even when draconian provisions for imposition of the so-called internal emergency even in the absence of external threat or war and the dismissal of elected State governments even while they enjoyed majority support in the respective legislatures were incorporated in the Constitution, the *raison d'être* for a civil liberties movement had not been felt or recognised. This drawback has its converse also. The tendency has grown among citizens with deeply felt grievances to take recourse to extra-legal methods to seek their redress.

When the People's Union for Civil Liberties (PUCL) was launched under the inspiration of Jayaprakash Narayan during the 1975 'emergency', the movement had virtually no social agenda. The attitude to the social dimension of human rights of some of the parties and groups, viz., the RSS, was ignored. Also, following the end of the emergency it was business as usual although the Janata Party leaders heading the Government were no better respectors of civil liberties than their predecessors and also a kind of upsurge by the Jats directed against the Scheduled Castes had been in evidence in western Uttar Pradesh.

It was only in the late 1980s and 1990s that the non-official human rights movement regained its social dimension steadily. Violent, secessionist agitations, with modern weapons supplied from across the border and often inspired and directed by overseas intelligence agencies, raised the spectre of terrorism as never before. As a backlash, the government armed itself with sweeping powers virtually doing away with the rule of law. The Terrorist and Disruptive Activities (Prevention) Act, 1987 (TADA) which has since been repealed is an example. There was a proliferation of paramilitary organizations often manned by raw recruits who were nearly trigger-happy. Regular troops were also deployed against insurgents in the North-East, Punjab, and Jammu and Kashmir. The helpless civilians of the affected areas had been caught between the ruthless terrorist and security forces inadequately aware of the constraints of the rule of law. The net result was that overseas human rights organizations, the Amnesty International and its US counterpart, Human Rights Watch (Asia), partly piqued by denial of access to the affected areas started publishing damaging accounts of the human rights situation in India. They were naturally grist to the mills of propaganda of Pakistan which has a psychological dimension to its proxy war in Jammu and Kashmir.

It must be noted in this context that a woodenly bureaucratic approach of the Government of India, especially during Rajiv Gandhi's Prime Ministership, also contributed to India's discomfiture in international human rights fora. National human rights organizations like the PUCL and respected civil rights activists like Justices V.M. Tarkunde and Rajindar Sachar were not also allowed to visit the Kashimir Valley but also a campaign had also been launched to fault the human rights activists on patriotic grounds, saying that they were championing the cause of secessionist terrorists. If the Indian human rights activists had been allowed into the affected areas of Kashmir, their findings even if unflattering to the administration would have dented motivated criticism by international agencies. The situation in Jammu and Kashmir was particularly bleak in this respect when Jagmohan Malhotra, a bureaucrat (now he is a BJP member of the Lok Sabha), was governor of the benighted State. He had not only let loose unbridled repression on all protest activity in Kashmir, thus aggravating armed militancy, but also arbitrarily dissolved the State assembly to snuff out a possible political solution to the problem of alienation of the people of the Valley. When he was replaced in the middle of 1990 by a seasoned IPS officer, efforts had begun to mend the situation. Justice Tarkunde and others were allowed into Srinagar. A team of senior journalists headed by B.G. Verghese had been commissioned to inquire cases of excesses by the security forces.

Then came the establishment of the NHRC as a statutory body under the Protection of Human Rights Act, 1993. Initially, there was skepticism, more abroad than at home, about the effectiveness of an organization established by government and inhibited by constraints built into the legislation governing its operation. But by its record during the last few years the Commission has dispelled such misgivings, with its skeptical foreign agencies like the Amnesty International and specially the Human Rights watch of New York acknowledging its dedication to the cause of human/civil rights and determination to expose and book violators of citizens' rights to life and liberty. The commission has also boldly sought enlargement of the ambit of its operation and listed the amendments needed for the purpose in the law. Most importantly, even when the Commission's plate is full with as many as 6,987 cases received for its disposal between March 31, 1994 and March 31, 1995, it has not neglected its social obligations by undertaking and promoting research in the field of human rights and realizing that "in a society such as ours, the indivisibility and interrelated quality of human rights—whether civil and political or economic, social and cultural—is self-evident. Nowhere is this link more keenly felt than in respect of (the) Scheduled Castes and Scheduled Tribes, and the status of minorities, a link that the Constitution itself recognizes."

The victims of police high-handedness and arbitrariness, especially in the rural and tribal areas, are the socially oppressed and, as the annual report of the Commission has noted, women. Dr. Ram Manohar Lohia said that the Scheduled Caste and Scheduled Tribe women are doubly oppressed, by the superior castes and plains people respectively and by their own men. Apart from such denial of civil rights by the authorities and other citizens, there is also the basic social injustice due to aberrations built into the Hindu society, viz., the caste system and the practice of untouchability. The tribal people are invariably shortchanged and exploited by the plains people. The forest department personnel, of all ranks, look upon the generally unlettered tribals as fair game for infliction of all kinds of injustice and even violence. It is a kind of racism.

Dr. Ambedkar thought that statutory safeguards in the shape of reservation of seats, proportionate to the number of SCs and STs in the population would lead to the social uplift of Harijans as well as Girijans (children of mountains). In the teeth of opposition by M.Ps representing the upper castes, he incorporated in the Constitution drafted by him a provision for reservation of seats in the legislatures as well as institutions of higher studies. It worked well during the period of Nehru but when Lal Bahadur Shastri became Prime Minister the constitutional provision for reservation of seats for SCs and STs was scheduled to lapse. Extension of the duration of the reservations had been surprisingly smooth. There was agreement among major parties that the concession should continue almost indefinitely. In fact, there was a competition among political parties in advocating continuance of the reservations because by then the value of what are called SC and ST 'vote banks' had been realized by politicians who had tasted relatively easy access to power by tapping the 'vote banks'.

A further fallout, perhaps not anticipated by Dr. Ambedkar, has been extension of the principle of reservations to all kinds of 'backward classes' so that the very concept of reservations as a manifestation of affirmative action has been vitiated. In some of the States the quantum of reservations has touched the 80th mark, disregarding the Supreme Court ceiling of 50 per cent of the total seats—in universities and government employment—for reservation. In the process, the handful of citizens who could not claim reservation on the basis of caste are embittered by denial of opportunities for higher education—in spite of their performance in competitive examinations—or are economically disadvantaged despite their belonging to the upper castes. Thus, both natural and economic justice are circumvented in the name of social justice. Meanwhile, following a Supreme Court judgment, a bogey has been created in the name of exclusion from the benefits of reservation of the 'creamy layer'—families or categories who have benefited from the reservation system. There are also demands and suggestions for extension of reservations to Muslims not because of bulk of the people of the community is socially backward and economically poor but because they are not Hindus. In short, ninety years after the Indian polity had rejected the sectarian Muslim demand for separate electorates and fifty years after the practice had been eliminated in independent India the spectre is reappearing.

Against this background, the human rights movement should put the problem of injustice to and exploitation of the SCs and STs in the correct social perspective—as a means to undoing the centuries-old injustice to the Dalits and the tribals and of ameliorating their socio-economic position in society. The paternalistic and purely ethical approach which Gandhiji had brought to bear on the subject to awaken the traditionalists among the upper castes to their social responsibility has to be replaced by a pragmatic attitude of integrating the Dalits and the tribals into the community on the basis of equity and justice.

REFERENCES

1. Michael Brecher, *Nehru: A Political Biography*, OUP, 1959.
2. *Crisis and Credibility*, Press Council of India, Lancer Paper 4, New Delhi, 1991.
3. National Human Rights Commission, Annual Report, 1994-95, p. 7.

29

HUMAN RIGHTS EDUCATION: INDIA'S HERITAGE

R.M. Pal

Indian scholars and human rights activists have been talking and writing, apropos of human rights violations, about India's glorious past of 5000 years, written in gold, and pleading that the past must be revived to usher in a new India where the values of tolerance, non-violence, friendship for all, equality, respect for the human being, human dignity and rights, and freedom will be respected and cherished. They, however, leave us in the dark as to which past is to be revived/reborn, of which we can be proud; and which one needs to be buried. Obviously we want to revive that past which will help India come into the inheritance of the blessings of modern civilisation. This means that we have to resist the temptation of reviving an imaginary Golden Age of India's past.

Furthermore, as Professor Romila Thapar puts it:

"The supposed perfection of the past has hampered our understanding not only of the social processes but also of our own cultural identity.... An analysis of the totality of Indian society today has to account for a variety of transitions taking place and involving tribal groups, peasant groups, and, at the most articulate level, the change to industrialisation. The nature of these changes will often involve a basic change of social values. The confrontation can no longer be evaded as it once was by recourse to the theory that our concern has always been only with things spiritual, or by an escape into the past. But the process can be facilitated by an awareness of the past, deriving from a realistic assessment....It is only the awareness that history is made by an entire people into its total activity, which can bring us nearer to explaining the past in its concrete actuality. And, this, after all, is the ultimate purpose of historical investigation."[1]

At the fag end of the twentieth century we cannot afford to go round in circles of ideological confusion. We need to raise our voice of reason and wisdom, discover our old literature, philosophy, and civilisation to make us wiser and constantly remind us of our journey forward. This is how Europe recovered from the savagery of the Dark Age and many of the crudities of the Middle Ages. The idea behind revivalism/rebirth (I use these two words interchangeably, for the sake of convenience, even though they mean different things) is to look at our past, that past which can guide us to respect the individual's dignity, and to build a future of which we can be proud. In the process we should have no hesitation, indeed we must be brave, in discarding those aspects which hamper our progress, like, for example, the theories of *Karma*, Transmigration of Soul, *Maya*, the principle of division of society into castes, the form which the system of exploitation assumed in the bygone days that was declared to be the creation of God, the 'spiritualist' culture that seeks to persuade the poor, the depressed, the oppressed, and the exploited to reconcile their lot to suffering, sacrifice, love, and voluntary poverty—all that signify complete surrender, and absence of the spirit of revolt. We must be brave to discard these even if they are backed by scriptures—indeed, we must bury such scriptures.

The highest appreciation of our past would be to find out how it could generate in us the spirit of revolt against social injustice and human rights violations. Indeed, a very large canvas, and a huge agenda for our historians in the above context, to prepare a course of study based on our heritage for human rights education to be taught in schools, colleges, and universities.

As regards tolerance, respect for human rights, dignity of, and respect for, the individual and his/her freedom, that have been part of our heritage, one need not be a great sophisticated scholar or historian to know that even the philosophies of religious movements in the not-too-distant past, not to speak of the materialist philosophy of ancient India,[2] incorporated such values. Regrettably, the human rights intellectuals and activists have hardly taken note of these movements, possibly because of the fact that most of these originated from, and were inspired by, the lower strata of society. And also that, to quote Romila Thapar again:

"The cultural identity which we have forged in recent times has been that of a Sanskritic upper caste, or else its equivalent in a Persian upper caste. Yet these identities are as elitist as the English speaking identity of contemporary Indians...(The fact remains that) the common features of religion for the majority of Indians lie in the worship of the mother goddess and fertility cults and in the teachings of what have come to be called the devotional or *bhakti* sects and the 'sant' and the '*pir*'. Emphasis is continually given by historians to the spread of Hinduism as reflected in the Sanskritic tradition and to the spread of Islam symbolised by the *Quran*. Yet, so little recognition is given to the fact that in the practice of religion it is the local cult, the non-Sanskritic tradition, which is often predominant."[3]

It is in this context that I give below a summary account of this non-Sanskritic tradition with special reference to the medieval age (this period should not be confused with what is known as the Middle Ages in Europe), that is, before the advent of European learning which came to India with the British. I suggest that contributions made in this period can inspire human rights activists in their work, and also scholars and educationists including the Government of India appointed National Human Rights Commission (NHRC), and the National Council of Educational Research and Training (NCERT), involved in the task of framing courses of study for human rights education.[4] The NCERT with the active support of the NHRC has brought out a Source Book on Human Rights Education which contains summaries/excerpts from various UN Charters and Covenants, and also from our own Constitution. One wonders, however, if a mere textbook reading of constitutional provisions and UN Charters can develop a human rights culture which is what the

NHRC's stated objective is. Furthermore, are not these already taught in the Civics, Political Science, and Law courses?

II

During the Buddhist period, interest in man, man in his own image, and man's affairs on this earth, unlike interest in gods and goddesses and good life in heaven after death, this earth being a vale of tears, became the primary concern of thoughtful men and women. Buddha rejected the caste system.[5] Human sufferings made Prince Gautama restless and he left all luxuries and comforts of the king's palace in search of remedies for all human miseries on this earth. The basic tenets of Buddhism are non-violence, non-hatred, and friendliness to all. Emperor Ashoka who become a devoted follower of Gautama Buddha took to the non-violent, humanitarian and humanist philosophy of Buddhism. Also, he became a great champion of freedom and tolerance. He pleaded for universal tolerance. One of the most significant contributions of Buddhism was the introduction and spread of secular education—education for all. Organised universities came to be established under the direct influence of Buddhism.

There were other non-Vedic sects—like the *Nath, Yoga, Siddharcara* who too, like the Buddhists, found the key to all religious mysteries in the human body itself:

> "The position of the *nath-panthi siddhas* and *jogis* in Hindu society needs to be understood. Most of the *non-panthi siddhas* and *jogis* belonged to the low castes, opposed caste-based inequalities, denounced the religion of works favoured by the Brahmins, and did not favour image worship."[6]

Women played an important part in these sects, particularly in the *tantra*.

There are other folk religions/sects which came into prominence in the medieval period: the well-known *Bhakti* movement, and the Baul movement in Bengal. They are remarkable for their simplicity, directness, and for preaching and practising tolerance, love, and friendliness.

Bhakti, the path of devotion, implies a belief in the Supreme Person, not in a Supreme *Abstraction*. It is, therefore, a very straightforward and unsophisticated belief. This movement has non-Aryan roots; in fact, according to some scholars, it originated in the Dravida country. It was opposed by the Brahmins for a long time because of its utter disregard for caste divisions, religious rituals and ceremonies.

The tradition of Bhakti has played an important part among the Tamils as mentioned in the works of the *Alvar* saints, most of whom came from low castes. In the beginning the movement was restricted to the lower strata of society who were oppressed by the Brahmanical religion. At a later stage, Vaishnavas of even higher castes hailed their literature. One *Alvar* saint, Andal, belonged to a low caste; she was accepted as a religious leader by the society in general. This is an indication of the popularity of the Bhakti movement. The great scholar Ramanuja, the best known exponent of this movement, was influenced and inspired by the "works of the Alvars, which were collected by the disciples of Ramanuja at his special request, and from which Ramanuja himself drew much inspiration and food for his system of thought."[7]

At this point, a brief look at the advent of Islam in India is necessary. In India, Islam led to a series of responses. We can ill-afford to ignore them as also the creative influence of Islam. An analysis of the Muslim conquest of India is of practical value today, and will help Indians—both Hindus and Muslims—appreciate the positive results of the Muslim conquest of India. (This is necessary, among other reasons, for a solution of the communal question which has been one of the major sources, along with the caste system, of human rights violations.)

It may be noted in this context that Europe came out of the shackles of the Dark Ages and the Middle Ages, and entered the civilised era by learning from the Muslims. It is equally true that a large number of Hindu reformers, largely of the Bhakti movement in medieval India, who revolted against orthodoxy, were considerably influenced by the Muslim conquest and its social effects.[8] The devotional Bhakti movement and the Islamic Sufi movement both have much in common. In mediaeval north India mysticism was the product of both the Bhakti movement and the tradition of the Sufis. One important aspect of this mysticism is its complete independence from orthodox scriptures. These teachers practised and taught tolerance.

The interaction of Bhakti and Islam, specially the Sufi idea, gave rise to a number of progressive movements with the core philosophy of tolerance. Human rights educationists should give the utmost importance to this aspect. It is regrettable that it has, with a few notable exceptions, been generally studied in isolation. It should, therefore, be emphasised in our textbooks that "relations between Islam and the religions of the area (South Asia) were marked by mutual understanding and tolerance. This spirit of mutual understanding, tolerance and cooperation were, to a large extent, promoted by the rise and spread of Sufi and Bhakti ideas."[9]

Our students must be reminded over and over again of what Rabindranath Tagore said: "the Sakas, the Hunas, the Pathans and the Mughals—all have been merged into one body", with a view to combating the religious frenzy that has been playing hovoc in our country. We must remind ourselves of the forgotten fact of history that

> "a distinctive feature of the thought and life of the peoples of the South Asian region is their adherence to the tradition of tolerance, syncretism and coexistence, (and in this context) the coming of Islam was an event of outstanding significance for the history of this subcontinent. This syncretic and humanist tradition in South Asian society and social thought is remarkably portrayed in the following poem of Kazi Nazrul Islam:
>
> *I sing the song of equality/Where all barriers have crumbled,/All differences have faded,/And Hindus-Buddhists- Muslims-Christians/Have come together and have merged./I sing the song of equality.*"[10]

In short, we must remind ourselves over and over again that a pluralistic society can flourish only if its basic value remains tolerance. We must also remember that tolerance and pluralism are not the same thing.

III

Namdeva and Tukaram from Maharashtra, the former a tailor, and the latter a peasant, made the Bhakti movement increasingly acceptable to the people. Namdeva taught:

"The stone image speaks not, see the Lord within. The *Tirthas* (holy pilgrimage) cannot wash away sins; clean your heart instead. Fasting and other observances are futile unless your being is purified. What can ceremonies do if love awake not in your heart"?

In Bengal, the well-known Vaishnava poets, Jaidev, Vidyapati, and Chandidas, as also Chaitanaya popularised the movement. The Bhakti movement during this period spread to almost all parts of India.

Though the movement did not succeed in breaking through caste barriers, the very fact that many of its leaders belonged to lower castes, and also that it believed in the equality of men, must be taken note of by human rights educationists.

In the fourteenth century, Ramananda (1370-1440) challenged caste divisions, revolted against traditional religious rituals and started preaching in Hindi, and not Sanskrit which was the preserve of the upper castes. His thought is well reflected in the following words:

"Wherever I go, I see water and stone; but it is you who had filled them all with your presence. In vain do they seek you in the Vedas... (*Guru Granth Saheb*)"

Ramananda had twelve important disciples. They all belonged to low castes. One of them, Ravidas, was a cobbler. "The recitation of the Vedic *Mantras,* even for many millions of times, will not satisfy the pangs of that longing (to see You)", sang Ravidas (*Guru Granth Saheb*). The most famous disciple was Shaikh Kabiru Din Momin Ansari, popularly known as Kabir, a Muslim weaver. The Sufi and Bhakti traditions of the Islamic and Hindu religions blended in his teachings. He struck at the very roots of ritualism and superstition. "O God, whether Allah or Rama, I live by Thy name," sang Kabir. Since Kabir composed songs for the common people he chose Hindi. "Sanskrit is like water in a well; the language of the people is a flowing stream," said Kabir. A married man, with a son and daughter, Kabir did not practise celibacy and asceticism. He practised and preached the gospel of universal tolerance and was one of the exponents of the idea of an India without any communal discord. Kabir gave the utmost importance to human equality and denounced inequality based on caste, station, and wealth.

The founder of the great Sikh religion, Guru Nanak, was greatly influenced by Islamic and Sufi ideas. Sikhism is known for its simplicity, and this was derived from Kabir's teaching. Both Kabir and Guru Nanak found a common link between Hinduism and Islam. The supreme significance of Nanak was that he was the harbinger of Hindu-Muslim unity, for he sought sincerely to reconcile Islam with Hinduism as the following verse will show : *"Guru Nanak Shah faqir/Hindu Ka Guru aur/Musalman ke pir."*[11]

Dadu, a Muslim cotton-curder, was another of Kabir's outstanding followers.

> "When I look upon the beauty of this Universe, I cannot help asking, 'How, O Lord, did you come to create it? What sudden wave of joy coursing through Your being compelled its own manifestations ? Was it really due to a desire for self-expression or simply on the impulse of emotion? ... That is why Your Universe ... has charmed me so. ...Dadu has no desire to know; he is satisfied to remain enraptured with all this beauty of Yours, and to rejoice in it with You",

so sang Dadu—so very different from the hair-splitting and complicated intellectualism of *Jnana* and *Karma*.

The story of such mystics of the Bhakti movement is long. I have given a very brief introduction to this movement in the foregoing with a view to bringing before human rights activists and educationists the positive aspects of our past.

V

Bauls are not known outside Bengal. The philosophy of the Baul movement lies in the simple man's (*sahaj*) search for the "man of his heart"—his God. The movement traces its origin to the fall of Buddhism and Vaishnavism.

Bauls are like the wind (*Baul* means wind, *vayu*)—always free, not tied to any religious traditions. They accept no caste division; they do not worship any special deity nor do they accept any temple or mosque. Baul devotees belong to the lowest strata of both Hindus and Muslims. "What need have we of other temples, when our body is the temple where our spirit has its abode?", they sing.

They do not observe asceticism, nor do they believe in celibacy. Earthly love, they maintain, helps them to feel Divine love, and harmony between material and spiritual needs. The following Baul song contains the core philosophy of the Baul movement:

> *"That is why, brother, I became a madcap Baul./ No master I obey, nor injunctions, canons, or custom / Man-made distinctions have no hold on me now./ I rejoice in the gladness of the love that wells out of my own being./ In love there is no separation, but a meeting of hearts for ever./ So I rejoice in song and I dance with each and all./ That is why, brother, I became a madcap Baul."*

One of the most famous Bauls, Faqir Lalon Shah, sang thus:

> *"Everyone asks Lalon what is your religion!/ Lalon says, I know not what it is./ If a male is circumcised, you know he is a Musalman;/ But how would you identify the religion of a female?/ A Brahmin male is identified by his poita (sacred thread);/ But how would you identify a Brahmin female?/ One holds rosary in hand, the other wears tasbi (bead) in his neck,/ That is how one's religion is known ; /But at moments of birth and death do these signs remain?/ People everywhere talk and gossip about religious differences./ Lalon says, I have dropped all polemics about religions in free market."*

I may add that Rabindranath Tagore was greatly influenced by Kabir and translated many of Kabir's poems into English in collaboration with Evelyn Underhill. Guru Nanak, too, left a lasting impression on Tagore's mind. Tagore was also greatly influenced by Bauls like Lalon Faqir and Gagan Harkarai. He composed many songs under their influence.

REFERENCES

1. Prof. Romila Thapar, *The Past and Prejudice*, National Book Trust, New Delhi, 1975, pp. 60-63.

2. The school of philosophy, *Lokayata*, considered physical sense data to be the only source of knowledge. It challenged the whole of Hindu metaphysics, and rejected after-life and reincarnation. This rejection is found elsewhere too. In the *Ramayana* a Brahmin, Javali, advises Rama thus: "I grieve for those who, abandoning the pleasures of the world, seek to acquire merit for felicity hereafter and sink to an untimely death, I do

not grieve for others, men waste food and other precious things by offering them up yearly, as sacrifices in honour of their departed ancestors. O Rama, has a dead man ever partaken of food? If food that is eaten by one, nourishes another, then those who journey need never carry provision on the way. Relatives might feed a Brahmin, in his name, at home! O Ramachandra, these scriptural injunctions were laid down by learned men, skilled in inducing others to give, and finding other means of obtaining wealth, thus subjugating the simple- minded. Their doctrine is, 'Sacrifice, give in charity, consecrate yourselves, undergo austerities, and become ascetics.' O Rama, be wise, there exists no world but this, that is certain! Enjoy that which is present and cast behind thee that which is unpleasant! Adopting the principles acceptable to all, do thou receive the kingdom offered thee by Bharata." (*Ayodhya Kanda*) (Quoted by K.M. Sen in his book, *Hinduism*, Penguin, 1961, pp. 63-64)

3. Romila Thapar, *op. cit.*, p. 6.

4. I have not dealt in this essay with the short-lived Renaissance that was ushered in India, specially in Bengal and Maharashtra, under the direct influence of European learning and philosophy and which gave rise to a large number of reformers and reformist movements, intellectual-activists, and political thinkers whose contributions have been recorded and acknowledged by most historians. Contributions made by European learning and philosophies in the field of human rights, civil liberties, and individual liberty have been significant, and they find elaborate mention in textbooks.

5. The Hindu caste system, in the context of human rights, must be dealt with in great detail, for it represents inequality and has played an important role in the stratification of Indian society—particularly because of its so called 'divine' origin. The caste system, by its very nature, goes against respect for an individual's dignity and freedom to express himself. Further, the caste system had a racial origin, in its association of castes and colour, cf. for example, an important verse in the Mahabharata: Bhrigu explains the nature of castes to Bharadvaja, "Brahmins are fair, Kshatriyas are reddish, Vaishas are yellowish, and the Sudras are black." What should be of interest for human rights education is how it is questioned by Bharadvaja: "We all seem to be affected by desire, anger, fear, sorrow, worry, hunger and labour ; how do we have caste differences then?" (*Santi Parva*)

That in ancient India, the caste system was repudiated is also illustrated by a number of characters in the Mahabharata: (i) the story of King Yayati and Devayani—Devayani a Brahmin marries Yayati, a Kshatriya, with the consent of her father, Guru Shukracharya, (ii) Vidura, one of the wisest men in the Mahabharata and also described as the very incarnation of Dharma, was the son of a Sudra woman, (iii) Rishi Vaisishtha was born of a prostitute, (iv) Parashara was born of a *Chandala* woman. Another example of argument against caste divisions, from the *Bhavishya Purana*: "All human beings have the same Father, and children of the same Father cannot have different castes."

6. Prof. Satish Chandra in *Cultural Interaction in South Asia*, Hamdard Institute of Historical Research, New Delhi, 1993, p. 103. Human rights educationists should find this book useful in preparing reading material for school students. It is a collection of papers written by scholars from South Asia, presented before a Colloquium organised by Jawaharlal Nehru University, New Delhi, Hamdard Institute of Historical Research, New Delhi, and Jamia Hamdard, New Delhi, in 1991. The three papers, "Aspects of Society and Social Thought in South Asia: The Syncretic and Humanist Tradition" by Prof. Salahuddin Ahmad of Dhaka University, "South Asian Sufis and their Social Linkage" by Prof. Riazul Islam, Prof. Emeritus at Karachi University, and "Interaction of Bhakti and Sufi Movements in South Asia" by Prof. Satish Chandra of Jawaharlal Nehru University of New Delhi, deserve special mention in the context of human rights education.

7. S.N. Dasgupta, *A History of Indian Philosophy*, Vol. III, 1940.

8. In spite of the fact that Islam had played out its progressive role before it penetrated India, Islam was welcomed as a message of hope and freedom by victims of the Brahmanical reaction which had overthrown the Buddhist revolution resulting in a state of chaos in Indian society. How is it that the Mohammedans, though not large in numbers, managed to rule a vast country for such a long time, and millions of people converted themselves to the new faith? The fact remains that Mohammedans satisfied certain objective requirements of Indian society. The historian Havell (not an admirer of Islam, he is a great admirer of ancient Hindu culture) in his book, *Aryan Rule in India*, writes: "It was not the philosophy of Islam, but its sociological programme which won so many converts for it in India. The victorious progress of Islam in India is not to be accounted for by external reasons. It was mainly due to the political degeneration of Aryavarta which set in after the death of Harsha. The effect of the Musalman political creed upon Hindu social life was twofold: It increased the rigour of the caste system and aroused a revolt against it. Islam made the Sudra a free man and potentially a Lord of the Brahmins. Like the Renaissance of Europe, it stirred up the intellectual waters, produced many strong men, and some men of striking originality of genius. Like the Renaissance also, it was essentially a city cult; it made the nomad leave his tent and the Sudra abandon his village. It developed a type of humanity full of *joie de vivre*." (Quoted by M.N. Roy in the book, *Historical Role of*

Islam, Ajanta, 1990 reprint, Delhi, pp. 84-85.) M.N. Roy wrote this book in jail during the period 1930-36 to indicate the way to a solution of the Hindu-Muslim problem in India. This book deserves to be read by human rights educationists as also by members and officials of the NHRC.

9. Prof. Satish Chandra, *op. cit.*, p. 100. What Prof. Satish Chandra writes with special reference to Tulsidas, the chief exponent of one trend of the Bhakti movement which was devoted to Rama, should be specifically noted by human rights educationists even though *Hindutvavadis* will take objection to Prof. Chandra's comments and views: "Tulsidas laid considerable stress on the need for social and political stability with the framework of which alone religious duties could be properly performed. The basis of this was his belief that the overwhelming sections in society consisted of people with wicked and evil propensities...Social control implied the maintenance of a reformed caste system in which people did not transgress their prescribed duties...Tulsl's own approach was fundamentalist or traditionalist in the sense that he based his teaching on the scriptures which, along with the Brahmins, were to be respected and were to be regarded as the bedrock of religion. He also strengthened and revived the tradition of image worship, the deity being worshipped and treated with the deference due to a person of high status. The tradition of reincarnation was automatically reaffirmed." (pp. 109-110)

10. Prof. Salahuddin Ahmed of Dhaka University in *Cultural Interaction in South Asia, op. cit.*, p. 37.

11. J.N. Sarkar, *Thoughts on Trends of Cultural Contacts in Medieval India*, Calcutta, 1984, p. 102.

PART II

STATE OF HUMAN RIGHTS IN INDIA

30

THE PROBLEM OF GRADED INEQUALITY

G.S. Bhargava

The *PUCL Bulletin* has, from time to time, dealt with the question of caste system and human rights violation in our society. This question does not appear to have been taken up by intellectual and political party leaders with the seriousness it deserves even though there has been a lot of talk in recent times about social justice. The outcome of the recent assembly elections in Uttar Pradesh is widely seen as a Dalit upsurge in a relatively backward area of the country. But the reaction it evoked from politicians and others including Dalit leaders suggests a superficial approach to the basic problem of "graded inequality" in Hinduism. Sanctified and sanctioned by the scriptures, it has been institutionalised and has even spread to Islam and Christianity as practised in India.

Dr. B.R. Ambedkar who is being widely deified by all sections of political opinion had put his finger on the source of unending social stratification and injustice in India and sought a radical solution to it. His approach was both conceptual and practical, gradualist and revolutionary in the sense of churning the Hindu society. But neither the political leadership of his time, including Gandhi and Nehru nor the religious leaders of Hindus were equal to the intellectual task set before them by Dr. Ambedkar. For instance, his studied criticism of Hinduism and its religious texts including the Vedas was virtually ignored by Hindu scholars. When Gandhi disputed Dr. Ambedkar's assessment that Hinduism rested on the bedrock of caste and should, therefore, be renounced if it could not be radically reformed, he did not question the inequity of the system or Dr. Ambedkar's indictment of it. He also conceded that everything contained in the scriptures was not authentic but at the same time claimed that "only saints and seers" could interpret the scriptures and not Ambedkar and himself.

His argument that the religion professed by saints could not be totally devoid of merit was as much a rationalisation of the caste system as the interpretation of Dr. S. Radhakrishnan that caste was "a process of fostering unity in the midst of diversity". According to Dr. Radhakrishnan, "The Hindu gods, Upanishadic philosophy, the concepts of *karma* and the journey of the soul through successive births and the mechanism of accommodating tribal gods and totems as variations of the Hindu gods and goddesses provided a loose-knit framework of unity. Without creating great racial disturbances, the Hindu spirit brought about a great racial harmony".

Dr. Radhakrishnan's explanation might be valid during the period of consolidation of Hindu society in the face of external threat, if one left out those treated as outcastes; but Hinduism as it operates now is marked by the caste system, providing social legitimacy and religious sanction to the deprivation and exploitation of the lowest castes. As Dr. Ambedkar had pointed out, it was not mere division of labour but of labourers also, permanently and forever Prof. M.S. Gore who has written an illuminating book on Ambedkar's ideology and its social context (*The Social Context of an Ideology: Ambedkar's Political and Social Thought,* Sage Publications, 1993) endorses Dr. Ambedkar's view that "in the present context, it has become a major source of social strife and an obstacle in the development of a healthy democratic polity".

Prof. Gore's study is significant for its detailed account of the origin and development of Ambedkar's ideas, in their social and political context, and in analysing them against the background of other interpretations including those of Gandhi and Dr. Radhakrishnan. His description of Dr. Ambedkar's assessment of the caste system is helpful in understanding the basic malaise of the Hindu society even today in the wake of urbanisation and modernisation. Dr. Ambedkar hit the nail on the head when he brought out the correlation between social status and caste. To quote from Prof. Gore's account of it, "a Hindu could not change his status, because he could not change his caste. If he lost his caste, he would lose his status but he could not acquire a better or a different status. This might happen, for example, when an individual married outside his or her caste. Such an individual suffered status ambiguity even in urban areas and would find life difficult in a rural context".

Further, there was no element of choice in the caste. One was born into it. Often the name of the caste became a part of the individual's surname. Religious sanction not only sanctified the system but "prepared the individual to uphold religious beliefs—independently of pressure from the group". "The sacred inspired in the individual the sentiment of reverence and deference. One should probably add that it is the sacred nature of caste sanction that accounts for the guilt felt in transcending caste norms. This internalisation often makes group pressure unnecessary".

It is true that more and more Hindus, especially in the urban areas, do not normally practise their religion. But at the same time, they do not renounce in practice the caste system, especially as it applies to the lowest stratum. There is very little social interaction between the upper castes and the Dalits. Intermarriages are even more rare. The caste system also reflected class cleavage in Hindu society, but without the antidote of social mobility available in western societies with their relatively open hierarchies. There is also the economic dimension of availability for upper caste farmers and landowners a readymade source of cheap labour. As Barbara Joshi has highlighted in her writings, "any effective struggle for equality in India must confront the caste component of high-caste actions and attitudes".

Among the short-term remedies proposed by Dr. Ambedkar is the principle of reservation or weightage for the Scheduled Castes in education and employment. His plea for separate electorates was bitterly opposed by Gandhi and rejected by the Congress. So there is no Constitutional provision for it. But thanks to the numbers-based democracy in the country, the Dalits have come to be reckoned as a force in the political arena. Mrs. Indira Gandhi in her time had successfully cobbled a coalition of Brahmins and the Dalits in large parts of north India. But its political benefits for the Dalits were meagre; nor did it make a dent in the caste system. The status and economic position of the Dalits had not effectively improved.

The more recent upsurge is significant for the awakening and political consciousness it generated among the Dalits. Their joining forces with the backward castes—who are as much a part of the exploitative caste system as the superior castes—will be similarly a palliative as far as the social amelioration of the Dalits is concerned. They continue to be seen inherently illegitimate competitors for much prized white-collar and professional positions. Even a symbolic step like the addition of Dr. Ambedkar's name to that of the Marathwada University in Maharashtra is being used to inflame caste tensions, with the Marathas spearheading the resistance and wreaking violence on Dalit homes and hearths. The authorities either treat it as a law and order problem or as a key to the Dalit vote bank.

Dalit leaders and their associates also play the political game, even if it be with greater justification. There is no effort to spread Dr. Ambedkar's ideology to underpin the upsurge of the Dalits and to prepare the Hindu society for the necessary abandonment of the caste system. With the result that efforts to promote the interests of the Dalits—socially and politically—are dubbed casteism and counter-revolutionary, while retention of the caste system, even if with reduced rigidity, is hailed as promotion of unity among the Hindus. In this context, political manoeuvres and vote banks do not promote social justice. [February 1994].

31

HUMAN RIGHTS TRODDEN UNDER FOOT

R.M. Pal

If there is one thing which has been made clear by Ayodhya on 6th December, 1992 is that those who cherish political freedom and civil liberties have been made irrelevant, at least for the time being, by political reaction and social/religious barbarism. There has been violation of all standards of morality, justice and freedom ; everything has been done in the name of *faith* meaning divine sanctions. Acts of barbarism and violence have been committed and justified in the name of *faith,* thus placing premium on ignorance and making the masses easy of exploitation. Religious sentiment has come very handy. The perpetrators of violence in Ayodhya have sought to prove, indeed have succeeded in doing so, that man made laws have no validity. They (Hindutuavadis) have waged war upon all that is fine and valuable in human culture. What we have withessed in Ayodhya is an appeal to violence, to emotion, to passion. And this kind of appeal inevitably leads to cruelty, madness and gangsterism.

Excesses that were committed in demolishing the Mosque, and subsequent cruelties inflicted in a large number of places, to put down "Muslim lies" and "secular lies" are not accidental, but the logical and deliberate acts of a policy. The object of this policy seems to be the destruction of the weak and the triumph of the strong. The panacea for all evils, according to the *Hindutvavadis,* is the annihilation of the weak. The underlying philosophy hardly needs any further elaboration.

Will those cherishing civil liberties and respect for human beings fight this war and this philosophy? If they do—it is regrettable that activists have not given importance to this aspect—there are some unpleasant but pertinent questions to be seriously thought over by them.

It is maintained by almost everyone including human rights activists that India's past was a glorious one and our tradition has been one of tolerance and non-violence (*ahimsa*). Well-meaning intellectuals and distinguished columnists and editors make ex-cathedra statements like: India has 5000 years of civilization written in letters of gold—of tolerance; hatred, bigotry, deception and lies are no part of Hindu tradition. But they are silent on why we have started disintegrating and have declined into barbarism?

Does our history confirm all that is being said about our past? Or, is it a mere accident that suddenly we have become intolerant and violent? "We gloss over the fact that the practice of untouchability is an extreme form of intolerance", and also that religious persecution and intolerance in our past was not infrequent. The persecution of Buddhists and Jainas is hardly ever mentioned, or is dismissed as minor sectarian rivalries.

We hear a lot about the practice of secular politics but hardly any mention of secular morality. As if one is possible without the other?

We have paid a very heavy price by ignoring such uncomfortable ground realities while exclusively concentrating on only those aspects of our past, such as "mutual intellectual borrowings in certain philosophical schools" and co-existence of "diverse religious sects", with the only intention of proving that our past was tolerant and non-violent. Can such selective reading of history help us in fighting the war that has been waged in the name of Hindutva? (Actually the establishment intellectuals confuse pluralism with tolerance; these are very different).

Another question which needs to be investigated relates to the religious identity of Hindus. We did have a Brahmin identity; but did we have a Hindu identity? Or, are these two the same thing? Lumping together different sects under one umbrella does not seem to have helped us even though this erroneously called 'Hindu identity' was made use of to forge the spirit of nationalism, and to create a nation-state.

Along with violence and intolerance India did have glorious chapters, like Buddhism, Jainism, Bhakti movement, and other systems of materialist philosophy—and Bhakti and Sufi movements should make us proud, but that does not seem to be of any importance and pride to anybody. No attempt has been made to revive that glorious past. The great secular epic, the *Ramayana* was converted into religious literature by the Brahmans, and Rama had been made an *avatara* of Vishnu, and this has been accepted as the true *Ramayana* and as our tradition. Why reject the Jaina version of the epic *Paumacaryam* as our tradition? Just because the exponents of the Brahman version dismiss this as falsehood because in this version Ravana has been portrayed differently? These and such other innumerable happenings in our past need to be investigated so that we get to know what traditions we must follow and what we must reject.

Coming to the modern age, how many of our thinkers and politicians have approached the problem of communalism on a scientific line? Even Mahatma Gandhi and Jawaharlal Nehru during the days of independence movement put the question in cold storage saying that once the British leave, the problem will be automatically solved. Mahatma Gandhi, at times, found the atmosphere too "foggy" for him to see clearly. If it was foggy then, it has been made intractable now. Our leaders have made use of shibboleths, albeit pious, to solve the communal problem, which along with the caste system is a major cause of human rights violations. This problem cannot be left to politicians; they can never succeed in solving this problem, for, among other reasons, party politics in our country has been reduced to only scramble for power. It is time therefore that human rights activists take up the questions of Hindutva and the communal problem with greater seriousness than they have done so far, and make efforts to make their presence felt. [January 1993].

32

WHICH CRY OF AGONY WAS SHRILLER AND SEARING TO THE SOUL?

R.M. Pal

At a seminar recently a very difficult question was posed : Which was the area of worst human rights violations during 1995? Difficult to say which cry of despair and anger is more evocative.

What should alarm us the most, however, is the increasing incidence of violence against women: rape, trafficking of women and girl children, bride burning and dowry deaths not to mention female infanticide. Then there are children who have been deprived of education by not being put to school at all or withdrawn from studies after a time. Outside the gender-biased violence, there are custodial violence and murder; and a community like the Muslims being under constant threat and living in fear; and upper caste crimes against Dalit men and women. It is indeed a long list which is difficult to arrange in the order of heinousness. In each case victims are hurt and deprived. The experience is evaluated not by the numbers of victims but by the intensity of suffering inflicted.

It is in this context we refer to the widely known cruelties inflicted on Mrs. Bhanwari Devi. That she was raped in the presence of her helpless husband is searing to the soul. But what happened in November, 1995, is more painful, more shocking and disturbing; people with sensitivity will find the cry of agony of the victim shriller.

Five persons were accused of gangraping Mrs. Bhanwari Devi, a *saathin* (social worker) working with the Women's Development Programme of the Rajasthan Government. She was subjected to this cruel humiliation and torture because of her attempt to prevent a child marriage, which was indeed her official duty. But it is against upper caste feudal tradition, specially in Rajasthan. All the accused in the alleged gangrape were acquitted by the District and Sessions Judge of Jaipur in November, 1995. Some of the reasons for the acquittal, as reported in the press, are shocking and disturbing. The judge said that taking into account the age of the accused—they were all middle-aged—it is inconceivable that such people will indulge in rape, for middle- aged persons are ipso facto "respectable citizens" and, therefore, cannot commit such a crime. Which means that rapists are usually teenagers. Which further means that no case can even be instituted against non-teenagers!

Another reason advanced by the judge is that the accused belong to the upper castes—one of them is a Brahmin—and, therefore, could not have raped a low caste woman (Mrs. Bhanwari Devi belongs to a low caste). It is hardly necessary to add that upper caste men are known not only for subjecting lower caste men and women to the curse of untouchability but also compelling, in some areas of the country, low caste girls to have sex with them, even on their first wedding night.

Can another cry of agony be shriller than that of Mrs. Bhanwari Devi?

By way of a footnote, we may refer to another incident, as reported in a section of the press. The Indian Trade Promotion Organisation (ITPO) decided to give saffron coloured shirts to *safai karmacharis* (sweepers) as part of their uniform. The Shiv Sena branch of Delhi and North India issued a statement saying: "We will not tolerate such insults. They deliberately made the *safai karmacharis* wear saffron, the colour symbolising saintliness, to hurt Hindu sentiments. We have noticed that even now the *safai karmacharis* in ITPO are wearing saffron coloured clothes. If the organisers do not change this, we will have to resort to active protests and demonstrations".

Such incidents are indicative of the fact that Constitutional provisions by themselves cannot put an end to the hierarchical mindset which persists in our society resulting in violation and abuse of rights and infringement of civil liberties. Our human rights groups and activists will have to put their heads together to find out ways and means to face the situation. [17 Dec. 1995].

33

INTOLERANCE

R.M. Pal

Intolerance is one of the primary causes of human rights violations and infringement of civil liberties in our country. Indeed, intolerance threatens the very existence of a civilised state and society.

Communal and caste hatred, both products of intolerance, can create havoc (as we commented in the editorial note of the last August, 1997 issue of the *PUCL Bulletin* while referring to the culture of intolerance and hatred exhibited by Hindutvavadi intellectuals).

Since then a new controversy has arisen with the publication of a book [*Worshipping the False God* by Arun Shourie] which denigrates Dr. Ambedkar. The author of the book dismisses Dr. Ambedkar's criticism of Hinduism as "caricature" and "calumnies", and is also rather dismissive of the perpetual suffering of the depressed section of our population for centuries, and Dr. Ambedkar's fight for their right to be human. The author also charges Ambedkar who, according to him, did not fight for India's independence and whom he equates with Jinnah as an "accomplice of imperial politics"; and that Ambedkar's disagreement with Gandhi is an indication that he was "anti-national". (The author of book does not recognise the fact that fascism is a dangerous cult; and that Dr. Ambedkar was in the company of those freedom loving leaders and intellectuals who waged war against fascism. They maintained that if the fascists were not defeated in the second World War, human freedom could not survive and in that eventuality, the question of Indian Independence would not arise. India would remain a perpetual slave to fascist powers. It was war between fascism and democracy. So Dr. Ambedkar took a strong stand in favour of full Indian support for British War effort. To say that Dr. Ambedkar was anti-national, is indeed blasphemy).

The author of the book however, does not, refer to what Gandhiji thought about Dr. Ambedkar: "He has every right to be bitter. That he does not break our heads is an act of selfrestraint on his part. ... Dr. Ambedkar has had to suffer humiliations and insults which should make anyone of us bitter and resentful. Had I been in his place, I would have been as angry. ... We shall be unfit to gain Swaraj so long as we keep in bondage a fifth of the population. ... In the history of world religions there is perhaps nothing like our treatment of the suppressed classes. ... What crimes for which we condemn the government as Satanic have not we been guilty of towards our untouchable brethren? We make them crawl on their bellies. ... Verses from scripture cannot be above reason and morality. ... Caste Hindu well wishers of untouchables have no right to speak for them", and so on. The author of the book completely ignores "the extremity of intolerance", in the words of the historian Romila Thapar, "implicit in the notion of untouchability we glossed over by regarding it as a function of caste and society".

Dalits are very angry over the book. In one angry outburst of intolerance, on 2nd August, in front of the Ambedkar statue on the lawn of Parliament House, a few Scheduled Caste MPs burnt the book and demanded its proscription by the Government. This incident and behaviour exhibits the same culture of intolerance referred to above, which is totally unbecoming of any civilised society, and utter disregard, if not contempt, for freedom of expression and the values associated with this freedom.

If one is offended by a book, the only sane and civilised method is to fight an ideological battle, and not a physical one. It is in this context that the role played by forty prominent Dalit intellectuals of Maharashtra must be commended. They have decided to counter the arguments put forward in the book and the forces of intolerance and hate campaign referred to in the editorial note of the August issue of the *PUCL Bulletin*, on the intellectual plane, and not by a totally indefensible act of burning a book or demanding its proscription. These forty intellectuals, apart from holding aloft the torch of the values of freedom, have shown the path to a wider social tolerance which is what the people of a socially complex country like ours must practice. [16 August, 1997].

34

ACADEMICS RENEW ANTI-RESERVATION STIR

R.M. Pal

The anti-reservation (in effect, anti-affirmative action) agitation in 1990 found active promoters in print media as also university, college and school students and academics, particularly in Delhi and other parts of North India. It became a mini-industry. It was revived, mercifully for a brief period, in 1993 after the Supreme Court judgement upholding the government action on the Mandal Commission recommendations. Now, once again, it has surfaced, in a fairly big way, in Delhi University.

Anguish and pain prevent one from giving a detailed description of the raw materials of this "industry". However, a summary account of the finished products is necessary for an analysis of the background of the current revival of the anti-reservation stir among academics of Delhi University.

The V.P. Singh Government's decision in 1990 to implement the Mandal Commission's recommendations had brought about a situation in Delhi University in which any discussion on the assumption that a coin has two sides became impossible. At a meeting of academics and students of the university an invited speaker was not allowed to have his say in support of reservation. The editor of a national daily, *The Indian Express*, went to the extent of exhorting students to take to the streets and they did. This was despite the fact that no political party had opposed the recommendations.

Colleges and faculties of the university held meetings to voice their opinion on a directive issued by the then Vice-Chancellor who, despite claiming to be a human rights intellectual, had expressed reservations about affirmative action, albeit in a language of honey and sophistry. The decision was already written on the walls: it would be disastrous for the country; it would give rise to casteism, and so on. This writer was present at a meeting where faculty members were asked if they had read the Mandal recommendations; no, they had not and yet stuck to their "identities". The Delhi University Teachers' Association (DUTA) took up *Mandal* on the trade union level and waged a regular warfare. This writer is unable to recollect any occasion during his long association with the university when the DUTA or any other teachers' organisation had taken up an issue of social justice and waged war against the inequities in our society. But when it came to opposition to reservation the inhibition ceased.

The verdict given by many editors, distinguished columnists, and academics in 1990 may be summarised thus : The government has created a situation in which there would be caste war; the administration will collapse; if the stir continues India will not survive; V.P. Singh has embarked on the task of dividing the country as did Jinnah, and he is another Hitler in the making, and therefore he must go—and he went. History was created by the festival of fireworks being celebrated not on the Diwali day, but on the night of V.P. Singh's resignation, with crackers bursting throughout the night while the light kept burning.

It is against this background that the recent stir in Delhi University, mostly by teachers owing allegiance to the BJP and the Congress party, against reservation of teaching positions for Scheduled Castes and Scheduled Tribes should be viewed. The other dominant group in the university led by the CPM, though not against affirmative action, is, however conspicuous by its silence, for fear of being thrown out of power in the next DUTA elections. Clearly, social justice and affirmative action to eradicate inequities are not on the agenda.

It may be recalled that the university took the decision (which is now part of a University Ordinance) in April, 1996, that 22.5 per cent of teaching and non-teaching positions in the university and its colleges be reserved for SC/STs. It is painful to recollect in this context that at a meeting of the Academic Council of the university, to discuss the item on the agenda on two or three occasions earlier—some faculty members went to the extent of saying:

Mother goddess Saraswati's clothes will be desecrated if the policy of reservation is adopted (literal translation of what was said in Hindi).

It is equally painful that no one present at the meeting thought of reminding them of what Abraham Lincoln had said in the context of slavery : it is dangerous to nurture a society and nation of half-slaves and half-free.

During the period April to October, 1996, hardly any effort was made to make the university decision of reservation effective. It is in the light of this non-implementation of the law that the University Grants Commission (UGC), reportedly under pressure from the concerned Parliamentary Committee, issued a letter on October 29, 1996, asking the university authorities to launch a special recruitment drive to fill the teaching and non-teaching positions reserved for SC/STs.

It is significant that although the UGC took the decision to write to the university on July 31, 1996, it prevaricated for four long months to communicate the decision to the university; in fact the letter has not yet reached the university (on November 12 at the time of writing this note). The contents of the letter were, however, made known to the leaders of anti-reservation teachers on or about October 29, 1996!

One of the arguments advanced by teachers, including well-known "Marxist" and "progressive" faculty members, is that academic standards will suffer if SC/ST teachers are appointed. "Implementation of the UGC decision would result in collapse of standards of instruction and research activities in the university system," they announced majestically, and warned that if the UGC "does not withdraw its letter, there would be intense unrest on the campus". No one has, however, said a single word about the increasingly and alarmingly falling standards in spite of the fact that the academic community has always been dominated and controlled by the upper and forward castes.

The fact remains—it should be obvious to all thoughtful men and women—that the upper and forward castes are bent on maintaining the status quo; they are determined to fight back, whenever the situation demands, any struggle for social justice and affirmative action. The North Indian educated middle classes (whom Rajni Kothari calls "the lumpenised middle class") feel threatened, not because they would be deprived of jobs, but because their caste identities would be at stake. One may recall in this context that a large number of banners were put up in Delhi in 1990, mostly in women's colleges, to assert their identity.

We are not particularly concerned with the question of reservation and politics involved in the controversy. We do feel concerned, however, about the fact that a large number of communities in our country have had their social status fixed for all time to come. This fact, too, has been summarily dismissed by anti-reservation faculty members of Delhi University. You refuse to accept the given social status, you are dubbed a casteist! These scholars do not accept the fact that every human being given favourable conditions, is capable of developing unlimited powers of intellect and will; and that those conditions have not yet been created for those who deserve them the most.

It is a great pity that universities which ought to be centres for initiating movements for progress have embarked on the dangerous path of leading us to the dark age of history. [30 Nov. 1996].

35

"ANCIENT WRONGS" AND THE NATIONAL HUMAN RIGHTS COMMISSION

R.M. Pal

During the last four years since the National Human Rights Commission (NHRC) came into being, it has focussed, to a fair extent, on violation of human rights by the organs of the state, the police, the paramilitary forces and others. It has a more exacting task ahead. (It is particularly important to take note on the fiftieth year of the *Universal Declaration of Human Rights*—the celebrations of which started on December 10, 1997—Article I of that document which states that all are born equal). That is the task of redressing societal wrongs which are more deepseated. The Dalits (SC/STs), together with other deprived sections like women, children, and the minorities, must be enabled to reap the rewards of independence which was ushered in fifty years ago. They must be provided all help in their bid to eliminate every type of discrimination. This is possible only in a non-caste, non-hierarchical society.

Basically, the Dalits' struggle is a struggle for human rights, human dignity. If they succeed in their struggle, as they must, it will prove a blessing for the entire nation—not merely any group or community. The dominating section of our people must, therefore, adopt a strong position against caste hierarchy, communalism, anti-minorityism, gender prejudice which are the major sources of societal human rights violations, or "ancient wrongs" as the NHRC put it.

With growing awakening among the Dalits who constitute a sizable section of our population and the Dalits' persisting alienation from the mainstream, if caste identity remains intact, the very concept of integration, assimilation, patriotism—in short pride in being an Indian, pride in being involved in nation-building—will be undercut. Making the dominating section respond to the national need is a veritable challenge because this section continues to assume innate superiority that its members being clever, intelligent, educated, cultured, and refined deserve what they have. They want the others to take shelter under their dominance and seek sustenance at their mercy. In such a social atmosphere, developing the culture and values of human rights which the NHRC is committed to promote will remain a distant goal.

The dominating section must rise to the occasion and declare that India does not accept the commonly held belief that caste hierarchy and the social system based on it have been beneficial or benevolent.They must demolish the structure of hierarchy so that there is no discrimination on this score. This step alone will help create a culture of human rights.

It is the task of the NHRC, in our understanding, to act, in cooperation with enlightened social activists and NGOs, as the philosopher-guide in helping the peple to help themselves with a view to creating a new man, a new woman and a new society where the values of human rights and freedoms and human dignity are universally respected.

These values and the respect for other fellow beings cannot be legislated. But the NHRC has the mandate to put the issue in the proper perspective both before the government and the society. As people living in this geographical territory, that is, India, it is in our interest to live together. But we cannot live together if we continue to think and act in terms of caste hierarchy. The NHRC can, if it can summon up the will, contribute considerably towards breaking the walls that have stood rock-like for centuries. We know it is a difficult and daunting task—the more so because these walls were not created by accident but by some of the most sophisticated scholars and "wise men". It is precisely because of this that pioneers like Buddha, Rammohun Roy, Ishwar Chandra Vidyasagar, Mahatma Phule found it hard to have a dialogue with such "scholars" and law-givers. With the result that the culture and values of human rights and civil liberties which these great and good men espoused have not yet taken roots in our country. Our soil is not yet ready to receive the seeds of these values. It is one of the tasks of the NHRC to prepare the soil.

The "ancient wrongs" have not disappeared. How do we go about in bringing a change in the situation ? First, the dominating section must have the knowledge of the "ancient wrongs" and must accept the need for their redressal and removal. Again, it is the task of the NHRC to impart this knowledge to them, for without such knowledge, the NHRC and social activists cannot chalk out a course of action for their future.

It is in this context that the NHRC must have platforms where concerned people can have a regular dialogue. India is celebrating the golden jubilee of its independence. It is only proper that the dialogue must start during the evocative phase of our history so that the people are enabled to look at our social problems with the purpose of assessing to what extent discrimination, prejudice, and human rights violations have been on the increase in the last fifty years. [15 Oct. 1997].

36

RIGHTS OF THE CHILD: EDUCATION

R.M. Pal

I have written extensively on the subject of compulsory basic education apropos of the basic human right of the child, published in the *PUCL Bulletin*, the *Mainstream*, the *Radical Humanist*, *Janata*, a number of national dailies including the *Times of India* and the *Pioneer*. One of the main reasons given in all these writings for non-fulfilment of the provision of Article 45 of our Constitution (free compulsory education upto the age of fourteen), is the middle class mindset. So that if the illiterate children and child labourers belonged to the upper strata of society illiteracy and child labour would have been eradicated long ago. As is known, almost the entire child labour force belongs to Scheduled Castes and Scheduled Tribes, Dalit Christians, the Muslim minority, and girls. I give below a few extracts from some of these write-ups. Since these articles were written on the same subject (over the period 1990—98) there are bound to be repitions of arguments.

The first editorial note, "A Basic Human Right" was written in 1990 (*PUCL Bulletin*) before the Supreme Court judgment making Article 45 a part of the fundamental rights and Professor Amartya Sen's thesis was enunciated by him in a lecture in Delhi in 1995 and then in the book, *India: Economic Development and Social Opportunities* by Jean Dreze and Amartya Sen.

The expressions, primary, elementary, and basic education mean education upto the age of fourteen, i.e. upto standard VIII as provided by the Constitution—R.M.P.].

* * *

A Basic Human Right—September 1990: There is one field ... which does not appear to be in the priority list of human rights organisations—education and schooling of children. ... It was stipulated by our constitution makers that children upto the age of fourteen will be given free and compulsory education. ... The attempts made by Union and State Governments since the time India attained independence indicate that education is not a subject which deserves top priority. The government has, however, spent huge amount by way of setting up Commissions and Committees which in turn have produced voluminous reports. Some of these Commissions started with the assumption that anything that was recommended by any Commission during the British regime must be scrapped—for example, the Sargent Commission Report. ... The fact remains that an increasing number of children are growing as illiterates. ...

It is said that parents don't send their children to schools because of economic reasons—they want their children to add to the family income and therefore they either do not send their children to school, or children drop out after a year or two. This is at best only half-truth, and half-truth is more dangerous than falsehood. ... Even where schools function, the physical condition is deplorable—there are no desks, no drinking water facilities, no lavatories. You visit any Corporation and Government schools in Delhi and you find that children in primary sections are not provided with desks; they are required to squat. Children from poor families do deserve better physical environment than in their places of residence where they have no amenities of life. Let them have some amenities at least in their school where they can feel happy, and if they are happy they may not drop out. [Sept. 1990].

* * *

"The Child" (written on the occasion of Children's Day 14 November, 1992) went on to say: In the scheme of things that obtains in India, any talk of abolition of child labour, women's progress, uplift of the depressed sections of our people, is futile. Even our first Prime Minister whose birthday 14 November is celebrated as Children's Day put the utmost emphasis on heavy industries, big dams, and technological achievement. And now, the government is concerned with making the country, not the people, "prosperous" by adopting any method which will enable it to get money from funding agencies and governments from the West. The government clearly is not concerned about the people.

Look at our priorities. Elementary and primary education (upto the age of fourteen) which should have been on the priority list, is not in that category. The percentage of children going to school in our country is much less than in many underdeveloped countries including those in Africa. The drop-out rate, too, is much less in those countries. Our government has money for everything, but not for compulsory education. One does not have to be an economist to understand the simple fact that economic prosperity, or for that matter any development, is just not possible without education. Furthermore, abolition of child labour will be possible only when children are sent to school. As an example, we may refer to Kerala where child labour has been on the decline because of increasing literacy.

The government's stated stand in the matter can be summarised in one sentence: It is not possible to abolish child labour in view of the economic situation of the country. Given this approach, the question of introducing compulsory education for childern upto the age of 14 is ruled out. And in that event, abolition of child labour too will remain a distant goal. In fact, it is not on the agenda of the government. How does one explain, therefore, the fact that we have a very large number of children working full-time even in prohibited industries under the most inhuman conditions?

Regrettably, the human rights organisations working for abolition of child labour, especially in industries like carpet weaving in Mirzapur, have not applied their mind to the educational aspect of the problem. One activist here and another there may succeed in getting children out of the industry, but what happens to them later ? That does not seem to be anybody's problem.

Abolition of child labour does not mean that children are not to help their parents in their work. Their work, alongwith schooling, and not at the cost of schooling, at this age can prepare them for the task ahead.

It is often said that child labour will disappear when poverty is eradicated. This is putting the cart before the horse, for poverty can be tackled only when children are educated. Promoting school enrolment is the only way out. [14 Nov 1992].

* * *

One Quarter Free Three Qquarters Slave: 15 June 1995. The greatest tragedy—a wholly avoidable one—that has befallen our country is the non-implementation of the programme of universal primary education and not putting this social welfare programme first on the list of priorities. For this the builders of the new India during the period 1947 till the mid-sixties are squarely to blame. [Except Kerala, the picture is grim all over. In U.P., for example, one-third of male children and more than three-fifths of female children are illiterate. It is the same in respect of school attendance for India as a whole, more so for U.P. In rural areas more than quarter of boys and more than half the girls have never been enrolled. India is not only behind China, Sri Lanka and South Korea, but also behind "low income countries" (as defined by World Bank) including sub-Saharan Africa (see also, Amartya Sen's D.T. Lakdawal Memorial Lecture under the auspices of ISS, a summary of which was published in the April, 1995 issue of the *PUCL Bulletin*; and also ILO Reports)]. Idealism of any kind has since the mid-sixties been replaced by utterly vulgar scramble for power, and diabolical political activities. In such a foul atmosphere progress of any kind is unthinkable.

Our leaders, almost totally and perhaps deliberately, chose to forget the fact that it is, to use Abraham Lincoln's words, dangerous to have a nation which lives half-free and half-slave. In fact, in the case of India it is not half, but more than three-quarters of India that consist of slaves. Our leaders also chose not to take any cognizance of the fact that slavery thrives on illiteracy—and that the precondition for any progress, apart from cultivating a culture of respect for the human being, in any field including realisation of civil rights, is the eradication of illiteracy and the 'divinely ordained' hierarchical order of our society. Non-recognition of this basic fact has rendered India vulnerable in almost all fields.

Our leaders did not adhere to the very simple and rational approach : first thing first. The first thing was to make the one social welfare programme, namely universal and compulsory primary education, successful. (Article 45 of the Constitution, had directed the State in 1949 "to endeavour to provide within a period of ten years from commencement of the Constitution, for free and compulsory education until they complete the age of 14." It took another five decades for the Supreme Court of India to appreciate the fact that nothing has been done and that the provision of this Article be made part of fundamental rights. Again, there is no indication of any action that is to be taken against the State for violating this right.) If we had successfully carried out only this welfare programme, all other problems would have remained under control and India would have been on the march forward. (As an example, we may refer to Kerala where because of high rate of literacy employment of children has been on the decline.) Instead, the stark reality today is one of intractability.

Illiteracy has many adverse affects: the freedom and welfare of the people; social change; health care; large scale female infanticide (only very recently an NGO has given a detailed account of this inhuman and criminal act in four districts of Bihar); abysmal poverty; economic disparity; population control; eradication of social evils like discrimination based on caste and sex; child marriage; child labour (India contributes the largest share in the child labour force in the world—it exists *not* because of poverty; it is all the more tragic to note the fact that almost 90 per cent of child workers employed in the notorious match factories in Sivakasi are girls)—the list is indeed vast. These problems will remain intractable so long as children are not sent to school—their only rightful place. (See also Amartya Sen referred to earlier).

In 1947 India's destiny was designed by leaders many of whom were intellectuals; they were well-versed in world history. They knew, or ought to have known, that the emperor of Japan in the 1870s concentrated on only one welfare programme with a view to tackling all other problems—he introduced universal primary education; that Britain too realised its importance and made primary education compulsory about the same time. Our leaders knew that, that is how they achieved a break-through in population control. They also knew that the evil of child labour disappeared from these countries, thanks to their successful implementation of this one single welfare programme. And yet our leaders exhibited a singular lack of will to make this successful in our country. Is it because it has not been our tradition to care for the poor, the deprived, the depressed?

Today the Government of India, through the NHRC have started publicising introduction of human rights education as a subject in schools and colleges. The reason for this public relations activity is well known—pressure from funding agencies and countries because of human rights violations. Conviction does not appear to be a factor. Otherwise the government and other concerned agencies and institutions would have shown a sense of urgency—this sense of urgency is conspicuous by its absence even on the part of human rights activists—in ensuring that all children received *at least* basic education. We have known over these years that shibboleths have been our leaders' and planners' mainstay.

Lack of funds is often cited as the main reason for failure in this sector. The country has money, however, for all "programmes". The Prime Minister went to France the other day with a large retinue. Agreed, the cause was laudable—to give a lecture on Mahatma Gandhi. One wishes, however, the Prime Minister and other politicians had indulged in a little less hypocrisy by following Gandhi's teachings and programmes, here in India, one of which is his basic education scheme (popularly known as the Wardha Scheme of Education) which aimed at imparting elementary education to *all* children. (We dare not mention Gandhi's insistence on observing morality in politics!). We have the money, for example, to send teams of ministers and members of Parliament on a world tour with the ostensible purpose of assessing the use of Hindi in our Missions abroad—the whole tour costing about rupees one crore. We have crores to spend on "security" of VVIPs, both present and past. There is no dearth of money for our foreign mission people who are "required" to live in style, observing all pomp and show, hiding under the carpet the reality of India's poverty. Funds have never come in the way of ministers visiting foreign countries—according to published reports, no less than 21 ministers have been on foreign trips or would be travelling abroad during this summer. This number does not include the President, the Vice-President, and the Prime Minister. One non-functional Cabinet Minister (on perpetual medical leave with pay) is being sent to London for medical treatment. There is no problem in spending money lavishly on our M.Ps and state legislators—they enjoy almost everything free of cost; over and above these they get a handsome pension for life after they have served a term of only four years. Add to all these the scandalous and diabolical scams involving thousands of crores of rupees. Who can say India is a poor country!

Well, everything except children's education is unavoidable expenditure; compulsory primary education can wait, for the abuse of the child is God's gift! Human rights activists may consider whether it is possible to bring about a change in the scenario including that of human rights so long as this wilful and criminal neglect of the child persists. [15 June 1995].

* * *

Universal Primary Education—the Odd Subject in India: 14 Dec.1996. The Supreme Court, 1996 while ordering the setting up of a corpus fund to be known as Child Labour Rehabilitation-cum-Welfare Fund with a Rs. 25000 contribution by the employer of a child in a hazardous industry, and giving a number of other rulings to end child labour, directs the government to ensure compulsory primary education for all children, and expresses the sentiment, "We have the fond hope that the closing years of 20th century would see us keeping the promise made to our children by our Constitution about half a century ago".

What is significant is that a similar sentiment was expressed, and more or less similar directive given by the Supreme Court in an earlier judgement in February 1993 while giving a ruling that primary education must be considered a fundamental right. The Supreme Court said then, while lamenting on the failure to achieve the goal in terms of Article 45 of the Constitution, namely that universal primary education be introduced within the stipulated period of ten years from the commencement of the Constitution: "Does not the passage of 44 years, more than 4 times the period stipulated under Article 45 convert the obligation created by the Article into an enforceable right? In this context we feel constrained to say that the allocation of available funds to different sectors of education in India disclosed an inversion of priorities indicated by the Constitution. ... Be that as it may, we must say that at least now the State should honour the command of Article 45. It must be made a reality—at least now". (Which ought to mean in effect that the government cannot take shelter under the provision of Article 45 of the Directive Principles of State Policy of the Constitution which is not justiciable—the provisions in the Fundamental Rights chapter are justiciable.)

Our rulers, since that judgement in 1993, have done precious little to fulfill "the fond hope". In fact, it does not even seem to recognise the fact that compulsory primary education is a social welfare programme not to speak of taking steps towards implementing it. Yes, after the judgement, some noise was made regarding midday meal to be provided to school children: and recently there have been a lot of advertisements on the TV about adult education. There is no doubt that it is very essential, but this is no substitute for compulsory primary education.

When the present rulers is the Deve Gowada Government came to power at the Centre about seven months ago, they made some noise about primary education, but soon after, officials in the education ministry announced that it would not be possible to implement this programme by the end of 2005 A.D. The only step the government is going to take now, it is reported, is to appoint a committee of legal and administrative "experts" to examine the possibilities and feasibility of making universal primary education a fundamental right in the Constitution and how to make this right operative. Obviously, the government seem to have conveniently forgotten the earlier Supreme Court ruling which made this subject a fundamental right!

We may, therefore, draw the attention of all concerned—the Supreme Court, the various international agencies, the government, human rights groups and activists, and groups working in the field of eradication of child labour—to the utter insensitivity on the part of successive governments during the last half a century. Prof. Amartya Sen, an eminent economist teaching at Harvard, has commented on this aspect so succinctly: "Education is one of the odd subjects in India, to the importance of which tribute has always been paid in theory and never much in practice". Let us add that the State and other agencies including groups and activists involved in the work of eradication of child labour, do not seem to have accepted universal primary education as a social welfare programme. Prof. Sen adds (*Nationalism, Democracy and Development*, OUP: "Despite his [Pandit Nehru's] continuous use of the rhetoric of education for all, Nehru and the Party he led put very little emphasis in practice on universal education when they gained office. The implicit concentration on a seamless unity [of India] might well have hindered concrete efforts to remedy the deprivation of the educationally neglected". The present government which speaks of social justice as also "progressive" intellectuals and political activists, might note what Sen adds: "But the eradication of this deprivation is not helped just by admiring the non-elite and their role in history, while leaving unaddressed their real deprivation that continue into the present".

It needs to be repeated over and over again that illiteracy has all the adverse effects, and that no development of any kind relating to freedoms and welfare of the people including abolition of child labour, can take place without implementing this social welfare programme.

The Supreme Court will no doubt appreciate the fact that child labour will be abolished automatically once the child is sent to school, and nothing else can tackle the evil of child labour, and also that it is the duty of the state to implement this most important special welfare programme; all other measures that the court wants to be implemented are only accessories.

We hope the New Year will usher in a different culture, a different mind-set which will take up the issue of education a little more seriously and with the honesty of purpose it deserves.—[14 December, 1996].

* * *

Rights of the Child: The Education Challenge: There are hardly any takers in our country for the thesis that without imparting basic education to our children, no improvement in any field and no economic development is possible. The corollary is that the most atrocious form of human rights violations—child labour—cannot be overcome without the implementation of Article 45 of our Constitution, (which has been made part of fundamental rights by a judgement of the Supreme Court. Article 45 provides: "The State shall endeavour to provide within a period of 10 years from the commencement of this Constitution for free and compulsory education until they complete the age of 14 years (that is, upto Class VIII)".

Politicians and bureaucrats averse to or unable to implement a social welfare programme for the deprived sections of our people, know how to get away with it through the in-built escape route in the system. Over the years they have perfected and legitimised the art of doublespeak and the language of deceit and arrogance, like George Orwell's four-legged dictator who quietly changed the original thesis of the revolution, "four legs good, two legs bad" to "four legs good, two legs better" and from "all animals are equal" to "all animals are equal but some animals are more equal than others". Our political rulers and bureaucrats justify and rationalise non-implementation of Article 45 in the kind of language referred to above. Language of reason has been totally lost on them. I give below a couple of examples of such language as also of quibbling and backtracking which is insulting to millions of our illiterate people.

The first announcement made by Dr. Murli Manohar Joshi, an eminent RSS ideologue and present Human Resource Development Minister, even before the Prime Minister sought the vote of confidence in the Lok Sabha, was that all efforts will be made to provide education to children upto class 'V'—indeed, a "fresh" interpretation of the Constitutional provisions!

On another occasion, sharply reacting to India being called the "illiteracy Capital of the world, Dr. Joshi angrily retorted: "India has a very large number of literate people also. Why don't you talk about them? The literacy rate is 50 per cent, so we have about 48 crore literate people in India. Which is double the population of the U.S." Victims of human rights violation—deprivation of basic education—know why Dr. Joshi and his likes get annoyed when reminded that India's illiterate population exceeds the total population of the USA, Canada and Japan.

The mindset behind this kind of quibbling and false pride cannot be expected to implement faithfully this social welfare programme. So that a vast number of our people will continue to be deprived of this basic human right; and our country will remain deprived of all the benefits including economic development, social progress, population control, reduction in infant and child mortality rate, and so on.

Dr. Joshi and his ministry seem to have evolved a new scheme (reminiscent of former Prime Minister Mr. I.K. Gujral's scheme of making it mandatory for all fresh graduates to teach at least five children for receiving the Bachelor's degree). It is called the National Reconstruction Corps (NRC) which is to launch the literacy drive, because, Dr. Joshi said, "the ministry doesn't have enough money" to impart basic education to our children. Under this scheme, boys and girls in the age group of 18-21 who have passed their 10 + 2 examination will be employed to teach children and paid Rs. 1,500/- per month. (Source: *Outlook* magazine, 6 July).

Two short points in this regard. One, since the minimum qualification for teaching primary classes is 10 + 2 pass certificate, why not appoint them as regular teachers and pay them the prescribed pay and allowances? (The obvious answer, the Government doesn't have the money ! The government has not been short of funds for anything except the programme of basic education). Two, girls and boys having + 2 certificates are not equipped to teach students of classes VII and VIII—children upto the age of 14. So that the NRC cannot be a substitute for compulsory basic education as a fundamental right. NRC can be introduced in addition to regular schooling with full-time teachers, proper class rooms, and other educational equipment. Or, is it that Dr. Joshi has now finally decided to stick to his earlier announcement, namely, that primary education will be provided upto class V and not upto the age of fourteen? (Here again, we are reminded of Orwell's *Animal Farm* and the sheep chanting regularly the revised lessons and the animals in the farm begin to believe that these are the true lessons! They forget the original lessons, "all animals are equal", and "four legs good"!)

Dr. Joshi seems to have decided to put the Constitutional Amendment Bill, making free and compulsory elementary education a fundamental right (which was moved by the United Front Government) in cold storage. He and his ministry feel that it is not feasible to implement such a Constitutional provision.

This is further reinforced by another exercise undertaken by a Government of India Research Institute, the V.V. Giri National Labour Institute in Noida. It has prepared a draft bill, the title of which is "The Child Labour Rehabilitation Bill 1998—an Act to Prohibit and Regulate Employment of Children". Note, it is to regulate child labour! Furthermore, may one ask, what has happened to the number of Constitutional provisions and the 21 legislative enactments on the subject? Nobody, certainly not those in the Government, need be told and reminded that these provisions as well as the 1993 and 1996 Supreme Court Judgements have not made any dent in the Government's immunity from action. Such negative and futile exercise is undertaken because it is an unwritten and unstated fact that illiteracy, which is limited largely to the marginalised section of our society, does not find a place on the agenda of Government's priority.

I may add that even the founding fathers—the Constitution makers—did not attach any importance to this social welfare programme. It may be recalled that originally, the Sub-Committee on Fundamental Rights of the Constituent Assembly proposed that basic education be included in the list of fundamental rights, but subsequently it was rejected by the Constitution makers. One member said, "Is this a justiciable right? Suppose the government has no money?" Pandit Govind Ballabh Pant quipped, "It cannot be justiciable. No court can possibly adjudicate", so "this clause be transferred to Part II (Directive Principles of State Policy)".

Although this committee had self-acclaimed Gandhians like Mr. M.R. Masani, only one member, Mr. K.T. Shah had the courage of conviction to give a dissenting note. He said that if a right to education becomes non-justiciable, it "would remain as no more than so many pious wishes". He added that if it does not become "imperative obligations of the state towards the citizen, we would be perpetuating a needless fraud". Furthermore, he wrote in the dissenting note, "once an ambiguous declaration of such a right is made (justiciable), those responsible for it would have to find ways and means to give effect to it. If they had no such responsibility placed upon them, they might be inclined to avail themselves of every excuse to justify their own inactivity in the matter, indifference, or worse". Prophetic words, indeed! No surprise, therefore, that the operative part of Pandit Nehru's famous tryst with destiny speech was not meant to be implemented.

What is worse is that even NGOs, "progressive" intellectuals and activists like the Sarvodayists, radical humanists and other activist-groups do not place compulsory education at the top of their agenda. In April 1998, Mr. V.M. Tarkunde prepared a document on behalf of the Radical Humanist Association, "People's Minimum Programme for Prompt Action by the New Government", demanding that "resources should be made available to provide free primary education". [This article was published in *The Radical Humanist*, but radical humanists seem to feel paralysed when this question is raised!]

Mr. Tarkunde does not consider "compulsory education" to be a feasible proposition for legal and other reasons—reminiscent of what our Constitution makers said. Does he, too, like the HRD Minister, refer to "primary" education, that is, schooling upto class V? This dilution of Article 45 by the Minister and others cannot be the result of "forgetfulness". Mr. Madhu Dandavate, when he was Vice-Chairman of the Planning Commission—this subject is supposed to be on the agenda of the Commission—did not find time even to have an in-depth discussion on the subject, with experts, not to speak of implementing it. The former Prime Minister, Mr. I.K. Gujral, dispensed with the subject by making an announcement from the Red Fort that the provisions of Article 45 would be implemented. His government's performance in this regard was limited to the production of a totally unreadable report—to make elementary education a fundamental right, and more importantly, a fundamental duty without spelling out the responsibilities of the State for non-compliance.

What I want to stress here is that this is a typical middle class mindset, and it has never taken Article 45 of the Constitution seriously. I may also add that without a change in this mindset, implementation of this programme will continue to remain a distant goal.

Let us also give a quick look at the record of the West Bengal government, a self-proclaimed, most progressive one, whatever it may mean. The State has now been ruled by a CPM-led front for over 20 years. The literacy rate of the Scheduled Castes in West Bengal is 42.21 per cent of the total Scheduled Caste population of the State.—this ranks way behind that of most other states in India. The literacy rate of the Scheduled Tribes is worse, 27.78 per cent of the total Scheduled Tribe population in the State—again, way behind that in most other states in the country. With regard to Scheduled Caste and Scheduled Tribe female literacy, the percentage is much lower. West Bengal does not come anywhere near States like Kerala and Tamil Nadu in respect of overall literacy and education—it is in the company of Bihar and Uttar Pradesh.

II

It is in this context that we must take serious note of the report, *Human Development in South Asia 1998 : The Education Challenge* (written by the late Mahboob-ul-Haq, one of the best known economists of our times and Khadija Haq for Human Development Centre, and published by O.U.P.). The preparation of the report was promoted and funded by UNDP, UNESCO, the World Bank and a number of other international funding agencies. (It is sad to note that Mahboob-ul-Haq's sudden death in New York recently was hardly noticed in the media in our country.)

The report presents a dismal picture. I give below a very brief summary of the report as also a few statistics relating to India, which should make all thoughtful people sit up and work for a movement to compel the Government to implement the programme without diluting the provision of Article 45. Once this is done, all other problems like family planning, health care, economic development, successful management of local self-government, and so on will become tractable.

Summary of the report: South Asia has emerged by now as the most illiterate region in the world, and that income poverty is no barrier to the spread of basic education. If Sri Lanka and the Maldives could achieve over 90 per cent adult literacy rate, and if

Bangladesh could make rapid strides in this regard, why can't India make progress?

Political commitment to basic education in India remains both faint and fragile. With the result that India has the largest illiterate population in the world. Many countries which are poorer than India have managed a much higher rate of literacy: (1) Tazakistan—real GDP per capita income 1117 dollars, and literacy rate 98 per cent; (2) Kenya—1404 dollars, and literacy rate 94 per cent; (3) Vietnam—1208 dollars and literacy rate 78 per cent. In 1994, India's real per capita income was 1348 dollars but its literacy rate was 52 per cent. So that poverty of resources [the reason for not achieving literacy not only given by government agencies but also by intellectuals and activists prominent among them was no less a person than the well-known Gandhian educationist, the late J.P. Naik] is not the real reason for India's dismal performance in the field of basic education. [Mr. Naik maintained this in a report prepared for the Citizens for Democracy of which Mr. Tarkunde was General Secretary.]

Even in India, there are some States which have made rapid progress in this field, which in turn has ushered in improvements in other spheres like population control, health care, quality of life. Kerala whose per capita income is less than the all-India figures, has a literacy rate of about 90 per cent. The other extreme is that about three-quarters of out-of-school children live in six states—Andhra Pradesh, Bihar, Madhya Pradesh, Rajasthan, West Bengal, and Uttar Pradesh.

In short, India, the report points out, is still first in the world in terms of the number of total illiterate persons. According to official sources, female literacy is 26 percentage points below the male literacy, that is, there are 91 million more adult illiterate females than males in India. About 35 million children in the 6-10 age group do not attend primary school. 37 per cent of all primary school children drop out before reaching grade 5.

The report states: India's problem is that the task of providing elementary education to all children is massive. The task was made even more difficult when India spent less than 4 per cent of its GNP on education and then devoted less than one half of this expenditure to elementary level education. Both the low over-all spending on education and its distribution among primary and higher education make it extremely difficult for India to reach the goal of Universal Primary Education. The amount allotted to elementary education in India has fallen from 56 per cent in the First Plan to 29 per cent in the Seventh Plan.

According to statistics collected by the authors of the report, from official sources, vulnerable groups in India are often deprived of educational opportunities. The literacy rate varies from 90 per cent for rich urban males to a mere 17 per cent for poor, rural Scheduled Castes women. Scheduled Castes and Scheduled Tribes have a literacy rate of 40 per cent compared to nearly 60 per cent for higher caste Hindus. The enrollment rate of 6 to 14-year-old Muslim children is 62 per cent compared to 77 per cent for non-Scheduled Castes Hindus.

Let me conclude this summary by quoting the main thesis of the report: "Education leads to many social benefits, including improvement in standards of hygiene, reduction in infant and child mortality rate, decline in population growth rates, increase in labour production and an improved sense of national unity... It is certain that South Asian economies cannot hope to engineer a decisive breakthrough in development or to become the industrialisation tigers of the future without a generous investment in basic education and technical skills".

This thesis was also propounded by Jean Dreze and Amartya Sen in 1995 in their book, *India: Economic Development and Social Opportunities*. What they wrote regarding the wilful neglect of this programme deserves to be quoted : "In India, both ancient and modern biases shape our policies reflecting prejudices of class division as well as of traditional cultures. The difficulty in getting even left-wing parties [we have referred to CPM led West Bengal Governments performance!] interested in combating inequalities in education relates to the general social atmosphere in India, including the nature of the leadership of the different parties which takes some major disparities as simply 'given' and not particularly worth battling against in view of other—perceived to be more 'pressing'—"Challenges".

Some economists hold the view that basic education does not necessarily lead to economic development. They give the instances of Sri Lanka, Jamaica and Costa Rica where the literacy rate is very high but the economy has not grown very fast. These economists maintain that economic growth leads to widespread education, and not the other way. Which means, in plain and simple language, that eradication of poverty is the precondition for implementing this welfare programme of basic education. This amounts to putting the cart before the horse, for poverty can be eliminated only when the people are literate. Even if we accept their thesis for the sake of argument, does it mean that our people must remain illiterate, and that our children must be deprived of their basic right?

These economists also maintain that government should not be involved in education, both with regard to finance and provision of education. They do not take into account the fact that implementation of social welfare programmes is one of the primary duties of a democratic government. How can a poor country like India achieve the goal of universal basic education without the active involvement of government? The governments of Japan and Great Britain in the 19th century carried out this welfare programme and took care of the total financial obligation in this regard. The results are there for all to see. Today, there is no western country which is not wholly or solely responsible for school education. The private sector cannot implement this programme ; it can and should supplement as it is done in Kerala.

There is one factual error in the report. It states that the Government of India has made a Constitutional amendment to make "elementary education an inalienable right of all children", that is, fundamental right. It has not yet been done. The United Front Government had introduced a Bill to this effect. It is unlikely that the present BJP-led Government, as noted above, will pursue the matter. Which bureaucrat and which politician are interested in the poor and the deprived, and want the State to be prosecuted? [July 1998].

* * *

Nobel Laureate Amartya Sen's Theory of the Role of Basic Education: The whole country, from the President downwards has suddenly discovered a genius in Prof. Amartya Sen after he got the Nobel Prize in Economics.

The country is proud of Amartya Sen that he has brought glory to the country. Bengalis have hailed him as a great and "quintessential Bengali intellectual", yet others have written about his Marxism and his view about market economy, globalisation, and so on. A few have written about his concern for victims of famines and his theory that famines are caused not by shortage of food grains. The Bengal famine in 1943—one of the significant works of Amartya Sen is on this famine—in which more than three million people died without raising a finger by way of protest, was caused by hoarding of food grains. The government failed to handle this great calamity. (One wishes Amartya Sen took note of this total absence of protest).

All these are, no doubt, important aspects of Amartya Sen's studies and contributions.

Regrettably, the most important contribution of Sen has hardly been noticed by commentators including academics and politicians. This relates to the role and importance of basic education in economic development, which is immediately and directly relevant for India. It is on account of non-implementation of Article 45 of our Constitution laying down that the state is "to endeavour to provide within a period of ten years from the commencement of the Constitution, for free and compulsory education until they complete the age of 14". The Supreme Court in a judgment in 1993 made it a fundamental right. This law has been treated contemptuously by all successive governments including the present one. (It may be mentioned in passing that this journal *PUCL Bulletin* has been the only one in this country which has highlighted this contribution of Amartya Sen which he first elaborated in India in a lecture in early 1995—the *Bulletin* published a summary of his lecture in the April 1995 issue).

I have however written on the subject since 1990, stressing that the country cannot make any progress until all our children have received basic education.

Prof. Sen's theory, which was recognised by the Nobel Prize Committee, is that without compulsory universal education, no economic development is possible. He writes: "The remarkable neglect of elementary education in India is all the more striking given the widespread recognition, in the contemporary world, of the importance of basic education for economic development. Somehow the educational aspects of economic development have continued to be out of the main focus" in our country.

Sen has offered convincing reasons for the wilful and criminal neglect of basic education: "The traditionally elitist tendencies of the ruling cultural and religious traditions in India may have added to the political problem. Both Hinduism and Islam have, in different ways, had considerable inclination towards religious elitism, with reliance respectively on Brahmin priests and on powerful Mullahs. ... The elitist hold is quite strong in both these religions [even today]. This contrasts with the more egalitarian tradition of Buddhism". He adds that in our country both ancient and modern biases shape our policies reflecting prejudices of class divisions as well as traditional cultures, and that even left-wing political parties as well as traditional cultures are not interested in combating inequalities in our country.

Another significant thing to which Sen has drawn attention is that the contrast between importance given to higher education and neglect of basic education is "intolerably large", and this inequality helps to sustain social disparities. And, as we all know, social disparity gives rise to human rights violation. (The BJP Government has conferred *Bharat Ratna* on the nobel bureete Amartya Sen even though the Government has decided not to implement his thesis. What is surprising is that he didn't have even any eerie feeling while accepting the 'honour'!). [2 Nov 1998].

37

DALITS DESERVE APOLOGY

Air Commodore G.N. Baindur (Retd)

I am proud to be Bharatiya, and inheritor of the multicultural entity of Bharat which India is. I am also conscious and acutely aware of the wrong done to the majority of our people whether they are described as belonging to middle castes, lower castes or outcastes residing in urban, rural or forest localities.

For the Hindus who form the majority of the population, the sacred texts are the Vedas and the Puranas, which are differently referred to and interpreted by the various schools of philosophy. The completion of 5200 years since the beginning of Kaliyuga, and start of the 5201st year was celebrated on 18th March 1999. The Kaliyuga is supposed to have started during the reign of Parikshit, grandson of Arjuna. At the start of the Mahabharat war, when Arjuna declines to fight his own relatives ranged against the Pandavas, Shri Krishna enlightens him of the secret of creation and destruction to enjoin on him the duty to fight. The discourse is the *Bhagavad Gita*.

In chapter 4 Sri Krishna states, "Chaturvarnyam Maya Srushtam Guna, Karma Vibhagashah". That is the "four varnas were created by me, according to their innate aptitudes and tendencies and the action they perform". These Varnas are assigned specific duties and among them the "Sudra" is assigned "Paricharyatmakam Karyam" or the duty of serving the other three Varnas to meet their needs. [Chapter 18 stanza 44]. Whether this was as slaves or paid labour is not clear.

Among the eighteen epics or Puranas mentioned as major works, Srimad Bhagavata Mahapurana is the most venerated. In Book 7 chapters 11, 12, 14, 15 and Book 11 chapter 17 the characteristics and duties of different Varnas are elaborated. Inter-marriage is prohibited with the exception that when a person of a certain Varna desires to marry one from a different Varna he has to formally marry one of his own Varna first (chapter 17 verse 39). Further, men of a higher Varna are permitted to marry women of a lower order and not *vice versa*. These Varnas are presently known as castes. As described in Book II, discourse 17, verses 47, 48, 49 a Brahmana in distress may take to the calling of a merchant (Vaishya) or even live by the sword *but under no circumstances by service to a man of lower grade.* A Kshatriya too may live by the trade of a Vaishya or by hunting or by teaching. But *in no case by menial service.* Similarly a Vaishya in adversity may adopt the calling of Sudra and a Sudra may adopt the craft of an artisan (clarified by Manu the lawgiver as carpenters, weavers, barbers, washerman and tanners of leather and shoemakers).

While assigning duties to these castes, duties involving manual labour are exclusively assigned to the Sudra caste. In the Amarakosha, the Sanskrit language dictionary there is a separate chapter named Sudra varga. It not only lists all the words naming professions involving manual labour but also words naming the progeny of mixed caste marriages.

While it is permitted for a person of a Varna in the first three categories to perform the duties of a higher or lower Varna temporarily when facing hardship, the Sudra is not given this privilege. Further, certain people are described as untouchable. No wonder the essential element in a developed society *viz.*, dignity of labour, is missing among the higher castes who feel it is beneath their dignity to work on the farms, orchards or tend cattle in the fields, etc. Thus an army of "educated unemployed" of these castes in the rural areas migrates to the urban areas in search of so-called "white-collar" jobs preferably in Government service. Some of them take to criminal activities—including robbery and murder.

If this system of division into Varnas had existed prior to and after the start of the Kaliyuga, those belonging to Sudra Varna must have felt oppressed and revolted from time to time. Thus as is well known, more than 2500 years ago they opted for Jainism and

Buddhism as both these religions did not recognise the case system. Buddhism emphasises the way people act and behave among themselves as important recognising the eight-fold path of The Buddha as the guiding principle. Buddhism spread in India and across the frontiers to Sri Lanka, Central Asia, China, Japan and south east Asia after it had been adopted by Emperor Ashoka. Buddhism being mainly a religion of the downtrodden the scriptures of Buddhism were composed in their languages—Pali and Prakirt. They had to be translated into Sanskrit for the Brahmana scholars to refute them in debate and establish the supremacy of the religion based on the Vedas. Clearly this took a long time. During this time, great Universities of learning were established and flourished at Taxila (now in Pakistan) and Nalanda (Bihar). Scholars from China and other countries visited them to study the Buddhist religious texts. After Ashoka, the religion based on the Vedas started spreading once again. Probably by the beginning of the Christian era the Vedic religion started getting royal patronage to wipe out Buddhism from our country. The decline of Buddhism reduced the artisan and labouring classes to Sudra caste or made them outcastes again.

I have yet to find a definitive statement defining "Hindutva" as also "Hindu". When I was admitted in a primary school, I was described as a "Hindu". As I grew older I tried to understand the meaning of the term by reading the translations of and commentaries on the Vedas, the Upanishads, the Ramayana and the Bhagavata Maha Purana. None of them use the term "Hindu" to identify the natives of this land which is now described as "India that is Bharat".

Some historians say the term "Hindu" is corruption of "Sindhu"—the river that originates in the Himalayas and flows to the Arabian Sea. Records now available through satellite photography have established that over the centuries the rivers have changed course or in some cases stopped flowing altogether. So also this "Sindhu" river could have/has changed course many times as the tectonic plates collided and earthquakes occurred to relieve the stress in the earth's crust. In the absence of surveys and maps delineating the course of a river in the past we can only surmise it coursed through this channel or that centuries ago. So, two main questions arise: (a) Who is a "Hindu"—how to define him and if as some historians state the people to the west of the river called those to the east "Hindu" because "H" and "S" are interchangable sounds. Even today Jugoslavia is called Yugoslavia in English. (b) The next problem is who is the "native" of Bharat? We can conclude in this context that those who are NOT Brahmana, Kshatriya or Vaisya by caste and do not follow the religious rituals and injunctions laid down in the Vedas and Puranas are the NATIVES of BHARAT now residing in urban, rural, forest or hilly areas.

A banner was displayed at the RSS office during the 60th birth anniversary of Shri Hedgewar recently who established it, proclaiming "Bharat Hindu Rastra Hai" in Devanagri script. The aptitude and attitude of many union ministers who belong to the RSS are thus based on the concept of one nation, one religion, one culture for all the inhabitants of Bharat. The followers of other religions are expected to follow the laws and customs laid down for the Hindus irrespective of what their own religious leaders and sacred scriptures prescribe. Further this approach manifested itself in the demolition of what are supposed to be symbols of rule by the adherents of other religions, particularly Islam.

The concept of "State" with well defined boundaries arose in the west around 1600 A.D. when the Westphalian treaty of the European kingdoms agreed on that definition. Until then the concept of nationhood was absent in Europe and the "Indian Sub-continent" as in Africa or the Chinese part of the Asian continent—small kingdoms fought mutually for supremacy, making and unmaking alliances. "Democracy" may have existed at the village level but not much beyond. Kautilya or Chanakya may have laid down his views on how to rule and rob but in practice no one bothered about it, as mostly even those who established themselves as "kings" of defined geographical areas were illiterate. Gradually when dynastic rule developed, sons were well educated in the arts, including dance and warfare and some also became recognised scholars in their own right. However, the whole area now loosely defined as "Indian Sub-continent" was never ruled by any one for any length of time. Therefore we can conclude there has never been a "Hindu Rashtra" and Bharat is a term applied to the Indian Union after partition in the hope it would draw attention to our past where caste distinctions or religious differences did not lead to conflict and chaos. Thus neither of the concepts of Akhand and Hindu Rashtra is valid.

Jainism and Budhism were practically banished from India, their place of birth. The fact that their scholars retreated to caves to study, meditate and practise their religion clearly indicates that they were persecuted by the rulers of the day. Thus, the Jains today constitute less than one per cent of the propulation, confined to western parts of Rajasthan and Karnataka.

Christianity came to Bharat in the first century A.D. while Islam came soon after it was established as a religion by Prophet Mohammad. With the advent of Christianity and Islam neither of which recognize caste divisions, the labouring classes opted for them partly to escape from the oppression of the caste system. Today, although the followers of Christianity are just about two per cent of the population, some Hindus feel rattled and have started campaigns of re-conversion of the Christians (and Muslims) to Hinduism. It is not clear to which caste the reconverted are assigned. If it is not to the first three viz., Brahman, Kshatriya or Vaishya, they remain to be Sudras—the down-trodden victims of discrimination.

In South Africa where Gandhiji initiated the struggle against racial discrimination with his weapon of *Satyagraha,* the African National Congress has finally succeeded in overcoming apartheid. The white supremacy President De Clerk handed over the presidency to Nelson Mandela peacefully. What is more remarkable was the establishment of the Truth and Reconciliation Commission chaired by Archbishop Desmond Tutu who submitted the report to President Mandela against the wishes of the ANC and Apartheid supporters.

We are celebrating the fiftieth anniversary of the day we gave ourselves a constitution democratic, republican. We should try to spare our children, grandchildren and generations to follow the conflict and misery arising from caste and religious difference. Let us have a free and frank discussion among the intellectuals and religious leaders to evolve a consensus on tendering a sincere apology for the wrongs done over the centuries by the upper castes to the rest and draw up a time bound plan of action to remove discrimination in practice. Let that be our tribute to the Father of the Nation on the fiftieth anniversary of the Republic.

A majority of the people who converted to other religions have done so to escape from the oppression of the upper castes though there have been instances of conversion by force. The hypocricy of the upper castes is seen when they proclaim abolition of untouchability by law while practising it. The caste system has over the centuries effectively disenfranchised the majority of the people denying them the opportunity for education and advancement so that after independence, the educated upper castes monopolised control of power.

As long as the upper castes claiming hereditary privilege continue to illtreat the lower castes, conversion to Christianity, Islam or Buddhism religions which recognise a single prophet and non-discrimination on account of birth will occur because all said and done human beings seeks to be recognised as humans and not treated as chattel.

I therefore, earnestly request the scholars, historians, sociologists, anthropologists and others who are knowledgeable on the subject to enlighten the rest of us on the causes leading to conversion and consequent social turmoil.

The new nations of Anglosaxon origin, the United States of America, Canada, and Australia having realised the wrong they have done to the "aborigines", have apologized openly to the natives and also agreed to compensate them to a reasonable extent for the wrongs done.

Similarly, we have a moral responsibility to recognise the wrongs done in the past—the wrongs continue to flourish even Today—and persuade the great Hindu religious heads the Shankaracharyas, the mathadhipathis and swamis to issue a joint declaration apologising for the past wrongs done to the Dalits. They should also issue edicts, if appropriate in their tradition, to punish those of their followers who seek to perpetuate inequality in our democratic, secular socialist republic. Further they should start a programme to make all Hindus realise the value of civil liberties and fundamental human rights enshrined in the constitution and honour them.

38

ALTERNATIVE MEDIA FOR DALIT LIBERATION IN INDIA

Henry Thiagaraj*

At the outset I would like to draw a distinction between the context of communication and contents of communication. The context deals with a vision, broader perspectives, principles that govern the contents, purpose, values like justice in communication, etc., whereas contents of communication deal with specific media specialties like print media, electronic media, audio-visuals, mass media like movies, T.V. Radio, spoken-word communication, Folk Theatre, etc.

So far as development communication in India is concerned the Fourth World people like Dalits have been left out of the communication process. Most of the communication in India has been elitist oriented; the upper caste people have always monopolised the field of communication. In segregated housing colonies Dalits languish without communication. Discrimination deprive them of the power of communication and condemns them to a dehumanised condition. In the process the communication skills of Dalits have always been suppressed. In South India, Dalits were at one time integral part of communication in society. The work "Paraiah" comes from "Parai", "to speak", to announce—to people Paraiahs were originally spokesmen of the Kings and rulers, as they communicated the decisions of the Court and the pronouncements of the monarchs to the people. Paraiahs were also great drummers, leading the procession of the kings, the leading band of war battles.

The great heritage of pariahs were suppressed by the dominant community; they were made to beat the drums for funeral processions; this led to the dehumanising process. In this exercise of dehumanising people, their heritage and communication skills were robbed. They were conditioned, brainwashed as their Karma made them to live a miserable life, denied of joy. As slaves they are to live in sorrow, condemned to their fate with no music and dance which the mainstream-dominant people enjoyed.

In the ancient region of Tamil Nadu, Ramanand area, one can see the rural Paraiah Drummers, still with their age old musical instruments like long pipes, different kinds of drums, etc. Great poets like the sage Valluvar, Avaiyar were Dalits and gave great values, golden words of wisdom and ethical valules to society. Therefore, it is important for us Dalits to re-discover our ancient heritage and in the process restore the dignity of the Dalits.

Communication is real power. It gives power over others. Those who own media like Newspaper, Television and Movie Studios, etc. wield enormous powers in society.

This power was denied to the Dalits, who became landless labourers.

Communication can be classified into personal, inter-personal and social categories. It can extend to national and international spheres to a great extent. The world has shrunk into a village—global village, thanks to communication. To day we have to think globally and act locally. News of local action is developed into a global communication. It is in this perspective the UN Declaration of Human Rights highlights the plight of the Dalits—the people of the Fourth World. It is to communicate the dehumanised condition of the Dalit people and the atrocities committed on them, we have launched the human Rights Education Movement of India which has two aspects: (1) First, humanising process of Dalits, to awaken them, to make them aware of their human rights, guaranteed by our Constitution and reinforced by the Universal Declaration of Human Rights.

It may be noted that out of 3,500 communities in India 900 are classified as Scheduled Castes. Among the "Chamar" community there are at least 62 sub-groups which are endogenous—yet there is no communication, especially social communication, among them. The bane of caste and caste consciousness really plays havoc on the human and social progress of our Dalit people. It is to break the barriers of man and man among dalits, to break the barriers between man and woman in society human rights education and humanising education is much needed among the people of the Fourth world. This humanising education for which humanising communication is required to create a new social order with justice and equality of people. A new humanity requires human communication which should become really free from the shackles which man has created for himself through social taboos.

I may quote Dr. B.R. Ambedkar on "WHO IS FREE MAN" : "I call him free who with his conscience awake, realises his rights, responsibilities and duties. He who is not a slave of circumstances and is always ready and striving to change them in his favour. I call him free, one who is not a slave of usage, of customs, of meaningless rituals and ceremonies of superstition and traditions, one who has not got blind faith in the teachings of saints and religious teachers, simply because these have been passed from generation to generation, whose flame of reason has not been extinguished, I call him a free man. He who has not surrendered his free will and abdicated his intelligence and independent thinking, who does not blindly act on the teachings of others, who does not accept anything without critically analysing and examining its veracity and usefulness in the light of the theory of the 'cause and effect', who is always prepared to protect his rights, who is not afraid of ridicules and unjust public criticism, who has a sound conscience and self-respect so as not to become a tool in the hands of others, I call him a free man. He who does not lead his life under the direction of others, who sets his own goal of life according to his own reasoning and decides for himself as to how and in what way life should be led, is a free man. In short a man who is the master of his own free will, him alone I consider a free man (Speech delivered on May 31, 1936 Mahar Conference held at Bombay).

Dalits have to be freed from fear for true liberation. Only the courageous will have the strength to break the chain of slavery—both mental and physical.

In order to express our real condition the Dalit liberation Education Trust has produced videos on the plight of Dalit Christians and published small books, and organised liberation camps to awaken our people. These are our attempts in Development communication both personal and inter-personal, with mass media emphasis like production of Audio—Cassettes in Tamil e.g.: Songs of Liberation entitled, "Open yours eyes" to see real world of knowledge.

Our Television caters mostly to the urban elites. Let me give the example of a movie entertainment scheduled on every Sunday which the rural and urban poor look forward to with great expectation. Suddenly this film programme is either shifted or cancelled for a live telecast of Wimbeldon tennis played in U.K. or cricket match in Australia—just to please the urban elites and ruling classes, while the poor in rural areas go disappointed. Do we really care for the poor?

I remember reading in the editorial page of a national daily an article by a woman activist which contained this sentence; '90 per cent of the prostitutes are Muslims'. What a way to preserve an identity!

The danger with the instant judgement of the media is that they can on the one hand increase a minority group's feelings of alienation and on the other encourage the majority group's sense of self-righteousness.

Media and Mandal : Two articles "Twice Born Riot Against Democracy" by Gail Omvedt (*Economic and Political Weekly* September 24, 1990) and "Mandal Mandir and Masjid : Dubious Role of the Media' by S. Shivanandan (Mainstream, October 20, 1990) have exposed shocking prejudices, cliches, untruths, incitement and manipulation by a section of the media.

"Certain basic issues raised by Omvedt need to be kept in mind: Opinion in the Mandal issue is totally predictable from caste status. The twice-born outnumber the Dalits and Shudras in forums which produce the 'war of words'. Those who oppose the mandal commission are invariably the twice-born, the high castes, plus Parsis and high caste Christians. These sources also attack the kulak lobby favoured by Mandal".

"A second strand is the lament over ignoring of 'merit' and its adverse effects on 'development', efficiency and marching into the 21st century. It's here that the worlds of the yogi and the yuppie meet—after all, an updated caste system is the best guarantee of the The New Economic Order."

"The curious fact is that when V.P. Singh played the game of the mainstream he was the darling of (most of) the media—postponing Punjab elections, taking tough line in Kashmir ("needs a smack of firm Government"—TOI), and towards Pakistan, and a soft line on liberalisation. But when he took a tough line on the 'Untouchables' he became an 'untouchable'.

An Alternative Press : The general pattern of press reaction seems to confirm rather than deny the Mandal thrust. Is major dissent— a modern "Buddhist" revolt—possible in the present media dispensation ?

"As Gail Omvedt says, the shudras and the Dalits need a press structure of their own". [*The Extracts are from on article on "Mandir, Masjid, V.P. and the Media—INDIAN EXPRESS dated Sunday, November 25, 1990*].

It is obvious the media in India represents the unjust world and we the dalits are the victims of injustice in the media world. Wherever we go injustice and oppression haunts us.

The curious fact is all our oppressors are a small minority. All the 120 cinema theatres in India screening three shows a day for 750 persons per show can reach only 3.20 per cent of our population. Similarly assuming one newspaper is read by 5 persons, only 3.33 per cent of the total population are covered by the circulation of dailies—as per the 1990 circulation figures. With 48.78 per cent illiteracy, the newspapers do not touch the fourth World people, the rural poor. The communication gap between the educated and the illiterates is widening despite all our development efforts! Our task is very clear: to empower our people, to create justice and equality in development communication to achieve real freedom and progress. We have to look for new paradigms of development of and communication in development—to create a casteless society, to ensure our children grow without caste consciousness. It is time we own television, newspapers to assert our human rights and to remedy the injustice we suffered. Let us face this challenge squarely!

39

NHRC'S CREDIBILITY AT STAKE

R.M. Pal

The existence of a human rights commission has brought hardly any change in the culture and climate of human rights in the country. We wrote on an earlier occasion when the publication of the National Human Rights Commission's (NHRC) annual report of 1995-96 was delayed (*PUCL Bulletin*, September 1995, "NHRC's Credibility at Stake") that the record of respect for human rights both by the administration and the people as well as of protection of civil liberties and human rights by the State, is depressing. We referred to two specific instances.

Let us examine the same instances. One, the NHRC does not seem to have taken societal violation on its agenda with the seriousness it deserves. It recognises the fact that "ancient wrongs" (to use NHRC's words) must be remedied. But, how? The NHRC is silent on this. In its 1996-97 report (two more reports due since then have not yet come out) the NHRC wrote: "Viewing the country in all of its complexity, the Commission believes that it has a special and inescapable responsibility to protect those who are the most vulnerable : Dalits and Scheduled Tribes, women and children, especially the girl child; the disabled...". Now, how does it propose to handle the problem, for example, of violations of human rights arising out of caste and religious intolerance, the victims of which are invariably Dalits, STs, and the minorities? The NHRC should be bold enough to give its verdict on the caste system even at the risk of becoming unpopular with the dominating section of our society.

It is not suggested, however, that the problem can be solved by the NHRC overnight for the walls raised by the hierarchical system have stood rock-like for centuries. But there ought to be a clear-cut recognition of the fact that caste divides, that it gives rise to divisiveness and dissension; and that under this system (which has by no means disappeared) "some are less equal than others" (again, to use NHRC's words); and therefore the system itself must be demolished. It is here the NHRC appears paralysed like most reformers and activists, both past and present.

Two, the NHRC knows that governments of all hues, as also all parties have treated with total indifference, if not utter contempt, the issue of violation of human rights. Let us give only one example of this mindset. Since the setting up of the NHRC in 1993, with a lot of fanfare, its annual reports have not been published on time. The 1997-98 report covering the period April 1997 to March 1998 (long overdue) has not yet been published—even though the publication of the report is mandatory, according to NHRC's own regulation. The publication of the 1996-97 report was also considerably delayed. The ostensible reason is that the reports have to be placed before Parliament before being made public. NHRC sources affirm that the 1997-98 report was submitted to the government a couple of months ago, but the Union Home Minister, Mr. L.K. Advani did not have the time to place it before Parliament before the Lok Sabha was dissolved. The 1998-99 report does not appear to have been written yet.

Which means the 1997-98 report is not likely to be published in the foreseeable future—a new government will be formed in September/October 1999. Furthermore, if past records are any indication, placing the report before Parliament will not be on the agenda of the new government for quite some time. The present government had all the time to take action on the report—obviously it was not an important issue for Mr. Vajpayee [Prime Minister] or Mr. Advani [Union Home Minister]!

What we wrote on an earlier occasion (referred to above, "NHRC's Credibility at Stake") remains valid: "That the government has been indulging in doublespeak with regard to human rights and civil liberties, is known; but what is not understandable... is the NHRC's role in the matter. Why should such a body like the NHRC submit to government's whims ? ...The provisions of *The Protection of Human Rights Act 1993* and *NHRC Regulations* [they should be read together] do not prevent the Commission from publishing the report. Section 20-2 of the Act prescribes : 'The Central and State Government... shall cause the annual and special reports of the Commission to be laid before each house of Parliament or the State Legislature respectively... along with a memorandum of action taken or proposed to be taken on the recommendation of the Commission and the reasons for non-acceptance of the recommendations, if any'. There is nothing in this provision to suggest that the Commission *must* wait until the report has been placed before Parliament. In fact, Regulation 17 (of the NHRC) makes it mandatory to publish it: 'The Secretariat of the Commission shall be responsible for the printing of the Annual Report and Special Reports with utmost expedition and in any case, not later than one month of the finalisation of the same' ... What was expected of the Commission is to establish its credibility by exposing the Establishment's doublespeak relating to human rights. Today the NHRC's credibility is at stake ... If the NHRC does not put its foot down at the initial stage, it, too will end up like other Commissions which are mostly sinecures."

Did the NHRC 'put its foot down' subsequently when reports were held up by government inaction? There is no mention even of NHRC's discomfiture or dissatisfaction, not to speak of protest, in its later reports. Persons close to the NHRC argue that apart from the legal bindings it has been the *convention* that all such reports are placed before Parliament before they are published. But surely, if the government does not respect this convention, why should the public be deprived of their rights ? Regrettably all conventions and constitutional norms and institutions are being destroyed in our country with ease by the bureaucrats and politicians, and with hardly any protest from the civil society and from organizations who ought to protest. If the present Chairperson, Justice Venkatachaliah and his colleagues do not stand up, the future of the Commission is bleak.

Furthermore, since 1993-94 successive governments have not had the time even to go through the recommendation of the Commission not to speak of taking any action. In fact, there has hardly been any debate and discussion on NHRC's reports in Parliament. Nor is there any record to indicate that the Opposition demanded any debate/discussion!

One example of the Opposition's concern for human rights may be noted. This writer was once asked by Justice Rajindar Sachar (former President of PUCL) to explain the provisions of the to an Opposition M.P. who was the spokesperson of his party (a party whose objective is social justice) in Parliament on human rights. Three precious hours on three different days were spent. When the subject came up in the Lok Sabha, the member spoke half-a-sentence! (14 May, 1999).

40

SOCIETAL VIOLATION OF HUMAN RIGHTS AND HUMAN RIGHTS EDUCATION

R.M. Pal

When we talk of Human Rights Education, the point of reference is human rights violation. What follows is in this context.

The National Human Rights Commission (NHRC) soon after its inception in October, 1993, embarked on the task of introducing Human Rights Education in schools, colleges, and universities, Obviously the NHRC acted in terms of Section 12 of *The Protection of Human Rights Act 1993*: "The Commission shall undertake, protect, and promote research in the field of human rights (and) spread human rights literacy among various sections of society and promote awareness of the safeguards available for the protection of these rights through publications, the media, seminars and other available means." One of the key words in this Section is "research". Let me add at once that research involves something more, much more, than a text-book study of our own constitutional provisions, international charters and covenants like the Universal Declaration of Human Rights (UDHR). To give just one example, Article 1 of the UDHR states that all are born equal and in dignity. Now, our divinely ordained hierarchical system is in contradiction with the provision of this Article. This needs research. More about this later.

Mr. Justice Ranganath Mishra, former Chairman of the NHRC, and now a member of Parliament (Rajya Sabha) got along very well with the then government headed by Mr. Narasimha Rao. He wielded power. All the ministries and departments and the UGC agreed to co-operate with the NHRC in introducing Human Rights Education as a subject. For whatever reason, none could annoy him ! (Well, I don't suggest that the Chairman of the NHRC should cultivate the Prime Minister! In fact, he should be a dissident intellectual).

I, however, wrote a brief editorial note in the *PUCL Bulletin* (August 1994), published by People's Union for Civil Liberties. I may reproduce the editorial :

"Civil liberties and human rights groups and activists have been talking about introducing Human Rights as a subject of study in schools and colleges, as also for law-enforcing agencies, security forces and the army. Some years ago, the University Grants Commission had set up a committee (Sikri Committee) for the purpose—nobody knows anything about the outcome. [The NHRC was not aware of the committee. When they read about it in my editorial note, they approached the University Grants Commission. The UGC was not able to trace any copy of the report! The NHRC then got in touch with a retired employee of the UGC, got him from Lucknow, paid his expenses! He was able to dig out a copy from a dusty corner of the UGC building!] The Delhi University Vice-Chancellor [Professor Upendra Baxi] known as a human rights intellectual has constituted a committee of teachers—not many of the names would inspire confidence—to go into the question of introducing the subject in the light of the recommendations of the UN Conference on Human Rights Vienna, 93—he does not make any mention of the provisions of the 'The Protection of Human Rights Act 1993'. And now, the National Human Rights Commission (NHRC) has started giving active thought to implement the provisions of Section 12 (under Functions of the Commission) of The Protection of Human Rights Act 1993. ...

"The Chairman of the NHRC, Justice Ranganath Mishra [wants] that human rights be taught as a subject right from primary school continuing upto the secondary level. The NCERT is engaged, we are told, in preparing a syllabus and study material. All this is fine, and needs to be done to promote the cause of human rights—the cause of freedom of the individual. It appears, however, that like everything else in our country, NHRC and research institutes seem to be in haste to introduce human rights as a subject of study, even though not much thought and research has backed the proposal. There has hardly been any discussion on the intellectual plane, any seminar, any get-together of people—not merely academics and theoreticians of great renown but also the sensitive, considerate, creative and committed to social justice who will make an earnest endeavour to create something that will endure.

"Let us give only one example of lack of adequate thought in this regard. One of the worst forms of human rights violations and infringement of civil liberties is caused by *Varnavyavastha* (the Varna system)—directly or indirectly. Indeed other widespread abuses like custodial rape, torture, and killing flow from this. How does one drive home the truth?—the Varna system is fine but untouchability is harmful? Well, even angels should fear to tread on such slippery ground where men like Gandhi and Ambedkar failed. The Constitution of India has prohibited untouchability : 'Untouchability' is abolished and its practice in any form is forbidden (Art. 17 under Fundamental Rights). There is no explanation however about the source of untouchability; and whether or not it is desirable to dismantle it to usher in a society where there will be social justice.

"What will be the scenario in a class room where the subject is taught by educators whose concept of social justice in relation to the Varna system is incompatible with what has been stated in the Universal Declaration of Human Rights, or even with the Fundamental Rights and Directive Principles chapters of our Constitution? We saw this during the anti-reservation stir—the English educated middle class and upper middle class intelligentsia in north India [including Marxists, communists and even humanists] had gone berserk over the issue of social justice. So that the children will be brainwashed by those whose concern for freedom and rights is different from what the Universal Declaration and other covenants have stated.

"Have we given enough thought to the question that concern for human rights, concern for the individual and his/her freedom is intimately connected with a particular way of life, that is, democratic way of life where the individual is not a mere cog in the wheel but is supreme, or that the dignity of the individual and an authoritarian culture are contradiction in terms; or even that we have inherited a predominantly authoritarian culture on which we have been wanting to graft a democratic system. We may perhaps recognize the fact that we have not yet prepared the soil—the soil is still not ready to receive the seeds that we want to sow. These are some of the questions which need to be given thought to before we set out to prepare our children to go through a formal course of study on human rights and human dignity."

The above note came to the notice of the NHRC and the then Secretary-General, Mr. R.V. Pillai responded: "Dear Dr. Pal, this is with reference to the Editorial 'Human Rights Education' in the *PUCL Bulletin* of August, 1994. The National Human Rights Commission is in agreement with the view that in preparing a curriculum for human rights education, there has to be involvement of not only academics but also individuals and organizations which are sensitive and committed to the issue of human rights. I am in the process of working out a list of organizations and individuals with whom the Commission could have a dialogue on the evolution of curricula at various levels. I shall be happy to receive any suggestions that you or the PUCL may have in this regard. Yours sincerely, R.V. Pillai".—*PUCL Bulletin*, October, 1994.

Well, I don't know of any interaction that the NHRC had with any non-establishment intellectual/activist or human rights group, except a seminar organized by the Delhi-PUCL with the support of the NHRC, the background paper of which was written by me. *This was the only brain storming session in which the NHRC had a dialogue with NGOs*. It is regrettable that the NHRC did not have any more dialogue with NGOs. (The seminar proceedings have been published by the Indian Social Institute, 10 Institutional Area, Lodi Road, New Delhi-110 003; price Rs. 40 under the title *Human Rights Education*). It has been a great loss—loss of the cause of human rights. I will refer later to what I wrote then.

I also requested some intellectuals to write on the subject—these were published in the *PUCL Bulletin*. I will quote from Professor Rajni Kothari and Professor Sibnarayan Ray, a little later.

Instead of having any dialogue with NGOs, the NHRC asked the NCERT to prepare a course of study. The NCERT produced a Source Book. It contains summaries of relevant portions of our constitution, international covenants, etc. If respect for human rights could be cultivated through these documents, we would have attained this long ago, for our students have been reading the constitution since the 'fifties!

According to the NCERT, "Human Rights Education is not an independent area in the school curriculum but its various aspects and dimensions have been integretated in the curricula of various school subjects and the education materials, particularly text-books based on them". The NCERT has been guided by what has been stated in the National Policy on Education adopted in 1986 (revised in 1992). The NCERT approach should be taken seriously. Instead of introducing a separate subject it might be desirable that school text-books, in all stages, deal with both societal and state violations of human rights.

The NCERT has brought out a large number of text-books on social sciences—civics, history, sociology etc., some of which could be read with profit by human rights educationists and students. But some of the text-books are misleading and the authors tend to indulge in half-truth.

Let me refer to only one such text book for students of class VIII. In the chapter, "The Caste System", there is no mention of those who are outside the four varnas (i.e. untouchable, known as Dalits). The authors of the book write, "some of the shudras were called 'untouchable' .... Mahatma Gandhi agitated against the inhuman treatment meted out to the people of the Shudra caste". It is hardly necessary for me to comment on this.

Among social reformers apropos of the caste system the authors of the book make reference to Ramanand, Kabir, Shri Chaitanya, Raja Ramohun Roy (writing his name, Ram Mohan), Ishwar Chandra Vidyasagar, Dayanand Saraswati and Mahatma Gandhi. "Mahatma Gandhi organised movements against caste discrimination". Did all of them fight against the caste system in an organised manner? I'm afraid there is a bit of distortion of history here.

There is no mention of the authority which prescribed the system.

In another chapter, "Untouchability", the authors write, "As you know, untouchability is a very common term and you also perhaps know what it means". Do girls and boys 12/13 years old know "what it means"? The writers then suddenly introduce the term, "Harijan", but there is no explanation.

The writers mention a few names who fought against untouchability, but Dr. Ambedkar's name is not there! (Did anyone fight against untouchability and the caste system more systematically and valiantly than did Dr. Ambedkar? Basically, he was a human rights intellectual-activist).

(It is hardly necessary for me to add that some text-books brought out by state governments and their education departments are horrendous and dangerous. The NHRC must scrutinize them).

In any case I have made brave, but futile, attempts to bring the NHRC closer to dissident intellectuals.

Let us be clear. Merely battling with either human rights violation by the State and to introduce human rights education only in this context, will not do. Nor will it serve any purpose if we confine outselves to a study of human rights in the legal context only. We have, in our country, highly knowledgeable scholars and academics who can keep us spellbound for hours by their oratory and erudition—telling us the exact numbers of Covenants, Conventions, Protocols, and so on, these are on their finger tips—and how many of them have been signed, how many ratified by different countries. These scholars have given us plenty of reading material on these information related subjects. But do we have material on the ground realities? The fact is that in the context of India the issue of social justice is very important.

There is, I am afraid, confusion of what the human rights agenda needs to be in a pluralist, multi-religious, multicultural (tolerance must not be confused with pluralism), and highly complex country like ours. We need to have an Indian movement that must provide an agenda for our society—here the State has criminally neglected to play its expected role in social welfare and social justice. Let me refer to the latest perfidy. The present government led by the BJP has decided to confer Bharat Ratna on the Nobel Laureate Amartya Sen. Fine, indeed. But this very government has declined to bring a Bill before Parliament making basic education a fundamental right, that is, the provisions of Article 45 of the Constitution which is now in the Directive

Principles Chapter. It must be added at once that the 1993 Supreme Court judgement has declared that the provisions of Article 45 are now fundamental rights. And yet the State takes cover under the plea that Article 45 is not justiciable. Well, in India the State "must have the right to break its own laws" as Goebbels proclaimed in Nazi Germany!

To get back to Amartya Sen and the Bharat Ratna. His thesis with regard to basic education has been made to pale into insignificance. Note what Professor Amartya Sen and his co-author Professor Jean Dreze write with regard to the non-implementation of the social welfare programme of basic education (it is their thesis that without universal basic education no development including economic, is possible): "In India, both ancient and modern biases shape our policies reflecting prejudices of class divisions as well as of traditional cultures. The traditionally elitist tendencies of the ruling cultural and religious traditions in India may have added to the political problem. Both Hinduism and Islam have, in different ways, had considerable inclination towards religious elitism, with reliance respectively on Brahmin priests and on powerful Mullahs. The elitist hold is quite strong in both these religions. This contrasts with the more egalitarian traditions of Buddhism. [There is an obvious reference to the hierarchical caste system]. The difficulty in getting even left wing parties interested in combating inequalities in education relates to the general social atmosphere in India including the nature of the leadership of the different parties which take some major disparities as simply *given* and not particularly worth *battling* against in view of other—perceived to be more 'pressing'—challenges." What are these "pressing challenges"?—Nuclear explosions; to spend about rupees one crore on a lecture; (One of the Prime Ministers, Mr. Narsimha Rao went to Paris only for one day to deliver a lecture on Mahatma Gandhi—Gandhi would have been happy if this amount were spent on basic education); to provide security guards to politicians at great cost—terrorists would even hate to go near some of these diabolical politicians not to speak of killing them and making them 'martyrs'); providing luxurious bungalows to the politicians and bureaucrats, and so on. We have money for everything, but not for basic education. I don't know if Amartya Sen had some eerie feeling on hearing the announcement! Look at the irony. You don't implement his thesis—introduction of compulsory education—but welcome him with a garland of Bharat Ratna, and Amartya Sen accepting it! Can there be anything more ludicrous than this. However, my congratulations to Amartya Sen! (Professor Sen has now been decorated!) In any case human rights educationists cannot ignore the problems of "ancient and modern biases" and "elitist tendencies and religious elitism of Brahmin priests and powerful mullahs" if we want to put a stop to human rights violation perpetrated on children by depriving them of their basic right—schooling.

In the context of Article 45 and child labour, when I look around I find that in my campaign (another campaign with grassroots activists which has now been started by Professor Jean Dreze of Delhi University should be supported actively by all those who are concerned about human rights) for implementation of Article 45—through my writings since 1990—I do not have the privilege of having the company of many—in fact, there are not many takers for the implementation of Article 45. (Let us not confuse the provisions of Article 45—compulsory basic education to children upto the age of fourteen with literacy, literacy campaign and adult education).

Let me add that those who maintain that this social welfare programme cannot be implemented for various reasons and yet, at the same time, bring out plans for eradicating child labour, indulge in unalloyed hypocrisy. Child labour is, of course, one of the most atrocious forms of human rights violation. What I have been stressing over the years is that deprivation of basic education is also a human rights violation—equally obnoxious and atrocious, if not more. This second aspect has been almost totally neglected, both by Indian NGOs and those from abroad. They have been concerned, rightly, with child labour; but they have hardly been agitated over non-introduction of universal basic education. Why? This must be investigated by NHRC and others who are engaged in human rights education. They might find that one of the reasons is the middle class mindset which would have taken this violation seriously if the victims belonged to their class—the NGOs too belong to this class; the fact is that the victims, almost all, belong to SC/STs, OBCs, the Muslim minority, and girl children.

The NHRC has recommended implementation of basic education in the context of eradication of child labour; it has taken up the violations of human rights—child labour—seriously and in right earnest. What I suggested to the NHRC is that it should start a movement, independent of child labour eradication, for implementation of the provision of Article 45 non-implementation of which is a human rights violation. If the point of reference is human rights violation, human rights educationists and authorities cannot ignore these aspects.

The NHRC recognizes that "it has a special and inescapable responsibility to protect" these "most vulnerable" sections, but does not spell out as to how they propose to go about. The importance of human rights education is to be recognized in this context.

Even a cursory reading of courses of study, and more particularly the reading material prescribed in various universities would leave no one in doubt that the NHRC, the UGC, research institutes have been in haste; not much thought and research has backed the preparation of courses of study and reading material. It has already become a mini-industry. [Even the Pune seminar is indicative of this. The UNESCO and NHRC have spent a huge amount of money reprotedly rupees seventy five lakhs. And, with what result?] In fact there is hardly any reading material on contributions made by India's human rights intellectual-activists. Even when they have made reference to them and movements in India, the list is selective and arbitrary. For example, some have referred to only Gandhi; some have presented Gandhi, Ambedkar and Dr. Lohia. One hardly comes across any reference to the medieval period, or to the 19th century renaissance, specially in Bengal and Maharashtra and contributions made by intellectual-activists of this period.

Let me briefly refer to a syllabus framed by a University—Post-Graduate Diploma in Human Rights.

The paper entitled, "Liberal Perspectives" prescribes the following thinkers: Rousseau, Thomas Paine, J.S. Mill, Diecy, John Rawls, Dwarkins, Russell. Two short points: One, why should our political science teachers be so allergic to other liberal thinkers including those form India? Second, philosophers like Bertrand Russell have different opinion about Rousseu.

There is another paper exclusively on Marxism in which the thinkers prescribed are: Marx, Rosa Luxemburg, Gramsci. Again, two short points. One, how does one resolve the contradiction between Marxism and human rights? Two, if one studies Mao, why to write off Lenin! (Is it because the Soviet Union has crumbled, and our Marxist teachers don't want to remember him!) How will a perceptive student reconcile to such an arbitrary list which does not include even Engels?

The paper on Indian heritage includes Gandhi, Ambedkar, Lohia, Buddha in this order. Obviously Buddha has been included as an afterthought. Mahavira has been left out. There is no mention of the mediaeval period the core philosophy of which is tolerance. Furthermore, to limit the Indian heritage to only Gandhi, Ambedkar and Lohia is an insult to a number of very distinguished human rights intellectual-activists of the 20th century. Has Lohia been included to please Lohiaete colleagues of the department! As if he is the only Indian socialist thinker who cared for human rights. M.N. Roy whose name does not appear is one of the very few philosophers who came down heavily on the ugly relics of the past which were, and still continue to be, major sources of societal violation of human rights (see, *Selected Works of M.N. Roy* Vol IV, ed by Sibnarayan Ray, OUP which includes, *The Philosophy, Profession and Practice of Fascism, The Historical Role of Islam*, and his essays on Indian sociology like karma, transmigration of soul, caste).

When one refers to socialist revolutions in former Soviet Union, East Europe and China in the context of historical perspectives of human rights as the syllabus referred to above does, is the reference directed at human rights violations or respect for human rights?

I may make a reference to National Law School of India University, Bangalore which has produced considerable material on the subject. Their material and syllabi, outline and references may be analysed in the light of what I have stated in this paper. I am not suggesting that our Universities have not given thought to the problems that I have mentioned. The Law School of India University has taken note of some of the problems.

The Indira Gandhi National Open University is making efforts to produce material on subjects referred to in this paper. Bombay University and Jamia Millia of New Delhi syllabi have taken note of some of the areas; other Universities too, I am sure, are seized of the problems. But unfortunately beyond a point we all seem to get scared, if not paralysed.

Let me mention, as a paradigm, what I presented in the background paper referred to earlier—*Varnavyavastha* and human rights violation and infringement of civil liberties. I referred to this aspect in the *PUCL Bulletin* editorial note quoted earlier. A former civil liberties activist of PUCL has written that there was an element of hatred in Dr. Ambedkar and that his conversion to Buddhism was a fraud. He is outraged and very angry that so many statutes of Ambedkar have been installed in the country. Why should he be called the architect of the Indian constitution? Why should be have criticised Gandhiji, and so on. How does one handle this mindset—of hatred and intolerance? Our institutions tend to keep this question of intolerance under the carpet. (It must be acknowledged by intellectuals, at least dissident intellectuals and seats of learning that Ambedkar was primarily a human rights intellectual-activist as I said earlier).

I may make a very brief reference to the practice of human rights within the school education system. The system does not acknowledge the fact that we had a horrendous past. If we do not accept this how can we close the door on this? I may quote from a presentation made by an academic of New Delhi's Jawaharlal Nehru University, Dr. Geeta Nambissan, on the basis of a field study, to the PUCL seminar referred to earlier : "Within the school it appears that Dalit students continue to experience social discrimination and this can be seen both in the official curriculum i.e., in the approved content of education and the hidden curriculum of schooling. Scheduled Caste communities and the experience of untouchability rarely form part of school knowledge. Textbooks are silent about Dalit communities ... Practices (untouchability) are rarely mentioned in school books or discussed in the classroom ... Children belonging to lowest castes continue to be discriminated within the school and blatant practices particularly in the attitudes of teachers and school authorities as well as in peer behaviour continue ... Given its background it is unlikely that human rights education in the abstract will bring about any significant change in the education environment provided for children belonging to these communities". (Some NCERT text-books refer to this aspect. I have referred to this earlier). Our universities, the UGC, the NHRC, (and even the NCERT) do not appear to have given much thought to the questions raised above.

We may take note of what the UN Committee on International Convention on the Elimination of all Forms of Racial Discrimination recommended in 1996 (and India is a signatory): The Committee recommended "a continuing campaign to educate the Indian population on human rights in tune with the Constitution of India and with universal human rights instruments, including the International Convention on the Elimination of All Forms of Racial Discrimination. This should be aimed at eliminating the institutionalized thinking of the high caste and low caste mentality". We have to go a little deep—how does one eliminate "institutionalized thinking?" Again, literature produced by NHRC and other educational bodies does not throw much light on this aspect. Let us be honest with ourselves: we cannot make any headway in transforming society if we do not face these questions boldly.

Let us take note of another area. Have we given enough thought to the question that concern for human rights, concern for the individual and his/her freedom is intimately connected with a particular way of life, that is a democratic way of life where the individual is not a mere cog in the wheel, but is supreme; or that the dignity of the individual and an authoritarian culture are contradiction in terms, or even that we have inherited a predominantly authoritarian culture on which we have been wanting to graft a democratic system? We may perhaps recognize the fact that we have not yet prepared the soil—the soil is still not ready to receive the seeds that the NHRC, the UNESCO, the UGC, the NCERT, have been sowing. This is what human rights education has to take care of.

Human rights education must teach us that it is our fundamental right to criticise authority—and in the context of societal violation of human rights, religious scriptures, divinities, avatars, prophets, saints, gurus and of course the holy loafers of our time even though they are patronised by our top ranking politicians. (Criticism does not mean condemnation). The scriptures and the divinities have the divine right to prescribe; but why can't we have the right to at least question them? Not many Hindus would openly question the "absolute truth" reportedly contained in the Vedas, or the Gita, or the great Puranas, or even the Manusmriti. Most Hindus accept Chaitanya and Ramkrishna as avatars; no Muslim can dispute the authority of the Koran or the Prophet; and no Christian will question the authority of the Bible.

Let me refer, as paradigm, to another area involving human rights violation and where tenets of human rights are in contradiction with traditional socio-cultural matrices. Our traditions—Hinduism, Islam, Christianity—see women as inferior to men, often on the authority of divine scriptures and sanctions. According to all socio-cultural traditions women are required to find their fulfillment in motherhood and domesticity. Their duty is to render service to the husband, his family, and to his children. In fact some of the scriptures have warned that if women enter public life there will be utter chaos and disaster. We are warned that society will break up if men and women forget the sacredness of marriage. The foundation of society would be shaken, we are warned not only by men but also by highly educated women, if women expressed dissatisfaction at the treatment accorded to them. How does one reconcile all these to the UDHR and our own constitution?

The human rights situation with regard to the woman and the girl child is most depressing. Crimes against them have been on the rise. There has been considerable decline in sex ratio—fewer females than males. Why is it so? This needs research. Why is it that 25% of the girls die before they attain the age of 15? If it is malnutrition, then why is it only in the case of the girl child? Why is it, again, that in some parts of the country parents resort to the most inhuman and cruel method to kill girl babies?

Not many, not even those women leaders who have been fighting for reservation refer to our religious scriptures that have considerably contributed to gender bias. For example, one scripture sanctions: "Let the bridegroom ask the bride to join him in sacred ritual with the prayer, let our union beget sons only ...". There was also the tradition of *Putreshthi Yagna* praying for *putra* and so on. We do not hear women's organizations demanding the burning of these ugly relics of our past. They are afraid of lie-hunting. Human rights educationists, the NHRC and the National Commission for Women, the Universities, the U.G.C., the NCERT, will have to take up this job of lie hunting which ought to be part of human rights education in India. They may take note of how a significant section of our opinion makers, both ancient and modern, have contributed towards human rights violations—by rationalising the irrational. They have fabricated many fables about the exalted position of women in our society to convince us and the world portraying them as goddesses. They remain silent on the codes of Manu which have advised men to treat women as their property and slaves; they brush aside the issue by saying that our society is governed not by the codes of Manu but by the Constitution.

This will not do. I appeal to you all, specially the NHRC, the UNESCO, the UGC, the Universities, the NCERT, the National Commission for Women, and social activists to go a little deep into the problems. I am told a meeting held in Bangalore in 1994, which was attended by representatives of NHRC and UGC did some plain speaking, specially on the aspect of our past, our traditions, and culture. But they did not, I am told, specifically take up the question of what is to be revived, and which to be rejected. Furthermore, we have to have reading material. I am not aware of any project handling the compiling of material relating to human rights and human rights intellectual-activists of India.

I know some human rights intellectual-activists who have been talking, very loudly indeed, and also writing with journalistic flourish that India has a glorious past of 5000 years—and that this history is written in gold. They want us to revive the golden past. Which past? —they are quiet. (I have often wondered whether our glorious past is not a great liability). They refer to tolerance and non-violence. Professor Romila Thapar has exposed this myth thus: "The insistence on the tradition of religious tolerance and non-violence as characteristic of Hinduism, which is built on a section of normative values emphasising Ahimsa, is not borne out by historical evidence. The theory is so deeply ingrained among most Indians that there is the failure to see the reverse of it when it stares them in the face. The extremity of intolerance implicit in the notion of untouchability was glossed over by regarding it as a function of caste and society." Actually, our establishment intellectuals and almost the entire middle class who glorify Hindu tolerance and Hindu non-violence actually confuse this with our pluralism.

In the context of intolerance I may refer to communalism which is one of the major sources of human rights violations in our country. Any scheme of human rights education must take this into account.

Yes, human rights intellectuals and activists do want to revive/create the values of tolerance, non-violence, friendship for all, equality, respect for the human person, human dignity and rights, and freedom—values of which we can be proud. Obviously only that past has to be revived, and the ugly rest buried, which will help India come into inheritance of the blessings of modern civilization. Which means that human rights educationists must resist the temptation of reviving an imaginary golden age of India's past. To quote Romila Thapar again: "... changes will often involve a basic change of social values. The confrontation can no longer be evaded as it once was by recourse to the theory that our concern has always been only with things spiritual, or by an escape into the past. But the process can be facilitated by an awareness of the past, deriving from a realistic assessment .... It is only the awareness that history is made of an entire people into its total activity, which can bring us nearer to explaining the past in its concrete actuality".

In the process of reviving our past which can guide us, we should have no hesitation in discarding those aspects which hamper our progress, like, for example, the theory of karma, transmigration of soul, maya, the principle of division of society into castes. This principle took the form which the system of exploitation assumed in the bygone days that was declared to be the creation of God. We must discard that 'spiritualist' culture which seeks to persuade the poor, the depressed, the oppressed, and the exploited to reconcile their lot to suffering, sacrifice, and voluntary poverty—all that signify complete surrender, and absence of the spirit of revolt. If our human rights educationists cannot take up this aspect we might as well not waste public money. Europe did it by ushering in the movement of Renaissance; we too can if only we shed a bit of our unnecessary arrogance.

We may examine the courses of study prepared by different universities, the NCERT text-books, and text-books prepared by State School Boards in the light of what we have discussed in the foregoing. I have gone through a few and I have found them wanting.

II

Let me give a few extracts from what Rajni Kothari wrote in the context of human rights education (see *PUCL Bulletin*, September, 1994, "Human Rights Doublespeak"): "It is an enlightenment that above all the educated middle class need the most if it is to come out of its present state of callous complacency. That this includes middle class students and even children is also granted. It is on the pedagogy needed for this purpose that there are two opposite stand-points, and it is best to be clear about which one is being pursued by those engaged in the very business of 'human rights education'. One is a pedagogy in which education is considered as an 'extension' activity, trickling down from established institutions of learning and reaching out to the communities, the people and the individual recipient. The other is a pedagogy that draws upon what is going on among the people—their struggles against hegemony and for due regard and dignity—and to structure the research, the teaching and even the training in the light of such 'education from the bottom up'. It is not until the former pedagogy draws more and more from the knowledge, insights and wisdom of the latter, including some sordid realities learnt from the latter, that genuine enlightenment on human rights and related matters will take place. There can be no genuine enlightenment (or education) on human rights in the abstract, distilled from 'the ivory towers'. It can only come out of engagement with real life situations; in this case situations of conflict and struggle, of the political process in dealing with them and of the knowledge and understanding that are gained from such engagement."

Professor Sibnarayan Ray's contribution, "Human Rights Education—A Few Reflections" appeared in the October, 1994, issue of *PUCL Bulletin*. Professor Ray raises a number of very important questions which must engage the attention of human rights educationists. He writes, *inter alia*:

"Can human rights be learnt and established without confrontation and conflict with vested interests and traditional authorities? In the past rights have involved major upheavals—social, cultural and politico-economic. Such upheavals are fraught with considerable risks, and often cause much suffering and damage. But can this be altogether avoided? Can piecemeal reform in which common-people may take an intelligent and effective part reduce the risk of highly explosive social convulsions? Can such social engineering or experiments in institutional changes be included in a Human Rights Education programme.

"All these issues require to be publicly discussed and debated. Not only professional educationists, but social workers, human rights activists and various other groups and individuals with some awareness of relevant issues and practical experience of working with people would have much to contribute towards evolving an appropriate educational programme. It will be an altogether wrong approach if some central body devises a syllabus and then imposes it on a school system which itself grew up in an authoritarian atmosphere. Human Rights is not an appendage to be added to an already excessively burdensome school curriculum. It may yet revolutionise our tradition-constricted society by first bringing new life into our moribund school system. But is that likely to be allowed or tolerated by the vested interests which are entrenched in the prevailing system? Can Human Rights Education hope to hold on to its objective and succeed without overthrowing the vested interests and radically altering the present system? These are issues which demand open and intelligent public discussion and are not to be settled by any fiat from the centre".

III

What follows is no more than a sketch and broad outlines and a few instances of what have been our heritage, i.e., India's contribution to human rights. Competent researchers can give shape to this sketch. I believe this is one of the most important tasks that the NHRC must undertake. [*The first part of the following sketch is a brief summary of a paper, "Human Rights Education: India's Heritage" presented at a national workshop, "Human Rights and Societal Changes with reference to SC/STs", jointly organized by DLET and NHRC, 3 and 4 August, 1996, in Chennai. This paper appears in Section I of this volume. I am conscious of repitition in presentation in spite of abridgement. The paper was originally published in the weekly,* Mainstream, *21 September, 1996 and subsequently in a number of collections and periodicals. The second part is a brief synopsis of a paper, "Rammohun Roy: The First Human Rights Intellectual-Activist of Modern India", presented at a national seminar on "The Place of Raja Rammohun Roy in the Intellectual, Social and Cultural History of Modern India", New Delhi, 10 and 11 February, 1998, organized by Raja Rammohun Roy Library Foundation Silver Jubilee Celebrations. The paper was published in the monthly,* The Radical Humanist *of December, 1998*].

We may start with an account of Buddhism, Jainism, and other scriptures which gave primacy to man and his welfare and non-Sanskritic Hinduism in the medieval period. During the Buddhist period, interest in man, man in his own image and man's affairs on this earth, unlike otherworldly interest, became the primary concern of thoughtful men and women. They did not consider this earth as a vale of tears. Buddha rejected the caste system. The basic tenets of Buddhism are non-violence, non-hatred, and friendliness to all. Buddha was a great champion of freedom and tolerance. One of the most significant contributions made by him was the introduction and spread of secular education and education for all.

The caste system had a racial origin, in its association of caste and colour. I refer to an important verse in the *Mahabharata*. Bhrigu explains to Bharadvaja: "Brahmins are fair, Kshatriyas are reddish, Vaishas are yellowish, and the Sudras are black". How it is questioned by Bharadvaja is of interest to human rights education: "We all seem to be affected by desire, anger, fear, sorrow, worry, hunger and labour; how do we have caste differences then"? That in ancient India, the caste system was repudiated is illustrated by a number of characters in the *Mahabharata*: (1) the marriage of king Yayati, a Kshatriya, and Devayani, a Brahmin; (2) Vidura, one of the wisest men in the *Mahabharata* and also described as the very incarnation of Dharma, was the son of a Sudra woman; (3) Vasistha was born of a prostitute; (4) Parashara was born of a *Chandala* woman. Another questioning from the *Bhavishya Purana,* "All human beings have the same Father, and children of the same Father cannot have different Castes" (See K.M. Sen, *Hinduism,* Penguin, 1961).

The school of philosophy, *Lokayata* considered physical sense data to be the only source of knowledge. It rejected after-life and reincarnation. We find this rejection in the *Ramayana,* too. A Brahmin, Javali advises Rama: "I grieve for those who, abandoning the pleasures of the world, seek to acquire merit for felicity hereafter and sink to an untimely death. I do not grieve for others, men waste food and other precious things by offering them up yearly as sacrifices in honour of their departed ancestors. O Rama, has a dead man ever partaken of food? ... O Ramachandra, these scriptural injunctions were laid by learned men, skilled in inducing others to give, and finding other means of obtaining wealth, thus subjugating the simple-minded. Their doctrine is, 'sacrifice, give in charity, consecrate yourselves, undergo austerities and become ascetics, O Rama, be wise, there exists no world but this, that is certain"! (see K.M. Sen, *Hinduism,* Penguin, 1961).

The medieval period: Professor Satish Chandra writes about non-Vedic sects: "The position of the *nath-Panthi siddhas* and *jogis* in Hindu society needs to be understood. Most of them belonged to the low castes, opposed caste-based inequalities, denounced the religion of works favoured by the Brahmins, and did not favour image worship" (*Cultural Interaction in South Asia,* New Delhi 1983).

The movement, *Bhakti* has non-aryan roots. According to some scholars it originated in the Dravida country. The works of *Alvar* saints are important in this regard. Most of these saints came from low castes. At a later stage even high caste people hailed their literature. One *Alvar* saint, Andal who belonged to a low caste was accepted as a religious leader by the society in general. This movement is characterized by simplicity, directness, preaching and practicing tolerance, love, and friendliness, disregard for caste division, religious rituals and ceremonies.

The great scholar Ramanuja, the best known exponent of this movement was influenced and inspired by the works of the *Alvars.*

The interaction of Bhakti and Islam, specially the Sufi ideas, gave rise to a number of progressive movements with the core philosophy of tolerance. In this period, "relations between Islam and the religions of South Asia were marked by mutual understanding and tolerance. This spirit was promoted by the rise and spread of Sufi and Bhakti ideas" (Satish Chandra, in *Cultural Interaction in South Asia*).

Namdeva and Tukaram from Maharashtra, the former a tailor, and the latter a peasant made the Bhakti movement increasingly acceptable to the people: "What can ceremonies do if love awake not in your heart?"

In Bengal the well known Vaishnava poets, Jaidev, Vidyapati, and Chandidas, as also Chaitanya popularised the movement. Ramananda challenged caste divisions, revolted against traditional religious rituals and started preaching in Hindi—Sanskrit was the preserve of the upper castes: "Wherever I go, I see water and stone; but it is You who had filled them all with Your presence. In vain do they seek You in the Vedas" (*Granth Saheb*).

Ravidas, a cobbler and Shaikh Kabira Din Momin Ansari, popularly known as Kabir, a weaver were Ramananda's famous disciples. Kabir struck at the very roots of ritualism and superstition: "O god, whether Allah or Rama, I live by thy name". Kabir composed his songs in Hindi. He practiced and preached the gospel of universal tolerance and was the most important exponent of the idea of India without any communal discord. He gave the utmost importance to equality and denounced inequality based on caste, station and wealth.

Guru Nanak was also greatly influenced by Islamic and Sufi ideas. "The supreme significance of Nanak was that he was the harbinger of Hindu-Muslim unity, for he sought sincerely to reconcile Islam with Hinduism as the following verse will show : Guru Nanak Shah fakir/Hindu ka guru aur/Musalman ke pir".

Rabindranath Tagore was greatly influenced by Kabir and translated many of Kabir's poems into English in collaboration with Evelyn Underhill. Guru Nanak, too, left a lasting impression on Tagore's mind. Tagore was also greatly influenced by the Bauls and composed many songs under their influence.

The modern period: In the modern period the first intellectual-activist was Raja Rammohun Roy (1772-1833). In his movement for freedom, social justice, and human dignity, he was influenced both by Christianity and Islam. The intellectual movement that the Raja heralded unfortunately paled into insignificance during the freedom movement, and the revivalists made their presence felt. Rammohun wrote on almost all aspects of our social, religious and political life and areas which were major sources of human rights violation in his time. He spoke the language of reason. He quotes Vasistha: "If a child says something reasonable it should be accepted, but if a Brahmin himself says something unreasonable it should be discarded as a piece of straw."

Rammohun was a champion of civil liberties and freedom. He stood up against the July 1827 Act which had introduced religious bias into the judicial system of India. The cause of compulsory basic education was sacred to him.

In the 19th century we had a galaxy of intellectual activists, rationalists and reformers who championed the cause of human rights, human dignity and freedom. To mention only a few: Ishwar Chandra Vidyasagar, Mahatma Jotiba Phule, Gopalrao Hari Desmukh, Agarkar, Sir Syed, and many others. In short, we should include an analysis of the short-lived Renaissance in Bengal, Maharashtra and a few other parts in the country which was ushered in under the influence of European learning and which gave the utmost importance to human rights.

In the 20th century, Mahatma Gandhi, Dr. Ambedkar, M.N. Roy and many others gave the utmost importance to human rights.

In conclusion I may repeat that research in the field of human rights must begin with the positive aspects of our heritage. We must guard ourselves against romanticising the past; we must raise our voice of reason and wisdom. What is most important is to accept the fact that the highest appreciation of our past is to find out how it could generate in us the spirit of revolt against social injustice and human rights violations and to inculcate this spirit. Our young students must no longer be deprived of the knowledge of the richness of our heritage. Together with the knowledge and learning from ancient Greece, the European Renaissance, and modern European ideas, we must see that our indigenous secular and human rights values and learning from our past blossom with a vigour and splendour surpassing all intellectual movements that I have referred to in the paper on Rammohun.

(A revised version of a paper presented to Asia and Pacific Conference on Education for Human Rights at Pune 3-6 February, 1999, organized jointly by World Peace Centre Pune; UNESCO, Paris; National Human Rights Commission; New Delhi; and Indian National Commission for Co-operation with UNESCO. An abridged version was published in the *PUCL Bulletin*, May, 1999)

LIST OF PARTICIPANTS AND OBSERVERS

Dr. Anand Kumar, Faculty Member,
Jawaharlal Nehru University,
New Delhi-110 067

Mr. A. Subramaniam, I.P.S.
Deputy Inspector General of Police
Protection of Civil Rights, Chennai.

Prof. Avinash Dolas, Faculty Member,
Millind College of Arts and Science,
Aurangabad-431 002
Maharashtra

Prof. Dr. Bhau Lokhande, M.A., Ph.D.,
Faculty Member, Nagpur University
Nagpur-400 014

Mrs. Christine Lazarus, Social Activist,
5-1-191/A, Flat No. 103, Hill Fort Apts.
Ritz Hotel Road,
Hyderabad-500 004.

Mr. Christudas Gandhi I.A.S.,
Secretary, Adi Dravida Welfare, Government of Tamilnadu
Chennai

Mr. D. Karunakaran
Consultant, CBM-SAROS
Bangalore.

Dr. D.L. Sheth
Member, National Backward
Classes Commission, and Faculty Member,
Centre for the Study of Developing Societies
29, Rajpur Road, Delhi-110 054

Mr. D. Manavalan, I.A.S.,
Additional Secretary, Ministry of Welfare,
Union Ministry, Government of India
Shastri Bhawan,
New Delhi

Dr. D.N. Sandanshiv
Former Member, Law Commission
Rahul Kunj, Kurla (E), Mumbai-400 024

Prof. D.R. Nagaraj, Senior Fellow,
Centre for the Study of Developing Societies
29, Rajpur Road, Delhi-110 054

Prof. G. Nancharaiah, Faculty Member,
Univeristy of Hyderabad,
PO Central University Campus
Gachibowli, Hyderabad-500 134

Prof. Gopal Guru, Faculty Member,
Department of Sociology, Pune University
Pune-411 002, Maharashtra

Mr. G.S. Bargava, Senior Columnist,
B-101, Gulmohar Park, New Delhi-110 049

Mr. Henry Thiagaraj
Managing Trustee,
Dalit Liberation Education Trust and Convenor
Human Rights Education Movement of India
Madras Chennai

Mr. I. Antony Nayagam
Chairman and Managing Trustee, SEED
1, Church Street, (T.N.)
Samadanapuram, Palayamkottai-627 002

Mr. I. Paulraj
Advocate and Human Rights Activist
147, Ambedkar Nagar, Perungudi
Madurai-625 022

Dr. Justus Devadas
Secretary, Educational Sponsorship Committe
Director, Public Affairs and Religious Liberty
Seventh-day Adventists
Post Box 2, HCF, Hosur-635 110, Tamil Nadu

Mr. Kathi Padma Rao, Educationist and Activist,
Ambedkar Colony,
Ponnur-522124 (Dist. Gantur)
Andhra Pradesh

Dr. Kancha Ilaiah
Faculty Member, Osmania University,
B-308, Anuradha Sadan
Adikamet, Hyderabad-500 044

Prof. K.S. Chalam
Director, Academic Staff College
Professor of Economics
Andhra University
Vishakapattnam-530 003
Andhra Pradesh

Justice K. Swamidurai
Retired Judge, Madras High Court

Prof. Kuppuswamy
Prof. Ambedkar Chair,
Dept. of Economics, University of Madras
Chennai-600 005.

Mr. K. Vijayakumar,
Documentation Coordinator
Human right Education Movement of India, Chennai

Dr. L. Mishra, IAS
Secretary, Ministry of Labour,
Govt. of India,
New Delhi

Mr. L. Elayaperumal, Ex. M.P.,
Founder and Chairman of
Human Rights Party
Kattumannar Koil
Chidambaram via, Vallalar Dist.-608 001, Tamil Nadu

Dr. Manohar Jilde, Faculty Member,
Millind College
Nagsen Vana, Aurangabad-431 002
Maharashtra

Mrs. Madhuri Pal
educationist, M-35, Greater Kailash-I
New Delhi-110 048

Dr. Maheep Singh, Former Faculty Member,
Khalsa College, Delhi University,
and Hindi writer.

Dr. Ms. Martha Gladstone
Women Activist
Initiatives : Women in Development
E2, B Block, 4th Floor
Parsn Paradise Apartments
109, G.N. Chetty Road
T. Nagar-600 017 (Chennai)

[illegible] zariah
[illegible] as, Church of South India
[illegible] oad, Chennai-600 086

[illegible] Mohini Giri,
[illegible] rperson,
[illegible] tional Commission for Woman
New Delhi-110 002

Mr. M.P. Murallidharaan
Advocate, Chennai

Ms. Mary Premila
Under Secretary to Government of Tamil Nadu,
Adi-Dravida Welfare Dept.
Chennai

Mr. N.L. Sao, Faculty Member,
Siddhartha College,
Bombay University,
Mumbai

Dr. Nirmala Arulprakash, Social Activist,
Chennai

Mr. N. Natarajan
Research Officer,
Office of the Director of the
Adi-Dravida and Tribal Welfare Dept.
Government of Tamil Nadu
Chennai-600 005.

Mr. P.A. Sangma,
Speaker, [at the time of the workshop] Lok Sabha,
New Delhi, (Inaugurated the workshop)

Rev. P. Mohan Larbeer
Dalit Activist, Tamil Nadu Theological Seminary
Arasaradi, Madurai-625 010, Tamil Nadu

Dr. Prakash Ambedkar, MP.,
168, South Ave. New Delhi

Mrs. P. Sivakami, I.A.S.,
Regional Director, ITDC
Anna Salai, Chennai-600 002

Mr. P.L. Mimroth, Advocate, Supreme Court,
Hony Gen. Secy,
Society of the Depressed People for Social Justice,
3360, Ranjit Nagar, Pusa Gate, New Delhi-110008

Dr. R.D. Maurya, Faculty Member,
Dr. B.R. Ambedkar National Institute of Social Science
Mhow (Madhya Pradesh)

Dr. R.M. Pal (Coordinator of the Workshop)
(Editor, PUCL Bulletin)
M-35, Greater Kailash I
New Delhi-110 048

Justice Ramakrishnan (Retd.),
Madras High Court, Chennai

Mr. Rama Mohan Rao, I.A.S.
Joint Secretary to Govt. of Tamil Nadu, Chennai

Mr. Ramamurthy, Economist,
Office of the DIG—PCR
Chennai-600030

Mr. Justice Ranganath Mishra,
Chairperson,
National Human Right Commission,
[Now Retired and Member of Parliament]
New Delhi-110 001

Mr. R. Balakrishnan, I.A.S.,
Director, National Commission for SCs/STs
Government of India
Shastri Bhavan, Chennai-600 006

Dr. R.K. Nayak, I.A.S.,
Secretary, Government of India
Ministry of Rural Areas and Employment
Department of Rural Employment
and Poverty Alleviation [now retired]
Krishi Bhavan, New Delhi-110 001

Dr. R.R. Sivalingam
Advocate, Human Rights Activist
Chairman-Island Trust
14-56 Club Road, Kotagiri,
The Nilgiris-643 217

Mr. R. Sampath, I.A.S.,
Managing Director, TADHCO,
Anna Nagar, Chennai

Mr. R.V. Pillai
Secretary General,
National Human Rights Commission
New Delhi [now retired]

Mr. S. Iyer, IAS
Special Tribal Welfare Scheme, Tamilnadu Government
Salem (Tamil Nadu)

Mrs. Sudha Ramalingam, Advocate
Gen, Secy, TN-PUCL
21, Tamil Street,
Padmanabha Nagar,
Choolai, Chennai-600094

Mr. S. Chalam
Deputy Secretary to Government of Tamil Nadu,
Adi-Dravida Welfare Department,
Chennai-600 005.

Prof. Sibnarayan Ray, well-known intellectual,
Research Director,
Indian Renaissance Institute, and former Head of Indian Studies Department University of Melbourne
Rudrapalash, 63, Purvapapalli
Santiniketan-731 235

Dr. S.K. Thorat, Faculty Member,
Jawaharlal Nehru University, New Delhi
New Delhi-110 067

Ms. Sashni Nayak, Research Fellow
New Delhi

Mr. Sam Devaanugraham,
Human Rights Education Movement of India,
Chennai

Mr. Virendra Dayal,
Member, National Human Rights Commission,
New Delhi

Mr. V. Karuppan, I.A.S., (Retd)
E-36, IV Main Road,
Besant Nagar, Chennai-600 90

Dr. V. Lalitha, M.A., Ph. D.,
Flat No. 102, Deva Ratna Apartments
Amba Garden Extension
Mehidipatnam, Hyderabad-500 028

Dr. Vimal Kirti, Faculty Member,
Nagpur University
Editor, Anguttar, 21, Subhash Nagar,
Hingna Road, Nagpur-400 022,
Maharashtra
Dr. Vimala Thorat, Faculty Member,
Indira Gandhi National Open University,
New Delhi

Mr. Justice V.S. Malimath
Member, National Human Rights Commission,
[now retired]
New Delhi

Ms. Y.D. Darshini,
Women's Coordinator,
Human Rights Education Movement of India,
Chennai

OBSERVERS

Mrs. Bader Sayeed, Member,
Minority Commission, Tamil Nadu,
Chennai-600 018

Dr. C. Julius Karunakaran
Development Consultant
Kamaraj Nagar, IVth Street,
Choolaimedu, Chennai-600 094

Dr. Nandi Joseph
Asst. Director, CLRI
66, Scientists Apts.
Block 5, CLRI Staff Quaters
Adyar, Chennai-600 020.

Mr. Ossi Fernendez
Human Rights Research Foundation,
Tamil Nadu

Ms. V. Geetha
Research Scholar, Chennai

Mr. S. Prabhu, I.A.A.S.
Chennai
Dr. Meera, Human Rights Activist
Chennai

Mr. Paranjothi
Chennai

INDEX